GENDER IN HISTORY

Series editors:
Pam Sharpe, Patricia Skinner and Penny Summerfield

The expansion of research into the history of women and gender since the 1970s has changed the face of history. Using the insights of feminist theory and of historians of women, gender historians have explored the configuration in the past of gender identities and relations between the sexes. They have also investigated the history of sexuality and family relations, and analysed ideas and ideals of masculinity and femininity. Yet gender history has not abandoned the original, inspirational project of women's history: to recover and reveal the lived experience of women in the past and the present.

The series Gender in History provides a forum for these developments. Its historical coverage extends from the medieval to the modern periods, and its geographical scope encompasses not only Europe and North America but all corners of the globe. The series aims to investigate the social and cultural constructions of gender in historical sources, as well as the gendering of historical discourse itself. It embraces both detailed case studies of specific regions or periods, and broader treatments of major themes. Gender in History titles are designed to meet the needs of both scholars and students working in this dynamic area of historical research.

The independent man

D0144860

MANCHESTER
1824

Manchester University Press

THE
INDEPENDENT MAN
CITIZENSHIP AND
GENDER POLITICS IN
GEORGIAN ENGLAND

⊷ Matthew McCormack ⊷

Manchester University Press
Manchester and New York

distributed exclusively in the USA by Palgrave

Copyright © Matthew McCormack 2005

The right of Matthew McCormack to be identified as the author of this work has been asserted by him/her in accordance with the Copyright, Designs and Patents Act 1988.

Published by Manchester University Press
Oxford Road, Manchester M13 9NR, UK
and Room 400, 175 Fifth Avenue, New York, NY 10010, USA
www.manchesteruniversitypress.co.uk

Distributed in the United States exclusively by
Palgrave Macmillan, 175 Fifth Avenue,
New York, NY 10010, USA

Distributed in Canada exclusively by
UBC Press, University of British Columbia, 2029 West Mall,
Vancouver, BC, Canada V6T 1Z2

British Library Cataloguing-in-Publication Data is available

Library of Congress Cataloging-in-Publication Data is available

ISBN 978 0 7190 7055 6 paperback

First published by Manchester University Press in hardback 2005

This paperback edition first published 2011

The publisher has no responsibility for the persistence or accuracy of URLs for any external or third-party internet websites referred to in this book, and does not guarantee that any content on such websites is, or will remain, accurate or appropriate.

Printed by Lightning Source

For J. E. M. S.

Contents

Figures

Acknowledgements

This book was made in Manchester, in more ways than one. I would like to thank members of the School of History and Classics at the University of Manchester (past and present) for their invaluable feedback and support, particularly Hannah Barker, Harry Cocks, Francis Dodsworth, Stuart Jones, Patrick Joyce, Rachel Rich, Nathan Roberts, Bertrand Taithe, James Vernon and Natalie Zacek. Frank O'Gorman deserves special mention for being an exemplary doctoral supervisor and a constant source of inspiration and gentle direction. Among the many people in the wider profession who have given me help and encouragement, I would particularly like to thank John Belchem, Arianne Chernock, Diana Donald, Karen Harvey, Robert Poole, Robert Shoemaker, John Tosh and Allen Warren. The staff, readers and series editors at Manchester University Press also deserve thanks for making the process of writing a first book far less daunting than it might have been.

I would like to thank the Arts and Humanities Research Board and the Economic and Social Research Council for the doctoral and postdoctoral funding, respectively, without which this work would not have been possible. I am grateful to the following institutions for permission to reproduce the following illustrations: figure 1 from the British Library, figure 2 from the John Rylands University Library of Manchester, and figures 3 to 5 from the British Museum, London. Chapter 5 contains material from my article 'Tobias Smollett's "Ode to Independence" and Georgian political culture', *British Journal for Eighteenth-Century Studies* 26:1 (2003); and Chapter 8 from 'The Independent Man: gender, obligation and virtue in the 1832 Reform Act', in Michael Turner (ed.), *Reform and Reformers in Nineteenth-Century Britain* (Sunderland University Press, 2004). These excerpts appear by kind permission of the publishers.

Finally, I would like to thank my family, especially Suzanne Jennifer McCormack (1946–2000), a truly independent spirit.

Acknowledgements

Introduction

I N 1833, EDWARD BULWER-LYTTON published his famous study of national manners and character, *England and the English*. In the opening chapter he noted: 'It is an old maxim enough amongst us that we [the English] possess the sturdy sense of independence; we value ourselves upon it; – yet the sense of independence is often but the want of sympathy with others'. He illustrated what he regarded to be the undesirable side to manly independence with the following anecdote:

> There was a certain merchant sojourning at an inn, whom the boots [a shoeblack] by mistake called betimes in the morning.
>
> 'Sir,' quoth the boots, 'the day's breaking.' The merchant turned round with a grim look – 'Let it break,' growled he, 'it owes *me* nothing!'

This episode, thought Bulwer-Lytton, epitomised the 'connection between selfishness and independence'.[1] Many other commentators over the eighteenth and nineteenth centuries would agree that this personal trait of 'independence' was characteristic of Englishmen. Indeed, 'the ideal of the independent man', notes J. G. A. Pocock, 'was one of the few subjects on which the age allowed itself to become fanatical'.[2] Most Georgians would not, however, have joined with Bulwer-Lytton in dwelling upon the negative aspects of a sturdy, defiant individualism. The idealised figure of the 'independent man' was instead long held up as the epitome of manliness, citizenship and national character. This study seeks to explore the important implications of this preoccupation with 'independence', particularly regarding political participation, understandings of personal freedom and the role of gender in political culture.

It is clear from Bulwer-Lytton's use of the term that 'independence' had significantly different meanings in the eighteenth and nineteenth centuries than it does today. Nowadays it is almost entirely used to denote the relationship of persons, institutions or objects to each other, although it retains positive connotations of impartiality (such as 'your Independent Financial Adviser'). In Georgian English, 'independence' was also used in this relational sense to denote freedom from obligation (or 'dependency'), but this freedom from obligation was far more emotive and had far greater evaluative implications. 'Independence' connoted not just autonomy, but the condition in which self-mastery, conscience and individual responsibility could be exercised. Only in this situation of 'independence', it was argued, could an individual be disinterested, incorruptible and impartial.

Whereas some of these relational connotations are still in the language, the implications of the term 'independence' regarding manners, masculinity, personal virtue and national character have largely been lost. Personal 'independence' concerned not just freedom *per se*, but a consciousness of liberty, a libertarianism that was supposedly inherent in all true Englishmen. We will see how personal freedom was a prominent aspect of a Georgian man's sense of his gender – as well as his social and political being – and this was commonly articulated in terms of 'manly independence'. It was also believed that this proud 'independence' manifested itself in behavioural and bodily terms. Georgians maintained that 'independent men' were easily identified, because 'independence' entailed an unmistakable sturdiness and directness of demeanour. In terms of social mores, admirers of 'independence' promoted a pointedly plain model of manliness, emphasising sincerity and straightforwardness. These qualities were all part of the English self-image, but 'independence' came to be seen as integral to Englishness and almost patriotic in itself.

Importantly, 'independence' was usually regarded as the epitome of political virtue and the criterion for electoral citizenship. There were several related reasons for this. Firstly, because this character type was widely held to be inherently English in an almost racial sense, the very workings of the political system were believed to be shaped around it. Most Georgians believed in an ancient political constitution, a perfect political arrangement that was ratified by the accumulated wisdom of the generations and centuries of usage. The constitution was the totem to which all political action had to be consistent: by and large, both proponents and opponents of change claimed to have the sanctity of the constitution in view, and constitutionalism remained a compelling political aesthetic and mode of argument well into the nineteenth century. This brand of constitutionalism emphasised that the political system was ideally adapted to the English character and conditions. For centuries, English writers had contrasted the supposed sturdiness of their indigenous stock with the miserable dependence of French peasants, suggesting that the former could only be governed and taxed with their consent. Eighteenth-century commentators from home and abroad continued to make links between the 'independence' of the English attitude and physique, and the individual freedom upheld by the political and legal system, attempting to ground England's revered constitution in the character of its people in an organic way.[3] William Cobbett, for one, approved of violent sports such as boxing, wrestling and bull-baiting for this reason: 'they tend to make the people bold: they produce a communication of notions of hardihood; they serve to remind men of the importance of bodily strength; [and] to keep alive, even amongst the lowest of people, some idea of independence'. This, thought Cobbett, encouraged men 'to preserve the independence and liberties of their country'.[4]

Secondly, Georgian theories of the constitutional structure were concerned primarily with the relations that subsisted between its various elements, and these questions were negotiated in terms of 'independence' and 'dependence'. 'Court' interpretations, commonly proffered by apologists for governments and monarchs, emphasised the power of the sovereign and the legitimacy of the executive's influence over the legislature. The alternative 'Country' interpretation propounded by critics of successive governments, on the other hand, emphasised the independent checks that balanced the constitutional structure: in particular, the power of the Commons to check the government, and of the electorate to influence the composition and conduct of the Commons. All branches of the constitution should retain the ability freely to check the conduct of the others, in order to ensure that government was carried on in the interests of all: namely, that property and political liberty would be preserved. 'Country' theorists also maintained that the *individuals* who participated in these institutions should closely guard their independence for this same reason. In the eighteenth century, when deference, patronage and preferment were facts of political life, and when freedom was more often understood as a granted privilege than as an abstract right, being free from dependence upon the will of another was of huge importance. As Marie Peters has noted, 'independence' was 'the only behaviour truly consistent with the theory of the mixed balanced constitution'.[5] Under pressure to justify the constitutionality of their actions, Georgian legislators, electors and polemicists commonly resorted to demonstrative shows of independence.

As we have seen, however, 'independence' was not just a question of autonomy. Great emphasis was placed upon the personal virtues and acquirements of these political actors. This was, to a large degree, due to the influence of neo-classical and 'Country' thinking upon mainstream political culture: an influence that was, I will argue, profound and enduring. These theories maintained that only virtuous and free individuals should be entrusted with political responsibility, and the shorthand for these criteria in Georgian English was 'independence'. This crucial term had a wide range of connotation and cut across a number of considerations that were felt to be relevant to political participation, including personal character, property ownership, conscientiousness, patriotism, responsibility, and so on.

All of these qualities related to the issue of manliness in some way and the concept of 'independence' was almost invariably gendered in the masculine in Georgian discourse. Historians have only recently begun to appreciate the importance of considerations of masculinity to the study of politics.[6] Men dominated the *dramatis personae* of traditional political history, but there was little sense that their gender was itself a worthwhile object of study. Much work has been done to reinstate the presence of women in eighteenth- and nineteenth-century politics, and this work has naturally been sensitive to considerations of gender.[7] The history of masculinity, however, has been relatively slow to address Georgian political life: ironically, it is now men who are in more need of rescue from the 'silence' of the historical record in this respect.[8] In particular, as I will show throughout this work, gender was central to the ways in which political life was defined: in terms of appropriate behaviour, modes of thought and – crucially – the type of person who should or should not participate in political life. The history of franchise reform is inseparable from considerations of gender, as historians of women's suffrage have long appreciated.[9] From the first calls for parliamentary reform in the eighteenth century until universal suffrage in the twentieth, British political life witnessed a debate about what sorts of persons could safely exercise the vote, and this was often articulated in highly gendered terms. Indeed, the story of the British parliamentary reform movement can be told in terms of how reformers gradually came to associate ever-humbler groups of men with the personal 'independence' that was required for citizenship, until the achievement of manhood suffrage in the late nineteenth century made the identification complete.

It is difficult not to tell the story of parliamentary reform in Whiggish terms, but this is not a narrative of progress, inclusion and empowerment. Until the early twentieth century, the notion of 'independence' could be employed to exclude more people from political, legal and economic entitlement than it included. Its most obvious exclusive implications were for women, and the debilitating cultural association of femininity with 'dependence' is an important theme of this study: in particular, we will examine the role of misogyny in radical culture, and how the question of women's political role was negotiated during the debates on parliamentary reform in 1830–32. But supposed *effeminacy* as well as femininity was also politically disempowering. Men who were younger, poorer, non-English or homosexual were similarly disadvantaged by the cult of the independent man. Understandings of who was capable of independence were constantly being renegotiated, but arguments for empowerment based upon 'independence' always required an 'other' in the form of a disempowered dependant. *In*-dependence is a negative term – the condition of *non*-obligation – so to argue that only *non-obliged* persons should participate in politics is to imply that supposedly *obliged* persons should not.

Existing historical writing on 'independence' fails adequately to address these considerations. Indeed, the importance accorded to the idea in Georgian writings has not been reflected in modern historiography, where historians have given 'the independent man' three or four entirely separate existences, without any sense that they may have been talking about a common phenomenon.

In works on the idea of 'independence' in the eighteenth century, the emphasis has been political, and often *high*-political. The independent man with whom most students of the period are acquainted is the independent country gentleman MP, as described by Sir Lewis Namier in the 1950s. The bucolic country gent disdained approaches from parties or patrons that might compromise his proud patriotic independence, which enabled him either to support his king or to stand up for 'Country' causes.[10] While undoubtedly a fixture of the mid-century political scene, however, conceptualising 'the independent member' as a discrete political type distorts the fact that the culture of manly independence was commonly drawn upon by persons beyond their ranks. In Victorian studies, by contrast, 'independence' has largely been considered in social terms. 'Independence' has often been examined in the context of the Poor Laws, where it was the Smilesian prescription of administrators and ideologues who sought to stigmatise those who depended upon parochial relief. Not that 'independence' did not inform working-class values: historians of labour and working-class politics have demonstrated that self-sufficiency and self-improvement were central to artisan culture.[11] More recently, there has been an appreciation of the extent to which this condition of worker independence was mythologised by contemporaries (and, indeed, by twentieth-century historians). 'Independence' is less central to Victorian political studies than it is to those of the eighteenth century. Indeed, it is largely within the histories of labour and of working-class radicalism that the 1867 Reform Act has been re-thought as an attempt to enfranchise the 'independent' portion of the male working class.[12]

I am seeking to bridge the gap between these two historiographies – the 'high-political' eighteenth century and the 'social' nineteenth – and to suggest that 'independence' was of great political *and* social importance, throughout this period and at all levels of society. By emphasising that 'independence' was a multifaceted and durable common culture, it is possible to turn our attention to long-term shifts in its meaning. The fact that different types of historians have tackled the concept in these two periods reflects some of the different ways in which the culture of 'independent' constitutionalism was used: to refer to different social constituencies, and in different senses. We will see how 'independence' was the boast of substantial gentlemen in the mid-eighteenth century, but would be conceived of far more widely by later generations. Indeed, when the history of 'independent' manliness is viewed in this broader perspective, it is the First Reform Act of 1832 – and not the Second – that becomes the pivotal moment in the transformation of the political idea of 'independence'. We will see in Chapter 8 how the reforming Whigs came to power with a firm notion of who should be admitted to the electoral system, an understanding that owed much to the eighteenth-century idea of 'the independent man'. Their Reform Act marks the moment at which this formerly elitist oppositional idea became the official criterion for mass political inclusion.

It is productive, then, to consider manly independence as a concept whose meaning and application shifted over a long period. As such, there is much to be learned from intellectual historians, particularly those who have emphasised the influence of classical republican ideas. Within classical political theory, 'independence' was the prerequisite of citizenship, and could only be possessed by substantial male householders of demonstrable virtue and martial capability. These ideas were reworked during the Florentine renaissance, and Pocock has argued that they entered anglophone thought through the work of the Civil War writer James Harrington, who merged Machiavellian republicanism with an idealised vision of England. Others place less emphasis upon Harrington, but agree that the eighteenth-century preoccupation with 'independence' was indebted to neo-classical conceptions of liberty and virtue.[13] Feminist political theorists, in particular, have underlined the masculinism and misogyny of a political tradition that emphasised virility and patriarchal mastery as the bases of political entitlement.[14]

This neo-classical thesis can be taken further. Firstly, the endurance of these ideas is often underestimated. Political theorists usually assume that classical republicanism was displaced by liberalism by around 1800, but this study will demonstrate that neo-classical tenets pervaded English culture well beyond that date: late-Georgian politics was conducted within a paradigm of virtue and corruption. Secondly, the social reach of these ideas can too easily be underplayed. Within the elitist parameters of the history of ideas, it would be difficult to imagine that 'independence' had any resonance beyond the privileged sphere of high-political ideologues, but I would argue that these ideas played an important part in how individuals of all ranks regarded themselves and their relations with others. Which brings me to my third objection: the fact that our sources are limited to representations does not mean that the significance of 'independence' at the time was limited to the linguistic. It is true that, to a certain extent, it was a political shibboleth, asserted by rhetoricians when the occasion demanded it: when Mr Gregsbury MP instructs Nicholas Nickleby how to write his speeches, he encourages him always to include 'a little compliment about independence and good sense'.[15] 'Independence' may well have been among the most over-used terms in the political vocabulary, but it was also a fundamental aspect of Georgian male identities and informed political behaviour in crucial ways. In order to get a purchase on this fundamental idea, we need a more nuanced understanding of political selfhood.

This study, then, is concerned with notions of the individual: how individuals relate to themselves, to others, and to the social and political world around them; how this affects the way that they behave; and how they are conceptualised, individually, relationally and as collectivities. Answers to these questions are necessarily elusive and contingent, in contrast to the certitudes of traditional political history. Nevertheless, in recent decades historical studies has become more sensitive towards these issues, and important shifts have occurred regarding how the self has been understood. It is understandable that Marxist social history and women's history should have focused upon the individual: aggregates of individuals, formerly at the periphery of historical description, were thrust to central stage. Their cultures, aspirations and worldviews, however, were rescued from 'the enormous condescension of posterity' in a characteristic way.[16] A straightforward elision was made from 'experience' of inequality, exploitation and opposed class interests, to 'consciousness' of the same: the relationship between social experience and identity was assumed to be reflective. In turn, the Georgian notion of 'independence' has often been interpreted in socially or economically reductive ways.[17]

In particular, there has commonly been a sense that 'independence' and 'dependence' were matters of class relations, and that the culture of manly independence was a product of the emergence of a class society between the mid-eighteenth and the mid-nineteenth centuries. This narrative of class formation also had a profound influence upon histories of sex relations. Women's historians similarly sought to understand women's oppression in terms of social structure and developed a complementary scheme, 'the emergence of separate spheres'. They argued that the emergence of a modern class society was characterised by the reinforcement of domestic patriarchy and the divergence of male and female spheres of activity: women were increasingly confined to domestic dependency, whereas bourgeois men exploited new opportunities to develop an 'independent' consciousness in the public worlds of work and politics. The metanarratives of 'class' and 'separate spheres' have recently been substantially revised, however, as critics have argued that both interpretations are empirically unworkable and theoretically reductive.[18] We will see that the concepts of 'class', 'public' and 'private' did indeed have important gendered meanings for contemporaries, but it is no longer acceptable to assume that an individual's consciousness resulted from their location within a social structure.

In recent years the more fluid notion of 'identity' has supplanted 'consciousness' in historical description. The epistemological flaws in reducing consciousness to one's position in a society structured by class or patriarchy have been exposed. Structuralism offered a productive critique of this 'reflective' conception of culture, arguing instead that we have to look at the categorical framework within which the individual renders the outside world comprehensible and meaningful. Post-structuralism, in turn, applies these insights less inflexibly, exploring how cultural practices construct subjectivity, and how the play of discourses interact with it. Significantly, gender history has taken place within this constructivist approach.[19] The process of cultural mediation is now the cultural historian's object of concern: culture has a formative role in how the individual and the world relate to each other, rather than just being the predictable product of this encounter. We should not, therefore, assume that the culture of 'independence' was the necessary product of an individual being in a state of party-political, electoral or social independence. Indeed, throughout *The Independent Man* we will encounter a wide range of men who loudly professed their 'independence', irrespective of their actual situations. We should not dismiss this as a false consciousness, or assume that they were dishonest. I would argue that it is far more revealing to explore why Georgian men felt the need to draw upon a culture of assertive autonomy, and to ask why this culture was so emotive, and what effects it had.

Fundamentally, the post-structuralist conception of the self is unstable. It is neither a predictable transhistorical 'given', nor reducible to a specific set of circumstances: it is contingent and always open to renegotiation. The term 'identity' encompasses this fluidity. One's understanding of one's own characteristics is impermanent: identity may be 'centred' artificially and temporarily, but has no permanent centre. This is relevant to the rhetorical practice of politics, which is often characterised by the use of discourse to fix that which is contingent or indeterminate. James Vernon and Patrick Joyce have recently made a case for a 'new cultural history of politics', embodying an understanding of how politics consists of 'a discursive struggle to empower people by imagining them as legitimately acting subjects around specific fixed identities'.[20] When political speakers and writers encouraged late Georgians to see themselves as 'independent men', it lent a purpose and a sense of agency and rectitude to their actions, and motivated support for their addresser.

Acknowledging the contingency of self-identity and social classification, therefore, can help us to think about the practice of politics in a new way. It also opens up the possibility of a new history of citizenship. Instead of being an instrumental legal category or a topic for the history of ideas, citizenship should be a matter of the self: we need to understand both how the legitimate political subject is defined, and how that individual experiences membership of the political nation and behaves within it. Much valuable work has been done on the Second Reform Act, scrutinising the language of the legislation and the debates around it in order to reconstruct how contemporaries went about 'defining the Victorian nation' in terms of gender, race and class.[21] There is now a need to open up a comparable debate in Georgian studies, so that the cultural history of English citizenship may be viewed in a broader perspective. *The Independent Man* is a contribution towards a new narrative in English political history, where gendered subjectivity is at the centre of the political historian's enquiry.[22]

The structure of the book reflects these preoccupations. Chapters 1 and 2 are introductory and thematic, and begin by asserting that notions of political virtue in late-Georgian England should be understood in terms of a highly gendered conception of obligation, a conception that owed a great deal to contemporary understandings of the family. The relationship of this ideology with political action is then explored, as we examine the role of 'independence' in the physical performance of political identities, particularly in the context of parliamentary elections.

Placing the notion of 'manly independence' at the centre of our understanding of electoral culture enables us to re-evaluate both the function of election contests themselves, and the nature of political citizenship in this period.

Chapters 3 to 8 take the form of a chronological narrative exploring how the meanings and application of the notion of 'the independent man' shifted over the course of the long eighteenth century. I seek to tell the story of 'the Age of Reform' in a new way. Instead of a heroic movement gradually turning the tide of public opinion and wresting political emancipation from an intransigent establishment, I examine how a wide range of political actors contested their understandings of the legitimate political participant – a project that was as much concerned with exclusion as with inclusion. At the beginning of this period, as at the end, the citizen was 'the independent man': it was the content and significance of this notion that changed. We need to comprehend this crucial debate if we are to understand the terms in which citizenship was defined in 1832, a definition that endured well into the Victorian era.

Notes

1 Edward Bulwer-Lytton, *England and the English*, 2 vols (London, 1833), vol. I, p. 10.
2 J. G. A. Pocock, 'Machiavelli, Harrington and English political ideologies in the eighteenth century' (1965), in his *Politics, Language and Time* (London: Methuen, 1971), pp. 104–47 (p. 127).
3 P. Langford, *Englishness Identified: Manners and Character 1650–1850* (Oxford: Oxford University Press, 2000), pp. 7–9.
4 William Cobbett, 'Boxing' (1805), in *Selections from Cobbett's Political Works*, 6 vols (London, 1835), vol. II, pp. 11–17 (p. 16).
5 M. Peters, 'The *Monitor* on the constitution, 1755–65: new light on the ideological origins of English radicalism', *English Historical Review* 86 (1971), pp. 706–27 (p. 715).
6 For example: J. Tosh, 'What should historians do with masculinity?', *History Workshop Journal* 38 (1994), pp. 179–202.
7 For example, the essays collected in K. Gleadle and S. Richardson (eds), *Women in British Politics, 1760–1860: The Power of the Petticoat* (Basingstoke: Macmillan, 2000).
8 The recent collection *Masculinities in Politics and War: Gendering Modern History*, edited by Dudink, Hagemann and Tosh (Manchester: Manchester University Press, 2004) seeks to redress this balance in the discipline more generally, but none of the contributors is concerned directly with Britain before the twentieth century.
9 A. Clark, 'Gender, class, and the constitution: franchise reform in England 1832–1928', in J. Vernon (ed.), *Re-Reading the Constitution: New Narratives in the Political History of England's Long Nineteenth Century* (Cambridge: Cambridge University Press, 1996), pp. 239–53.
10 L. Namier, 'Country gentlemen in parliament, 1750–84' (1954), in his *Collected Essays*, vol. II: *Crossroads of Power* (London: Hamish Hamilton, 1962), pp. 30–45.

11 For example: I. Prothero, *Artisans and Politics in Early Nineteenth-Century London: John Gast and His Times* (Folkestone: Dawson, 1979); K. McClelland, 'Some thoughts on masculinity and the "representative artisan" in Britain, 1850–1880', *Gender and History* 1:2 (1989), pp. 164–77; R. Grayson and A. White, '"More myth than reality": the independent artisan in nineteenth-century Sheffield', *Journal of Historical Sociology* 9:3 (1996), pp. 335–53.

12 C. Hall, K. McClelland, and J. Rendall, *Defining the Victorian Nation: Class, Race, Gender, and the British Reform Act of 1867* (Cambridge: Cambridge University Press, 2000); P. Joyce, *Democratic Subjects: The Self and the Social in Nineteenth-Century England* (Cambridge: Cambridge University Press, 1994).

13 Pocock, 'Machiavelli'; Q. Skinner, *Liberty Before Liberalism* (Cambridge: Cambridge University Press, 1998).

14 Carole Pateman, *The Sexual Contract: Aspects of Patriarchal Liberalism* (Stanford: Stanford University Press, 1988).

15 Charles Dickens, *Nicholas Nickleby* (1838–39), ed. D. Parker (London: Dent, 1994), p. 182.

16 E. P. Thompson, *The Making of the English Working Class*, 4th edn (London: Penguin, 1991), p. 12.

17 C. B. Macpherson, *The Political Theory of Possessive Individualism: Hobbes to Locke* (Oxford: Clarendon, 1962).

18 P. Joyce, *Visions of the People: Industrial England and the Question of Class 1848–1914* (Cambridge: Cambridge University Press, 1991); D. Wahrman, *Imagining the Middle Class: The Political Representation of Class in England, c. 1780–1840* (Cambridge: Cambridge University Press, 1995); A. Vickery, 'Golden age to separate spheres? A review of the categories and chronology of English women's history', *Historical Journal* 36:2 (1993), pp. 383–414; L. Klein, 'Gender and the public/private distinction in the eighteenth century: some questions about evidence and analytic procedure', *Eighteenth-Century Studies* 29:1 (1995), pp. 97–109.

19 J. Scott, 'Gender: a useful category of historical analysis', *American Historical Review* 91:5 (1986), pp. 1053–75.

20 J. Vernon, *Politics and the People: A Study in English Political Culture, 1815–1867* (Cambridge: Cambridge University Press, 1993), p. 5.

21 See note 12.

22 See, for example: Gisela Bock and Susan James (eds), *Beyond Equality and Difference: Citizenship, Feminist Politics and Female Subjectivity* (London: Routledge, 1992); Susan Kingsley Kent, *Gender and Power in Britain, 1640–1990* (London: Routledge, 1998); and the 'Gender and citizenship' special issue of *Gender and History* 13:3 (2001).

1

Gender, obligation and political virtue

I N MANCHESTER CATHEDRAL there is a memorial to Samuel Taylor
of Moston, who died in 1820 aged forty-eight. On the face of it, he
was the quintessential Georgian gentleman, serving as a JP and as a
Lieutenant-Colonel in the local volunteers, and his epitaph emphasised
the appropriate personal qualities:

> He was a Man of warm and generous Feelings;
> of unblemished Honour and Integrity;
> and with a most ardent Spirit of Loyalty;
> He maintained through life a firm Independence of Character.

In the eighteenth and nineteenth centuries, a man's virtues would commonly be evaluated in such a manner and be preserved for all time in a
public memorial like this. The personal qualities that Taylor's family
identified in him were typical of their times. Warmth and generosity of
feeling, honour, integrity and loyalty (particularly when it meant to one's
country, as it probably does here) were attributes that Georgians hoped
to identify in men of Taylor's class. The concluding virtue, however, was
arguably the most important: 'a firm Independence of Character'. This
was the guiding principle that he 'maintained through life'. Many
of Taylor's contemporaries would similarly have been preoccupied with
this consideration of independence. It moulded their conceptions of
themselves as men, as patriarchs and as citizens; it informed the ways in
which they related to their social betters and inferiors, their patrons and
clients, their family and acquaintances; and it influenced their behaviour,
from their most momentous political decisions to the minutiae of their
everyday lives.

This chapter seeks to explore why this was so, and the important
implications that this had for political and family life in particular. The
association of obligation with femininity and effeminacy informed the

eighteenth century's concern regarding the role of clientage in state and society, and we will see how the political careers of elite gentlemen were preoccupied with this need to preserve their 'independence'. As we approach the nineteenth century, however, it is the virtue of the electoral citizenry – rather than those whom they select – that dominates contemporary argument. Classical-republican argument emphasised the role of the independent householder-citizen in the polity, an ideal that meshed with English conditions since, in practice, voters were householders. Electoral citizenship, however, was increasingly identified with that station. Only the 'independent' male householder, reformers argued, could and should represent the rest of society in the public world. Although the relationship between them changed, politics and the family were inseparable in Georgian England.

Obligation and the gendering of public virtue

Georgians comprehended obligation in a particular way. Independence from obligation was regarded as a manly and honourable condition where conscience could freely be exercised. In particular, independence was the prerequisite for legitimate political action since only persons free from political obligations could act for the general good rather than with reference to sectional interests. Thus independent MPs, independent voters, independently wealthy gentlemen and independent artisans all asserted that they were in a privileged position and drew upon a broadly common culture of manly virtue and assertive individualism. Anyone who was subject to an influence or obligation that compromised their individual autonomy, on the other hand, was accused of being 'dependent' – a term with considerable force, connoting a degrading lack of manliness, virtue and free will. 'Dependence' upon a patron, an employer, a landlord, or the parish was enough to call an individual's manliness and freedom into question, and could undermine a claim to political legitimacy. This state of 'dependence' was the polar opposite of masculine 'independence': laudable in females, but contemptible – and supposedly effeminate – in adult men.

This imperative was felt most keenly in the factious, client-ridden and ruinously expensive business of parliamentary politics. John Perceval, the Second Earl of Egmont, for example, had some unfortunate early political experiences. In the 1740s he paid £1,000 to Prince Frederick on the understanding that he would come in for a Cornish borough, but the scheme fell through and he was left out of pocket. As he noted ruefully in a document he entitled 'Memorandum in regard to the Prince which may be necessary for myself to remember':

> I was fully convinced by this, and I had always formed the same opin-
> ion that a man's best dependence is on himself, and that to depend
> upon any other person is but the last resource. I was therefore resolved
> upon all occasions for the future to make my own way, as far as possi-
> ble without counting any other man's assistance but in a secondary
> manner, and rather to expect success by bringing other men to offer
> their aid, than to set out by courting their assistance.[1]

By the 1750s he was Lord of the Bedchamber and a prominent figure in
Leicester House circles, but his destiny remained tied to that of his royal
masters and he never realised his ambition of becoming prime minister.
Nevertheless, his personal declaration of independence is significant,
both with respect to his own values, and in terms of how he approached
a political system in which obligations to parties and patrons were often
a fact of life. Resolutions of this sort are common in private memoirs,
which were commonly written for the instruction of younger sons. A contemporary of Egmont, William Cavendish, Fourth Duke of Devonshire,
recorded how he responded when approached by the Duke of Newcastle
in 1760:

> That with regard to myself, I was determined to remain my own master;
> that I had so often declared both in public and private, that I would be
> free and independent; that I could not act any other part; that therefore
> I could enter into no agreement to go out with his Grace; that whenever
> the time came, I should judge for myself and do what I thought most
> for my own honour . . .[2]

As a Duke of Devonshire, he was above the financial exigencies of patronage, but the questions of party loyalty and personal connection had still
to be weighed against the value of manly independence.

Very different dilemmas were faced by those at the opposite end of
the social spectrum, but they were framed in a remarkably similar way.
The most tangible situation in which a humble man's political independence would be put to the test was the election contest, and the culture
of Georgian elections will therefore be a recurring theme in this study.
Questions of political obligation were apposite in an electoral system that
operated in a localised, face-to-face context, in which the candidate or
magnate was commonly a figure of considerable social and economic
power, and where voting was not secret. Voters commonly had to weigh
up their own political choices against those of a local patron, landlord or
employer, and were aware that they had to bear the consequences of these
choices. As we will see in Chapter 2, 'independence' was central to electoral culture and had several related connotations in this context. Voters

should be of sufficient standing and means that their political decision should not be unduly influenced by another: 'independence' implied a condition where conscience and public spirit could be exercised. Besides circumstances, 'independence' also suggested the strength of character that was required in order to exercise them – the manly spirit and love of liberty that would enable a voter to stand up for what he believed in, in defiance of the wishes of a patron or an election mob.

The precise relationship between patron and voter is a complex one. The gift relationship is highly political, and implicitly places the recipient in a position of obligation (and therefore dependence) upon the giver.[3] The mechanics and conventions of the Hanoverian electoral system, however, complicate the picture and it would be anachronistic on our part to condemn all political patronage as illegitimate. What radicals condemned as 'corruption' was often regarded by others as legitimate political practice. Electoral life was structured around customary expectations and, although a direct cash bribe would have been questionable, the acknowledgment of continued favour and service would not have been. Although the provision of free food and drink would fall foul of later reformers, 'treating' was an accepted part of the Georgian electoral carnival.[4] Furthermore, elections were regarded as an opportunity for local people to acknowledge their social leaders. Even the reforming Whigs of 1830–32 argued that electoral influence could take 'legitimate' forms, and was compatible with the independence of the individual elector. Nevertheless, reformers were concerned that poor voters could be swayed by the gifts (or threats) on offer. As the radical John Wade put it, a candidate could offer a '*ten-pound note*, to a man, almost shoeless and shirtless, who has not five shillings in the world, and whose rent-day, perhaps, or his wife's confinement, is hard at hand'. 'How is it possible', therefore, that 'the present class of voters can act independently?'[5] Typically for a late-Georgian reformer, Wade combines sympathy for the poor man's predicament with a conviction that he is nevertheless not qualified for political rights. Only independent men should vote, since only they were in a position to judge conscientiously on behalf of people who were not. In particular, a man who could put his family – and even his unborn child – in that position did not come up to the mark: as we will see, voters were increasingly called upon to prove their capacity for responsibility and government in the sphere of the home as the prerequisite for political empowerment.

The imperative for working men to support themselves and to avoid recourse to poor relief was conceived of in very similar terms. If a man applied to charity or the parish authorities, he was regarded as placing himself in an ignominious position of obligation, compromising his masculine honour. In the language of the debate on the Poor Laws, such men were demonised as 'paupers' or 'the undeserving poor'. Men who supported themselves and their families by their own labours, on the other hand, were idealised as 'the independent', even if they were poor. As Francis Knowles declared from the Shaftesbury hustings in 1830: 'the spark of independence burns yet too brightly in the bosom of the English peasant to let him kneel and crave the charity of his fellow men, so long as he has a single chance left of supporting himself by the sweat of his own brow!'[6] Peter Mandler rightly warns us that we should view such statements with suspicion. He argues that accounts of proud working men refusing relief are more likely to be patrician prescriptions of how the lower orders should behave, rather than objective descriptions.[7] Should we view accounts of voters declaring their 'independence' from bribery with similar scepticism? Certainly we should acknowledge the theatricality of the claim, but we should neither assume that they were being preached to, nor ignore these accounts if they were not telling the truth. It is more significant that Georgian men felt the need to draw upon this emotive culture of manly independence, and more productive from the historian's point of view to study this culture on its own terms. Knowles's speech may well have been part moral instruction and part election-time idealism, but it nevertheless gives us a telling insight into contemporary political and gender values.

The importance of spurning parochial relief was amplified during elections, since recipients were generally excluded from voting. According to the political theory of dependence, they were not free from political obligation and therefore could not act conscientiously for the general good. In reality, many voters deliberately stayed off relief during elections so that they could qualify for the vote, since patronal treating could be far more remunerative. Nevertheless, the debates over the Poor Laws and parliamentary reform were inextricably linked and have a similar chronology: the New Poor Law followed hard on the heels of the 1832 Reform Act, which formalised the exclusion of paupers from political representation. In a sense, both measures were concerned with inculcating 'independence' and demonising 'dependence' among humble citizens. Political and social self-sufficiency were inseparable, and both were evaluated in terms of gender.

Indeed, the pride associated with self-sufficiency (and the support of one's dependants) was increasingly identified with work. The place of 'independence' in masculine work values is a large field[8] – and probably worth a book in itself – but a few comments will suffice here in order to contextualise this discussion of politics. Belonging to a 'trade' had long been central to artisans' sense of esteem and self-identity, and directly related to their political personality. Artisans acquired their 'freedom' when they completed their apprenticeship, and in some 'freeman' boroughs this entitled them to the vote.[9] This freedom was a kind of inde- feasible property that made the artisan independent: once acquired, the freeman would always be able to support himself in work, so could defy his betters on the grounds that he could supposedly work elsewhere. Work also became increasingly important for men of middling rank. In particular, independence through work resonated with the Protestant work ethic and freed middling men from the ignominy of patrician patronage. Occupation became more important to male identities, as economic activity became increasingly identified with the political and civil public domain.[10] Work became a sphere in which men could prove their manhood.

In particular, middle-class men pointedly contrasted this ethos with that of their betters. Unlike men of the aristocracy – who claimed to be independent because they did not have to work – they asserted that true masculine honour consisted in achieving independence *through* work. As Stefan Collini has shown, this value became all-pervasive in Victorian England, when the struggle for independence in the marketplace was regarded as conducive to 'character'.[11] In many respects, 'character' was a similarly loaded term to 'independence', with a comparable range of con- notations including moral discipline, self-restraint, perseverance and duty. Both notions were therefore concerned with strength of personality and evaluated it in terms of manhood, but there were also significant dif- ferences. It was partly a question of different eras: arguably Victorians accorded 'character' a similar esteem to that accorded to 'independence' by Georgians. This suggests a shift of values, from a concern with public reputation and hierarchical relationships in the eighteenth century, to 'inner' virtue in the nineteenth. Independence itself took this course over the two centuries and becomes increasingly difficult to distinguish from character: as we will see in later chapters, evaluations of independence shifted from a preoccupation with circumstance to interior qualities that were not just accessible to the privileged few. The ideal of the inde- pendent man retained its resonance in the Victorian period. Although Victorians would hope to identify character in their public men, it was 'independence' that had the *political* genealogy and would continue to be the primary means of evaluating constitutional virtue and electoral entitlement.

In general, then, questions of political obligation and virtue were always evaluated in terms of gender, but the nature of that evaluation changed. Regency men still encountered the dilemmas of obligation faced by Egmont and Devonshire, but were not so preoccupied with the niceties of elite patronage and office. Indeed, the entire political game in which the latter had participated became anathema to their late-Georgian successors. From the mid-century there were calls for 'economical reform' to the systems of clientage and officeholding, with the dual aims of retrenching expenditure and curtailing the executive's influence. By the 1800s, this programme had evolved into the radical critique of 'Old Corruption', which linked the unbalancing of the constitution through patronage with the abuse of the electoral system, and evaluated both in terms of the moral degeneracy of the aristocracy and the exploitation of the working man. Radical publications like the *Black Book* described a nightmarish 'system' whereby the Crown and nobility filled 'every lucrative office' with their 'connexions and dependents'.[12] Regency radicals even appropriated the language of the Poor Laws to condemn the idleness, illegitimacy and effeminacy of the 'state paupers' who lived off the taxes and monopolised political power. The language of political entitlement, therefore, was related in complex ways to a whole host of other discourses – including those of party, patronage, honour, work and pauperism – but all were concerned fundamentally with gender, obligation and virtue.

Of these three related considerations, it was arguably *gender* that became the most important. The independent man came to be associated less with the trappings of elite masculinity – landed property and rank – and was instead identified more with maleness itself. This was both in terms of certain 'male' stations that were increasingly associated with political responsibility – namely father, husband, breadwinner and householder – and also with certain supposedly 'manly' qualities. As John Tosh has argued, 'manliness' came to be a dominant value in the Victorian period. Manliness was not equivalent to maleness – not all men were manly – but was a highly qualitative measure of male virtue, encompassing (often contested or contradictory) injunctions 'to work, to pray, to stand up for their rights, to turn the other cheek, to sow wild oats, to be chaste and so on'. This was sharply distinguished both with femininity and with polite, elite gentility, and the 'desired outcome was the "independent man"'.[13] Fundamentally, manliness and independence were within the reach of every man: they had to be earned through inner strength and mastery of one's circumstances.

A representative example of these Victorian ideals is the 1856 collection of poetry entitled *Lyrics: Love, Freedom and Manly Independence* by Hugh Buchanan MacPhail.[14] The poems themselves – such as 'Depend on Heaven!' and 'To One Who Would Make a Scotchman a Slave' – exude defiance, pride and strong feelings. The lengthy preface reads like a personal manifesto, where MacPhail recounts his own struggles against poverty and misfortune. He is obliged to thank his subscribers for their patronage, but pointedly does so in the language of sincere feeling ('the genuine expression of my inmost heart') rather than clientage. Indeed, the poet dwells at length upon what manly independence means to him:

> When I say manly independence, I do not mean that ghostly independence leans on birth, or rank, or wealth, for its sole importance and consequence in the world . . . that independence to which idiots may be born by title, or sheer blockheads, by accident, come to be possessed of by riches; but *the* independence springs from pure feelings and noble thoughts – asserts the royal dignity of man – the majesty of his nature, and the incentive to real brotherly kindness, genuine civility, and unaffected politeness.[15]

The Victorian model of independence, therefore, differed sharply from its Georgian predecessor, and this study seeks to account for this crucial transformation. As we will now see, this gendered understanding of virtue derived to a large extent from the family, both in a theoretical sense and with reference to contemporary domestic realities. Indeed, the notion of independence was profoundly affected by changing ideals and practices within the Georgian household. It was an understanding of independent manliness predicated upon sentimental domesticity, in particular, that influenced the remodelling of electoral citizenship in the Age of Reform.

The familial model of obligation and power

The distinction between 'independence' and 'dependence', and how this was morally evaluated, should be understood in terms of the metaphor of the patriarchal family. Within this model, the male household head controls, protects, dominates and represents the other members of the household, who are all dependent upon him. These dependants include his wife, children and servants. In symbolic terms, all of these dependants are conceived of in the feminine: even male minors, servants, or lodgers are not truly manly, as a consequence of their dependence. All the members of the household may be virtuous, but only the male household head is fully capable of the virtue of 'independence'. Within this scheme, only he is free from obligation and is therefore fully in command of himself, and is capable of full self-realisation and self-determination.

As Quentin Skinner and others have shown, this familial model of obligation was derived from the classical understanding of liberty and virtue. Only the independent man, the head of the household, is fully free and in possession of the manly virtues. This was commonly referred to by Georgian commentators in the Latin, as *virtus*: this connoted both virility and political virtue, underlining the link between sex and citizenship in republican theory. Only he should be admitted to citizenship, because everybody else in the household is 'dependent'. Even if no coercion is exercised by their master, they are fundamentally unfree because they depend upon his arbitrary will. They are thus in a degrading position analogous to slavery and are not free to pursue the public good, which is the object of citizenship in a free republic.[16] This familial model of obligation came to be profoundly influential in anglophone political theory.

Georgian political life was therefore gendered at its very heart, in terms of an evaluative scheme of obligation. The patriarchal family served as a powerful metaphor to evaluate a wide range of stations and relationships in the wider society. The critique of patriarchy has long been the objective of academic feminism. Originally conceived of as the transhistorical structure of male domination, recent studies have instead emphasised that patriarchy is a cultural practice that changes over time: as such, we need to historicise the patriarchal relationship.[17] In early modern Europe, gender roles and natures were regarded as hierarchical. According to Galenic orthodoxy, men were qualitatively superior to women, whose balance of humours dictated that they were necessarily weaker and more passive.[18] The notion that men should be *obeyed* by their womenfolk owed much to biblical and Aristotelian prescriptions. The Bible teaches that husbands should command and dependants should submit, because this is the law of God and man[19] – a teaching reiterated to eighteenth-century Anglican churchgoers in the form of the Homily on Obedience. Aristotle, too, stated that males and females had fixed, hierarchical natures and that wives necessarily obeyed their husbands.[20] Within classical-republican theory, only the male independent head of household is fully free and capable of citizenship, because all other family members are necessarily in a position of political obligation – dependence upon the patriarch, supposedly the most elemental obligation in human society.

Although the Georgian paterfamilias would not have put it so starkly, these notions were congruent with both the ideal and the reality of the eighteenth-century household. The extent to which home life was separated from the public world of work and politics, and how far women were consigned to the former and excluded from the latter, dominated

twentieth-century accounts of gender in Georgian England: 'the emergence of separate spheres' was the dominant narrative in women's history.[21] As we will see, the home and 'public life' were gendered in
importantly contrasting ways, but the 'separate spheres' orthodoxy is an
unhelpful context in which to study the independence/dependence
dichotomy. The notion that maleness and femaleness corresponded to
discrete spatial and sociological spheres is an empirical and intellectual
fallacy. Revisionist gender historians have largely concerned themselves
with the former objection by exploring exceptions to the rule, but the
assumption that practice and ideology related to each other in an
unmediated way has remained largely unquestioned. Men's and women's
conceptions of their own personhood were not determined by the zones
that they supposedly inhabited. The central Georgian notions of 'independence' and 'dependence' hinged instead upon the relative virtues and
capacities of men and women (and, indeed, other men), the relations that
existed between them and their different expectations of behaviour in
certain situations – situations that did not correspond to a sharp division
of (male) public and (female) private. Furthermore, we will see how 'separate spheres' was itself a political idiom rather than a reflection of social
circumstances: reformers emphasised the independence and domestic
mastery of humble men in order to make a moral case for wider male
access to political rights.

The related debate exploring changing notions of men's and
women's natures has been more productive, particularly regarding the
notion of 'sensibility'. From the late seventeenth century, proponents of
this anatomical and psychological notion emphasised the role of the
nerves in sense perception, and hence the importance of the environment
in the formation of character. Had the argument that all individuals
anatomically experience the world in the same way been followed
through to its logical conclusion 'sensibility' would have entailed equality
between ranks and sexes. Indeed, in the later eighteenth century, male
'feeling' would become modish and radicals would explore its egalitarian
implications. Its early popularisers, however, identified sensibility as a
feminine quality that was exercised in a more acute and morally responsive manner by women and cultivated persons.[22] For Lawrence Stone, this
culture of sensibility entailed a positive change in the status of middling
women, who were morally idealised and whose partnerships with their
husbands became more egalitarian and affective.[23] His stance has rightly
been much criticised by women's historians who have argued that the creation of the 'sentimental family' served to reinforce patriarchy.[24] Women
were conceived of as helpless creatures of sentiment, who lacked the

'sense', rationality and physical and mental strength of men, and should therefore be protected by their menfolk and shielded from the rough and demanding public world. The home was increasingly conceived of as a feminine sphere and the woman's contribution was to provide a nurturant retreat for her husband. As Elizabeth Sandford argued in 1831:

> domestic comfort is the greatest benefit she confers upon society: for happiness is almost an element of virtue; and nothing conduces more to improve the character of a man more than domestic peace. A woman may make a man's home delightful, and may thus increase his motives for exertion.

Although the home was supposedly the woman's sphere, sentimental ideology underlined the need for male authority within it. Prescriptive literature in this mould preached that women should be dependent upon their husbands. Sandford insisted that women should always 'show their consciousness of dependence':

> There is, indeed, something unfeminine in independence. It is contrary to nature, and therefore it offends. We do not like to see a woman affecting tremours; but still less do we like to see her acting the amazon. A sensible woman feels her dependence. She does what she can; but she is conscious of inferiority, and therefore grateful for support.[25]

In a sense, everyone in the house besides the householder was analogous in their dependency. Women were commonly conceived of as being childlike: whereas boys started the process of acquiring manliness with a ritual breeching, girls never left petticoats, a centuries-old symbol of their dependent position.[26] Boys' position within this scheme was ambiguous. Dependent and close to their mothers while they were minors, boys nevertheless had to make the uneasy transition to being in a position where they were independent and capable of having an establishment and dependants of their own. Separation from the feminine home space – and in particular from the mother – was central to this, and the increasing preference for sending boys away to 'public' boarding schools over home education can be thought about in these terms. As John Tosh has shown, fathers took an anxious interest in this process and had a duty to train their sons in manliness.[27]

Other household members were held to be comparably dependent. This obviously applied to invalids or poor relatives, but the position of servants is particularly interesting. Clearly below family members in the status hierarchy, they were nevertheless regarded as being dependent upon their master in a comparable way. Adult male servants had a particularly ambiguous position, since their status as dependent, kept persons was implicitly effeminising. Anxieties about their capacity for freedom of action, and possibly their manliness, ensured that they were among the last groups of male adults to be granted the franchise.[28]

The male adult householder was the only member of the household who was held to possess the requisite 'independence' to conduct its outside dealings: he should represent, protect and support those who are dependent upon him. James Mill famously employed this dictum when discussing the franchise in his *Essay on Government* (1820):

> One thing is pretty clear, that all individuals whose interests are indisputably included in those of other individuals, may be struck off without inconvenience. In this light may be viewed all children, up to a certain age, whose interests are involved in those of their parents. In this light, women may be regarded, as the interest of almost all of whom is included either in that of their fathers or of their husbands.[29]

We will see how commentators increasingly returned to this classical conception of the family in discussions relating to the franchise, in order to justify limiting electoral citizenship to adult men. Women were commonly grouped with minors, convicted criminals and the insane, as those who should be excluded from political rights on the grounds of 'dependence'.[30] This was not just the fact of their dependent relation with another: in sentimental terms, their dependence was inherent. Leonore Davidoff has shown how the emerging conception of the civil, legal, political and economic 'individual' should be understood in this way. Only a rational and free actor, capable of entering into contracts, was accorded a full personality in this regard.[31] Dependants, by contrast, were held to have no individual will or interest of their own. When a woman married, she ceased to exist as a distinct legal entity and – as Mill argues – was subsumed into that of her husband.

Fundamentally, a woman's right to own property was very limited. Widows, uniquely, were accorded many of the rights and opportunities of independent men (with the notable exception of voting): in a sense, they represented a continuation of their dead husband's civil, legal and economic personality, ensuring, for example, that family businesses were maintained. Married women, on the other hand – and it was expected that all women would be married at some stage of their lives – largely gave up their property and their rights separately to own any. In a sense, women *became* a form of indefeasible property when they got married.[32] This exclusion from the world of property was an important aspect of women's exclusion from official politics, since the 'independence' required for citizenship was partly predicated upon forms of proprietorship. Voting in the counties and in most boroughs required the fulfilment of a property qualification relating to the value of the voter's house or lands. As Sir William Blackstone noted in his *Commentaries on the Laws of England*, electors must have 'estates in lands or tenements' of a certain value 'because that sum would then, with proper industry, furnish all the necessaries of life, and render the freeholder, if he pleased, an independent man'.[33] Indeed, electoral citizenship continued to be based upon proprietorship until well into the twentieth century.

Property ownership may have enabled 'independence' but it was never simply a question of money. Nor was it a 'class' relationship between a producer and an exploiter. Property was only empowering insofar as it helped to free a man from dependence upon the will of another, by making him self-sufficient: a rich man could enter into constraining obligations, just as a humbler man could disdain them. Property – particularly landed property – entailed certain duties and moral responsibilities, particularly if dependants relied upon it for their support. It connoted a stake in the common weal, which would supposedly encourage public-spirited action. Fundamentally, an independent man should be the proprietor *of himself*. Self-command was associated with self-ownership, whereas to be 'owned' in any sense by another was both degrading and absolutely disempowering within the neo-classical paradigm.

These questions of obligation had important implications for self-ownership, rationality and subjectivity. As Clifford Geertz noted in 1974, the modern Western notion of the autonomous, rational, sovereign individual is unique among the world's cultures.[34] But not everybody in Georgian England was regarded as a sovereign individual: the extent to which persons were fully in control of their selves was hierarchical and evaluative. Only 'independent men' were held to possess full political subjectivity, and were fully in control of their homes, their consciences and their identities. In a sense, the 'dependent' were not held to be subjects at all – they were the objects of political action rather than its originators, the spectated rather than the spectator. They may have participated on the margins of politics, but it was seen as desirable to deny them the manly functions of judging and choosing.

Citizenship and the household

The household, then, had long been central to English political theory and practice. Indeed, Britain was conceived of *as* a nation of households.

This picture was reinforced by the work of social investigators and statisticians, who conceived of the family – not the biological individual – as the elemental unit of the state. Gregory King's famous social survey of the 1690s was based around the estimated number of 'families' in Britain, not population. Accordingly, King did not consider servants as a separate occupational group, absorbing them with the rest of the family under the household head. This procedure was followed by statisticians such as Joseph Massie and Patrick Colquhoun over the century that followed.[35] The latter was concerned with counting and classifying 'heads of families' and considered other members of the household only in terms of a numerical average: you have to multiply the two in order to get an estimate of the aggregate population. Their basis in numbers of households and householders was partly a consequence of the format of their sources – the Heart Tax returns (King and Massie) or a combination of Income Tax, census and Poor Law records (Colquhoun). Nevertheless, these were the surveys that contemporary commentators repeatedly referred to, and the first censuses of the nineteenth century also followed this format, basing the returns upon household occupants. In Georgian England, the *household* and the *householder* were the basic units of social conceptualisation.

The vocabulary of social classification in this period needs to be regarded in these terms. In eighteenth-century parlance, 'the people' did not connote the population, but the aggregate of substantial, independent, adult male householders. The utilitarian political writer George Ensor clarified this for his readers: 'By the people I do not mean the populace, but that body of thinking and industrious citizens who form the strength and credit of the nation'.[36] When elections 'took the Sense of the People', they supposedly appealed to this group. If Britain was a nation of households, its polity was, in turn, conceived of as a 'public' composed of the independent men that dwelt in them. Throughout this period, British political commentators were committed to a romanticised vision of 'a smiling land, not bestrode with overgrown palaces, but covered with quickset dwellings, every one of which holds a freeman, enjoying equal privileges with the proudest subjects of the land'.[37] The myth that England possessed a citizenry of sturdy independent yeomen, which would provide a bulwark against the abuses and excesses of government, was widely held. The radical paper *The Black Dwarf* reassured its readers in 1817 that so long as ministers 'collectively awe a nation of freemen', there was nothing to fear.[38]

This ideal householder-citizenry was increasingly equated with the parliamentary electorate. Although the plethora of borough and city

qualifications made the distribution of the franchise haphazard in practice, theoretically the vote was exercised by 'independent' heads of household. We have seen how this was partly a question of property ownership:
only a proprietor (in effect, the male householder) was self-sufficient
enough to vote freely. The household itself and the family relationships
within it, however, were also of fundamental importance. Indeed, the
man's public capacity was predicated upon the 'shadowy' private world of
the home.[39] In later chapters we will encounter a wide variety of radicals
and reformers who deployed these familial arguments, but it is worth
focusing here upon a single work. The reformer Thomas Oldfield began
a study of the representative system (including an account of every
constituency) in the 1780s, and his monumental multi-volume work *The
Representative History of Great Britain and Ireland* was finally published
in 1818. The work contains a wealth of factual information, but the chapter entitled 'General Observations on the Representation' is probably of
greatest interest to the student of political theory because he focuses upon
the gendering of electoral entitlement in unusual detail.

Oldfield situates the family in Georgian theories of political representation. The eighteenth-century theory of 'virtual representation' had
it that MPs represented the whole nation (indeed, the whole empire)
rather than just their constituents in any direct sense. This was long a
powerful argument against redressing the social and geographical
inequalities of the electoral system, since everyone in society was *virtually*
represented in parliament.[40] Late-Georgian radicals modified this line of
reasoning. Any notion of 'the people in parliament' was too abstract and
impractical, so only persons who lacked an independent will of their own
should be excluded from direct representation. Dependent people, on
the other hand, could be effectually represented by the person upon
whom they most immediately depended. Oldfield argues that the male
household head is the logical person to represent the will of the other
household members in the wider community: 'He is the natural guardian
and virtual representative, not only of his family and servants, but of all
those who depend upon him'.

Radicals cited the familial nature of this bond to prove that the
householder could be entrusted to exercise this power responsibly: male
citizenship was commonly justified in relation to the sentimental family.
Oldfield describes the householder in this way: 'He is necessarily the
master, and probably the father, of a family. In the first character, he has
personal credit and respect to maintain; in the second, he has given
actual hostages to society'. Radicals exploited the contemporary assumption that the father and husband would 'naturally' have the best interests

of their dependants at heart in their arguments for enfranchising humble men. This was commonly expressed in the most melodramatic terms: Oldfield suggests that even poor men needed political power to protect 'the virtue of their wives and daughters'. Furthermore, the station of householder was valorised in itself as a guarantee of the voter's character and responsibility: 'Such a station deserves confidence, and should be made respectable, that all men may be prompted and encouraged to rise to it. The relations and duties that belong to it are antecedent to all positive institutions, and constitute at once the basis and the security of civil society'. Oldfield therefore goes beyond instrumental reasons for enfranchising fathers and husbands and argues from first principles: the patriarchal family is the elemental unit of political life. Even propertyless men 'have yet wives and children, in whom they have a right'.[41] By equating political entitlement with the male stations of husband, father and householder, radicals were able to argue for a more socially inclusive (if gender-exclusive) franchise by undermining independence's traditional associations with property and rank.

In the ideology of radical reform, then, the political rights of men were fundamentally based upon their domestic relationships. The very fact that a man had dependants to govern and support morally underwrote his public role. 'Independence' therefore entailed domestic attachment as well as public freedom. George Ensor argued in 1806 that marriage was essential to the creation of an 'Independent Man': 'Marriage induces regular habits, tempers the passions, and renders man more complying, more feeling, and a better citizen; for he has stronger sympathies with the commonwealth'.[42] It is important to distinguish between obligation and attachment (be it a familial bond or a stake in a larger enterprise). Independence/dependence is a two-way relationship, but it is a hierarchical one that does not work the same both ways. According to republican theory, a person who has a dependant is empowered by the relationship, whereas the dependant is disempowered: only the independent person is free enough to pursue the general good, or that of their dependants. This did not necessarily translate into political practice. To a large extent, the household vote was seen as the family vote: many husbands consulted their wife about how the vote should be cast and women were therefore canvassed by candidates at election time. Nevertheless, the idea of the independent householder-citizen became increasingly important in late-Georgian politics, and came to have a significant bearing upon the reform of the electoral system in 1832.

The idea of the independent man, and the domestic dependencies by which his masculinity was importantly defined, therefore dominated

British culture. Although the household model derived from classical political theory, the Georgian ideal of masculine citizenship was also informed in crucial ways by contemporary familial practice. In many ways, the sentimental home became increasingly important during the Age of Reform, as radicals appealed to a notion of citizenship that would not exclude humble men. Over the course of the eighteenth and nineteenth centuries, citizenship continued to be evaluated in terms of obligation and virtue, but moved from a paradigm of rank and landed property to one of gender. By the nineteenth century, masculine virtue was evaluated, not in terms of circumstance, but of manly strength of character and 'natural' familial responsibilities. In a nation of households, it was the husbands, fathers and masters who should be admitted to official politics.

Notes

1 'Leicester House politics, 1750–60, from the papers of John, Second Earl of Egremont', ed. A. Newman, *Camden*, Miscellany XXII, 4th series, vol. 7 (1969), pp. 85–228 (p. 98).

2 *The Devonshire Diary: William Cavendish Fourth Duke of Devonshire. Memoranda on State Affairs 1759–62*, ed. P. Brown and Karl Schweizer, *Camden*, 4th series, vol. 27 (1982), p. 67.

3 A. J. Kidd, 'Philanthropy and the "Social History Paradigm"', *Social History* 21 (1996), pp. 180–92.

4 My discussion of electoral deference, and electoral culture in general, is indebted to the work of Frank O'Gorman: *Voters, Patrons and Parties: The Unreformed Electorate of Hanoverian England* (Oxford: Oxford University Press, 1989).

5 John Wade, *The Extraordinary Black Book* (London, 1831), p. 560.

6 'A Constitutional Reformer', *History of the Shaftesbury Election 1830* (London and Shaftesbury, n.d.), p. 5.

7 Peter Mandler (ed.), *The Uses of Charity: The Poor on Relief in the Nineteenth-Century Metropolis* (Philadelphia: Pennsylvania University Press, 1990).

8 See, for example, P. Joyce (ed.), *The Historical Meanings of Work* (Cambridge: Cambridge University Press, 1987); R. Grayson and A. White, '"More myth than reality": the independent artisan in nineteenth-century Sheffield', *Journal of Historical Sociology* 9:3 (1996), pp. 335–53.

9 R. Sweet, 'Freemen and independence in English borough politics c. 1770–1830', *Past and Present* 161 (1998), pp. 84–115 (p. 91).

10 L. Davidoff and C. Hall, *Family Fortunes: Men and Women of the English Middle Class, 1780–1850* (London: Hutchinson, 1987), pp. 199–205, 307.

11 Stefan Collini, 'The idea of "character" in Victorian political thought', *Transactions of the Royal Historical Society* 35 (1985), pp. 29–50. For a recent study of this powerful notion, see Nathan Roberts, 'Investigating Character in England, c. 1880–1914' (unpublished doctoral thesis, University of Manchester, 2002).

12 Wade, *Black Book*, p. 223.

13 John Tosh, 'Gentlemanly politeness and manly simplicity in Victorian England', *Transactions of the Royal Historical Society* 12 (2002), pp. 455–72 (pp. 459, 460).

14 On the relationship between Scottish and English notions of 'independence', see Matthew McCormack, 'Tobias Smollett's "Ode to Independence" and Georgian political culture', *British Journal for Eighteenth-Century Studies* 26:1 (2003), pp. 27–39.

15 Hugh Buchanan MacPhail, *Lyrics: Love, Freedom and Manly Independence* (Glasgow, 1856), pp. ix, xx–xxi.

16 Q. Skinner, *Liberty before Liberalism* (Cambridge: Cambridge University Press, 1998).

17 The debate over patriarchy is summarised in the 'Introduction' to R. Shoemaker and M. Vincent (eds), *Gender and History in Western Europe* (London: Arnold, 1998), pp. 1–22.

18 A. Fletcher, *Gender, Sex, and Subordination in England 1500–1800* (New Haven: Yale University Press, 1995), chs 2–4.

19 'Wives, submit yourselves unto your own husbands, as it is fit in the Lord' (Col. 3. 18).

20 Aristotle, *The Politics and The Constitution of Athens*, ed. S. Everson (Cambridge: Cambridge University Press, 1996), Book 1 (pp. 11–30).

21 For critiques of this historiography, see Introduction, note 18.

22 G. J. Barker-Benfield, *The Culture of Sensibility: Sex and Society in Eighteenth-Century Britain* (Chicago: Chicago University Press, 1992), chs 1 and 2.

23 L. Stone, *The Family, Sex, and Marriage in England, 1500–1800* (London: Weidenfeld and Nicolson, 1977).

24 S. M. Okin, 'Women and the making of the sentimental family', *Philosophy and Public Affairs* 11:1 (1981), pp. 65–88.

25 Elizabeth Sandford, *Woman, in Her Social and Domestic Character* (1831), 5th edn (London, 1837), pp. 2, 14. On prescriptive literature, see Davidoff and Hall, *Family Fortunes*, pp. 292–3, 321–7.

26 I am grateful to John Tosh for this observation on the significance of breeching. On petticoats, see Davidoff and Hall, *Family Fortunes*, p. 413.

27 J. Tosh, *A Man's Place: Masculinity and the Middle-Class Home in Victorian England* (New Haven: Yale University Press, 1999), p. 116.

28 L. Davidoff, 'Adam spoke first and named the orders of the world' (1990), in her *Worlds Between: Historical Perspectives on Gender and Class* (Cambridge: Polity, 1995), pp. 231–64 (p. 233).

29 In J. Lively and J. Rees (eds), *Utilitarian Logic and Politics* (Oxford: Clarendon, 1978), pp. 53–95 (p. 79).

30 See, for example, William Cobbett: *Advice to Young Men, and (Incidentally) to Young Women, in the Middle and Higher Ranks of Life* (1829), new edn (London, 1878), p. 317.

31 Davidoff, 'Adam spoke first', pp. 232–4.

32 T. Michals, '"That Sole and Despotic Dominion": slaves, wives, and game in Blackstone's *Commentaries*', *Eighteenth-Century Studies* 27:2 (1993), pp. 195–215.

33 William Blackstone, *Commentaries on the Laws of England*, 4 vols (Oxford, 1765), vol. I, p. 166.

34 C. Geertz, '"From the Native's Point of View": on the nature of anthropological understanding' (1974), in R. Shweder and R. LeVine (eds), *Culture Theory: Essays on Mind, Self, and Emotion* (Cambridge: Cambridge University Press, 1984), pp. 123–36.

35 R. Porter, *English Society in the Eighteenth Century*, revised edition (London: Penguin, 1982), p. 143 and the comparative statistical tables, pp. 366–9.

36 George Ensor, *The Independent Man: Or, An Essay on the Formation and Development of those Principles and Faculties of the Human Mind which Constitute Moral and Intellectual Excellence*, 2 vols (London, 1806), vol. II, p. 324.

37 *The Real Character and Tendency of the Proposed Reform* (London, 1832), p. 12.

38 *The Black Dwarf: A London Weekly Publication by T. J. Wooler* (12 March 1817).

39 Davidoff, 'Adam spoke first', p. 235.

40 Paul Langford, 'Property and virtual representation in eighteenth-century England', *Historical Journal* 31:1 (1988), pp. 83–115.

41 T. H. B. Oldfield, *The Representative History of Great Britain and Ireland*, 3 vols (London, 1816), vol. III, pp. 4–6.

42 Ensor, *Independent Man*, vol. II, p. 415.

2

'Act the part of Honest Independent Men'

IN 1809, AN ENGLISHMAN NAMED SIR JOHN CARR was travelling through mainland Europe. In a Spanish bar, he encountered an English naval lieutenant who was so embarrassed that a Spaniard had settled his bill that he chased after him to protest:

> He continued, with an oath, that he had never been treated so before, that he had never, hitherto, been under an obligation to any one, and would not put up with it. He then told the waiter, through an Englishman who spoke Spanish, that he insisted upon paying for his punch; the waiter refused to take his money, he remonstrated, the other still refused, and doubtless thought him mad, upon which the worthy, blunt, but mistaken lieutenant threw a dollar into the bar, and ran out of the house, declaring, much as he liked a Spaniard, he would be d—d before he would be under any obligation to him.[1]

Carr's anecdote would have been as comical in 1809 as it is now, but for different reasons. To the modern reader, the lieutenant is patently absurd, needlessly proud and possibly xenophobic. Georgian audiences, on the other hand, would have identified a peculiar resonance in this episode: affectionate, knowing humour might have been derived from an understanding of what drove the lieutenant to such behaviour. The lieutenant, like most Georgian men, evidently prided himself upon his 'independence', which he would compromise if he consented to such an obligation. As we have seen, the loss of independence jeopardised a man's virtue, manliness, liberty and even selfhood.

Carr's lieutenant serves to remind us that the horror of obligation implicit in the ideology of manly independence was not merely a tenet of political theory. It pervaded male values and identities, which could influence behaviour in important ways. In this chapter I will explore the place of 'independence' in male identities and political action. I will begin with a discussion of male conduct literature – which suggests some of the themes that will be examined in the following chapters – and will explore how 'independence' informed the *performance* of male identities. The second half of the chapter will then examine the culture of Georgian election contests, which provided a stage upon which men could bring these gendered political identities vividly to life.

Prescription, identity and performance

There is an appropriately large historiography on the prescriptive texts that were written for women and girls in Georgian England.[2] Male advice literature from the same period, however, has received relatively little attention.[3] Prescriptive works aimed at men took various forms. Besides periodicals (such as *The Spectator*) or novels with avowedly pedagogical intentions, there were three main varieties. The first and oldest was courtesy literature, which codified the forms of courtly gentility.[4] By the late eighteenth century, this genre was largely defunct and new forms of 'independent' gentility were being mobilised against the contrived behaviour that it had promoted: as such, I will not be concentrating on courtesy literature here. I wish instead to concentrate upon the second and third varieties: self-help texts, which instructed their readers how to improve their lives in religious, educational, economic, or career terms; and rhetoric manuals.

The second of these genres was commonly concerned with inculcating habits of independence. We have already encountered George Ensor's *The Independent Man* (1806). As he states in the opening sentence: 'It is the object of the following work to explain what should be the EDUCATION, the MORALS, the LITERATURE, and the PURSUITS of an INDEPENDENT MAN'. It begins as a guide addressed to parents, including strictures on pregnancy and breast feeding. Ensor takes a Lockean view of the importance of education and appropriate upbringing, insisting that 'children are fashioned by the teachers of their infancy'. For example:

> I am also of Rousseau's opinion, that those who have the care of children should only be cautious to preserve them from dangerous accidents: this teaches them independence and hardihood. I have known a child only four years old, thus educated, so superior to common accidents, that, having violently struck his forehead against an iron grating in the street, he ran . . . to the female attendant, beseeching her not to be grieved, for the ill which he had received was not great.

As he sees it, the independent man is made not born. Independence is an inherent personal quality rather than an accident of rank or fortune, but it is one that has to be created and constantly monitored. Although the conditions that Ensor describes are those of patrician society, this is an argument with socially egalitarian connotations. At the same time, however, it is also sexually exclusive: it is clear throughout that Ensor's ideal life-narrative is a *male* one.

Ensor addresses the reader directly when he reaches adulthood. Besides hardihood, the independent man is encouraged to cultivate the virtues of honesty, generosity and wisdom. In terms of property,

> moderate wealth serves personal independence, supplies the means of knowledge, and provides leisure and solitude, the parents of thought . . . Though men should not anxiously pursue the attainment of wealth, a poor man should look to independence, and all should practice œconomy: œconomy is the virtuous medium between prodigality and avarice, two vices strongly connected.[5]

These rationalisations of wealth and the virtuous mean are recognisably classical. Ensor also takes a classical view of citizenship, citing Aristotle in order to affirm that 'a citizen is chiefly formed for the commonwealth', and asserting that independent citizens should be able to defend their country. The primary calling of the independent man, however, is politics. As Ensor sees it, the apogee of a man's existence is to serve in parliament, and his manual provides detailed advice on how to achieve this without compromising one's independence. He warns against 'ambition', 'electioneering arts' and 'faction' and urges his reader only to seek a ministerial station 'without intrigue or mean compliance'.[6] *The Independent Man* therefore reminds us that politics and masculinity were inseparable in this period: manliness was important in political situations, but politics was also central to the business of being a man.

The radical writer William Cobbett also made significant contributions to the life-of-independence genre. Indeed, in living his own life through his voluminous writings, he presented himself as the exemplary independent man. 'From my very first outset in politics', he explained in his *Political Register*, 'I formed the resolution of keeping myself perfectly independent' – a stand that he expected his readers to admire and to emulate.[7] Through his undoubtedly egotistical productions, Cobbett *became* John Bull, the very embodiment of the independent freeborn Englishman.

Cobbett's works spoke very directly to his audience yet, remarkably, he cultivated both working and middling, rough and refined, readerships. His prescriptive works were targeted – in style, content and cost – at particular groups: therefore we have *Advice to Young Men . . . in the Middle and Higher Ranks of Life* (1829) on the one hand, and the part-works *Cottage Economy* (1821–22) and *The Poor Man's Friend* (1826–27) on the other. These seek to enable the reader to live a life of dignified self-supporting independence, like their author. To poorer readers he advises on industriousness, household economy and garden husbandry, and middle-class men are warned of the dangers of luxury, gaming, ill-chosen wives and patronage. All are preached the value of frugality: 'The greatest source of independence, the French express in the precept of three words, "*Vivre de peu*", which I have always very much admired. "*To live upon little*" is the great security against slavery . . .'. Happiness is to be found only in independence from 'what is called *interest*'. He clearly believes that the middle classes are in greater danger, for 'He who lives by a pursuit, be it what it may, which does not require a considerable degree of *bodily labour*, must, from the nature of things, be, more or less, a *dependent*'. The bodiliness of masculine independence is a recurrent theme in his writings. He exhorts his readers to be neither boorish nor simpering and servile in their manners. He believed that 'good food, and plenty of it, is not more necessary to the forming of a stout and able body than to the forming of an active and enterprising spirit': the traditional pleasures of beef, bacon and beer are preferred to foreign and unhealthy tea and potatoes.[8] And, as we have seen, Cobbett recommends hardy sports such as boxing, wrestling and bull-baiting to guard against '*effeminacy*' and to foster 'independence' of character.[9]

How should we regard texts such as *The Independent Man* or *Advice to Young Men*? Recent work on women's conduct literature reminds us that we should not take a 'command' view of prescription.[10] Reading practices were far more nuanced: we can certainly assume that, for most, Ensor's narrative from the womb to the cabinet would have been read for entertainment or wish-fulfilment rather than for a realistic life-plan. Others may have laughed at its piety, or quibbled with its dogmatism: this was neither a blueprint for, nor a 'reflection' of, Georgian society. Nevertheless, the fact that it resonated with so much of contemporary discourse suggests that Georgian readers may well have identified with its values. This was an *attractive* prescription that suggested many everyday techniques by which even humbler readers could ape the dominant masculine ideal of the day. (Perhaps there is a greater need to read against the grain in women's prescriptive literature, which was comparatively negative in its thrust: male conduct works were more aspirational and empowering, and so may be read more at face value for the meanings that audiences derived from them.)

Fundamentally, these works were far from unique,[11] and the story of a man's life-quest for independence recurs in contemporary representations. Many Georgian novels feature a young man of reduced circumstances who has to make his own way in the world and support his dependants, until he finally achieves independence and adulthood. We will encounter Roderick Random in Chapter 5, and De Vere and Coningsby in Chapter 7 (both of whom triumph by entering parliament as independent members); other famous examples include Tom Jones and Nicholas Nickleby. Narratives such as these enabled Georgian men to make sense of their lives, and to conceive of their own past, present and future in terms of a story in which the struggle for independence was the abiding theme. Samuel Taylor's epitaph serves to remind us that 'independence' was the guiding principle of a Georgian man's life-story. As we will see throughout this book, the prominence of 'independence' in private diaries[12] and public memoirs[13] are testaments to the power of this narrative. The life-story of 'independence' was central to male ontologies.

If conduct texts give a vivid impression of the centrality of 'independence' in the values of Georgian men, rhetoric manuals furnish us with further clues about what constituted 'independent' behaviour. In particular, they suggest the *bodiliness* of political action. There are several reasons why this consideration should be central to our enquiry. Since independence was commonly described as an inherent trait – rather than just an abstract ideal – we need to be able to understand its behavioural and corporeal manifestations. Our sources commonly give the impression that independence was read in this way, but do not feel the need to describe something that was apparently obvious to readers at the time. In this way we can try to understand how an 'independent' identity presented itself in actual political situations; and, conversely, the ways in which independence's very performativity enabled it to be constituted as an identity in the first place.

In the eighteenth century, rhetoric was regarded as a science as much as an art, with set rules that had to be learned. Success in public life, and politics in particular, was almost inconceivable without mastery of its primary medium, public speaking. As the conduct guide *Political Primer; Or, Road to Public Honours* put it, not all young men are 'from their station, independent of popular arts': most are required to employ rhetoric, the means of 'forming the natural impulses of others into a ladder for his ambition'.[14] The rhetoric manual promised to tutor the reader in these fundamental skills, and would have been required reading for a Georgian schoolboy with political ambitions.

1   John Walker, *The Academic Speaker . . . To Which are Prefixed, Elements of Gesture*, 3rd edn (London, 1797), plate 1. This copy has been defaced by a contemporary reader (note the long 's'). The speech bubble is illegible, but the caption 'A Stupid Ass' is not, reminding us that readers did not always take lofty prescriptions at face value.

This genre included works such as James Burgh's *Art of Speaking* (1761) and Hugh Blair's *Lectures on Rhetoric* (1783), but John Walker's simpler *The Academic Speaker* achieved great popularity and ran through several editions. Aimed at schoolboys, it sought to teach the bodily actions that accompany oratory, in order to achieve 'the exact adaptation of the action to the word, and the word to the action'. Besides detailed descriptions of the postures that are appropriate to particular emotions or emphases, Walker provides illustrations for boys to emulate (see figure 1). This may appear stilted, but the effect that he sought to achieve was 'plain, open, distinct, and forcible pronunciation'. Walker had reservations about theatrics as a medium for practising these techniques, and instead provided a selection of parliamentary debates, featuring such eminent orators as Wyndham, Pelham, Shippen and the Elder Pitt.[15]

Sources such as these are of interest because they suggest some of the ways in which the culture of manly independence may have manifested itself in behavioural terms. 'Independence' was a comment upon the character and physique of an individual – their inherent ability to resist dependence, as well as their place in power relationships – so we also have to turn our attention to posture, speaking style and physical behaviour. These are significant in themselves, but recent work in performance studies has also emphasised the role of physical action in the construction of identity. The standard sociological understanding of performing-one's-identity emphasised the artifice implicit in acting: action serves to hide the real 'I', which precedes and remains unaffected by the performance.[16] More recently, performance theorists have argued instead that the 'I' does not precede the performance, but that the self is brought into being in the process of the performance itself. Commentators such as Richard Schechner emphasise the productivity of performance, which contains strips of occurrences that are remembered and constantly recycled and recombined into new – but never entirely original – performances.[17] Even outside of theatre studies' very practice-orientated theorisations, there is a wider acknowledgement that identity should be understood as something that is performed. Judith Butler, for example, draws upon the notion of performativity to argue that the subject has to be spoken in order to be constituted as an actor, to be cognitively brought into being. Within this illocutionary understanding of speech, speaking – which is 'itself a bodily act' – is a kind of performance within which identity is enacted.[18] Performance, therefore, is inextricably tied up with the process by which identities are learned, articulated, and indeed constituted as 'identities' at all.

This focus upon bodily communication and the place of performance in identities is peculiarly appropriate to late-Georgian England. Not only was political behaviour in this period highly stylised, but I would even argue that politics and the theatre in this period shared a common aesthetic, with comparable plots, *dramatis personae* and moral schemes. In particular, we will see how descriptions of political behaviour are strikingly congruent with accounts of Georgian acting styles, both of which were notable for their 'bodiliness' and their formalised communicative conventions.[19] In both cases, virtuous action was equated with manly heroism, and this demanded a posturing, direct and declamatory manner. Moreover, both theatrical and political acting conformed to contemporary theories of expression, whereby the body expresses 'inner' feeling and

Servility

2   'Servility', from Henry Siddons, *Practical Illustrations of Rhetorical Gesture and Action; Adapted to the English Drama* (London, 1822), plate 37

conveys it in the most immediate way to an audience, who are able to read the stereotypical bodily signals and to experience an identity of sensation. As Peter Brooks notes, this was a culture in which gesture was valorised over language: 'Much late eighteenth-century reflection on the nature of language and its origins tends to the view that gesture is the first and ulti-mately the most passionate form of communication, that which comes to the fore when the code of verbal language lapses into inadequacy'.[20]

A prime example of this emphasis upon bodily legibility was Henry Siddons's *Practical Illustrations of Rhetorical Gesture and Action* (1822), a volume not dissimilar to Walker's *Academic Speaker*. This was a manual for actors, which instructed them how to perfect the bodily signs 'by which the interior modifications of the soul are manifested and made known'. Siddons included over sixty illustrations of the human 'passions', including 'pride', 'contempt', 'apprehension' and 'servility' (figure 2). The latter is particularly interesting in this context, since servile behaviour was the antithesis of independence: as we will see, visual depictions of 'the independent man' were often juxtaposed with its stooped, fawning and effeminate opposite. By illustrating the human passions, Siddons hoped to demonstrate how 'all the interior powers of man tend in a certain way to the exterior'.[21] This notion of rendering 'inner' truth 'out-wards' was an important element of late-Georgian ontologies. Whereas outer refinement and inner virtue could be separated at the beginning of the eighteenth century, later commentators strove to synchronise the two. The late eighteenth century in particular was a time when increasing emphasis was placed upon the emotional credibility of the political spoken word, suggesting that public and private virtue needed to be linked in order to serve the common good.[22]

There were many political occasions where participants were called upon to demonstrate their independence in some way, to make their sincere sensibility clear to all by demonstrative action. There was a con-tradiction inherent in *performing* one's independence, since this was a culture that lauded sincerity, directness and 'truth'. The culture of manly independence purported to be anti-theatrical, whereas it was in fact a highly stylised performance, and one that came to dominate elections in particular. The ritual nature of Georgian political and civic occasions should be placed in the context of a society decidedly uneasy with the idea of theatricality. There was a strong current of anti-theatricality in eighteenth- and nineteenth-century England, largely characterised by a moral Puritanism opposed to feigning of any kind.[23] This dread of muta-bility was bolstered from the late eighteenth century by the Romantic inclination towards inwardness, 'truth' and the natural. In this context, therefore, an anti-theatrical performance such as 'independence' is comprehensible: studied 'naturalness' is, of course, as performative as what it purports to reject.

Political speechmaking was an important opportunity to demonstrate one's 'independence'. Records of political speeches are often accompanied by accounts of how the speech was performed and these accounts commonly dwell upon the more bodily aspects of performance. An account of the Norwich election of 1830, for example, includes reports of the speeches and descriptions of how they were delivered. Gurney is described as 'stout, manly and bold', and Grant is comparably imposing: 'Mr. G's stature is lofty, and his deportment grave and commanding. – His voice and manner are alike dignified, and his style copious and rich. There is something peculiar in his manner of address that cannot fail to secure the attention of his hearers'.[24] Asides such as these serve as a salutary reminder to historians about the limitations of our materials and our methods. Much as there is to be gained from a 'linguistic turn', words had meanings beyond their textual interconnections. We may experience an election speech 'on the page', but that may tell us little about how the words were delivered and received. Dress, posture, accent, volume, timing, audience reaction and so on, were all crucial elements of a speech, suggesting that we need to employ an understanding of 'discourse' that encompasses more than language alone.

Caricatures of notable figures delivering speeches, for example, can tell us a great deal about the bodiliness of 'independent' behaviour. Clearly these present imaginative tableaux rather than faithful records of physical appearance, but – given Walker's and Siddons's prescriptions – it is fair to assume that comparable conventions were at play, and that caricaturists intended their audience to derive similar meanings from bodily attitudes. I have selected two examples, which illustrate some of the alternative models of 'independent' manliness that were current at the turn of the century. The first is of the backbencher Thomas Tyrwitt Jones, in a caricature by James Gillray of 1799, entitled 'Independence' (figure 3). Jones was a famously eccentric and vocal backbencher, regarded at the time as a symbol of 'independence and Old England'. He soon took his own line in Parliament, voicing his 'Country' prejudices against placemen, pensioners, standing armies, taxation, non-Anglicans and the French – many of which figure in his speech here.[25] Gillray's caricature pokes fun in an affectionate way: the benches behind him are empty, suggesting that no one was listening to his rant. The piece nevertheless tells us something about what 'independence' connoted in terms of bodily performance. Jones is stern, defiant, proud and direct: a 'doughty country squire' in the John Bull mould.[26]

I'm an Independent Man, Sir, — & I don't care That, who hears me say so —
I don't like 'Wooden Shoes'! no Sir, neither French Wooden Shoes, no nor
English Wooden Shoes neither! — and as to the tall Gentleman over the way
I can tell him, that I'm no Pizarro! I'll not hold up the Devils Tail to fish for
a Place, or a Pension! — I'm no Skulker! no, nor no Seceder neither! I'll not
keep out of the way, for fear of being told my own! — there's my Place, & Here I ought
to speak! — I warrant I'll not sneak into Taverns to drink humbug Toasts that
                                I am afraid to explain, not I!
                                my motto is, "Independence &
                                Old England!" — and That!
                                for all the rest of the World!
                                there, That! That! That!
                                        That! That!

3 James Gillray, 'Independence' (1799)

This model of 'independent' behaviour contrasts significantly with
that portrayed in our second example, Charles Williams's take on Sir
Francis Burdett's victory in the 1804 election for Middlesex (figure 4). Like

Jones, Burdett is depicted in the 'teapot' pose, as struck by actors when declaiming in heroic roles, particularly those who aped the statuesque style of Charles Kemble.[27] Our two caricatures, however, present us with two different teapots. Sir Francis lightly rests his left hand – in which he clasps 'the constitution of England' – upon his side, whereas Jones shoves his in the pocket of his waistcoat, misshapen by his considerable paunch. And whereas Jones threateningly raises his right arm in defiance of the world, Burdett's senatorial pose gives the impression of moral loftiness, integrity and legitimacy.

4   Charles Williams, 'The Triumph of Independence over Majesterial Influence and Corruption' (8 March 1805)

Sympathetic caricatures of Burdett often sought visually to identify the radical with classical republican libertarianism. Images of Burdett as a warrior-citizen made the link even more explicit.[28] Williams sticks with contemporary dress, but makes much of Burdett's Roman nose and elegant frame, and even his hairstyle is rich with political meaning. John Gale Jones noted the instance of a dance in Maidstone, when 'a young gentleman' was refused a dance with an aristocratic lady on these grounds: 'I perceive, Sir, from your hair (he was a *crop*), that your principles are different from mine; I must, therefore decline the honour you intend'.[29] Such was the politics of style in the 1790s. By the 1800s, neo-classicism was all the rage in men's fashion. Burdett's statuesque pose is underlined by his long shapely leg and what Anne Hollander describes as 'the ubiquitous Classical lunge – one leg bent in front, the other straight behind', an attitude copied from Greek vases and Roman mosaics. Men's breeches and waistcoats at this time gave the impression of long-leggedness, emphasising the prominence of the genitals.[30] While sexual attraction was clearly one motivation for this fashion, it also had political implications: *virtus*, of course, comprehended masculine virility as well as public virtue. Gillray, by contrast, emphasises the characteristically short-legged fashion of the eighteenth century in his send-up of Thomas Tyrwitt Jones. When we compare this pair of prints, it is Burdett who exudes classical-republican manliness. Burdett's deportment also contrasts forcibly with that of his opponent Mainwaring, cast in the mould of the cringing thwarted villain of popular theatre.

Both Gillray's Jones and Williams's Burdett are heroic and manly in their way, and the two have much in common. Both laud openness, patriotism and principled defiance. But these prints also illustrate two different types of independence. The former is in the bellicose and bucolic mould. Jones's large round hat, scruffy long coat and half-boots, together with his corpulent build and rustic directness, are suggestive of the eighteenth-century country gentleman. Nineteenth-century critics such as Thomas Babington Macaulay would commonly portray the Georgian independent country gentleman MP in this manner, as a self-consciously alien presence at the metropolitan centre of power who was addicted to provincial autonomies and the unrefined pleasures of the field and the table.[31] Gillray's humorous portrayal also suggests that *this* sort of independence was considered slightly ridiculous by the turn of the century, a form of licensed 'rudeness' that was by then a fond anachronism. We will further explore this changing image of the country gentleman in later chapters.

This is not to say that 'independence' ceased to be a prized personal quality, however, nor that 'independent men' were no longer regarded as the repository of national virtue and the bulwark against oppression. Williams's picture of Burdett presents a slightly later image of manly independence, and from the perspective of adulation rather than satire. The independent man remains heroically defiant, but does not lack cultivation, sincerity or moral character. Although Burdett is of higher rank than Jones, his independence is not primarily conferred by his acreage but by the strength of his conviction and the loftiness of his motives. Later generations would eschew the showy sexuality of Regency dress for plainer attire, but Burdett's demeanour pointed towards the future. Victorian politicians would similarly have to demonstrate their independence and manliness at the hustings and dispatch box, and would continue do so by means of bodily performance. It is interesting to note that Walker's *Academic Speaker* had a bearing on this later golden age of parliamentary oratory. It counted Gladstone and Disraeli among its admirers, and pictures of Gladstone speaking at school and in the Commons suggest that he put Walker's visual prescriptions vividly into practice.[32] The political world, therefore, should be regarded as a stage upon which masculine identities were brought into being.

Political manliness in action: electoral independence

The main opportunity for ordinary Georgian men to demonstrate their independence was the election contest. It was here that they were able to enact their political ideals in a tangible way and to put their 'Country' convictions to the test. The notion of 'the independent man' should be central to our understanding of the Hanoverian electoral system, since it dominated the language of election contests and sheds important light upon expectations of behaviour in this context. Conversely, the culture of elections should also be central to any account of manly independence, since late-Georgian understandings of political virtue and citizenship were fundamentally preoccupied with the exercise of the parliamentary franchise. Indeed, it was the *electoral* incarnation of the independent man that dominated Whig and radical thinking on parliamentary reform, so it is worth exploring this phenomenon in detail.

Electoral sources from this period are pervaded by the language of 'independence'. Voters and candidates alike repeatedly claim to be 'independent' and to be acting in an 'independent' manner; voters are conventionally addressed as 'the worthy and independent freeholders'; and everybody claimed that they had the 'independence' of the constituency itself in view. The student of this material, however, has difficulty finding in the historiography satisfactory answers to the question of what electoral independence *was*. On the one hand, psephological historians have regarded 'independence' as a pattern of voting behaviour and 'independent' as the type of voter who behaves this way. In order to render voting amenable to statistical analysis, such historians have often conceptualised electoral behaviour simplistically: as 'deferential' (voters who obey their superiors) or 'independent' (voters who do not, thus making the system 'participatory').[33] Historians of radical politics, on the other hand, have approached independence from the perspective of popular political ideas. Voters' insistence that they should be politically free, they argue, constitutes an immature radical consciousness, since they employed traditional methods to oppose local elites: it was therefore a stage on the way to genuine working-class activism.[34] A more nuanced approach is taken by Frank O'Gorman in his revisionist account of the pre-1832 electorate, *Voters, Patrons and Parties*. O'Gorman argues that 'independence' was an integral aspect of the Hanoverian electoral system, as both a type of conflict and as an ideology. He argues that the system was dominated at the local level by powerful interests, but that this was tempered by habits of independence among the electorate. In particular, in constituencies where interests sought the nomination of both seats, and where voters felt that their reciprocal relations with their patron had broken down, voters could mount an 'independent' protest by seeking a populist candidate to break the local monopoly.[35]

None of these three models defines electoral independence adequately. Fundamentally, they do not fit many of the constituencies where the language of 'independence' was all-pervasive. The psephological model is too clear-cut, since 'independence' was not incompatible with deference and all participants claimed to epitomise the former: are we to assume that objectively 'dependent' voters were being dishonest? Proponents of the second model are correct to consider 'independence' as an ideology, but the assumptions that 'independence' was an underdeveloped version of something else (proto-radical) and the expression of a social stratum (proto-class) are unhelpful.[36] O'Gorman's model is not universally applicable either, since relatively few contests fit the ideal-type of a 'third man' taking on an oligarch, whereas the *culture* of electoral independence was perceptible throughout the country. All of these models selectively impose the label 'independent' upon certain groups rather than examining participants' professions on their own terms, missing the richness of the notion 'independence' and of electoral culture more broadly.

More problematically, 'what' and 'why' remain unclear. Electoral independence should be considered alongside the broader culture of manly independence. 'Independence' provided a critique of obligation, which was conceived of in terms of a highly gendered model of freedom, honour and virtue. Voters maintained that if they were not represented effectually, they were subject to the arbitrary will of their governors. They thus become dependent, which absolutely compromises their liberty and dignity: as individuals, they cease to be genuine 'freemen'; as a borough, city, or county, they lose their honour, privileges and autonomy. Voters therefore drew upon a shared culture of manly virtue and individualism in order to legitimise the act of defying those who would seek to deny them their electoral freedom: this could take the form of supporting

O'Gorman's 'third man', but was also a culture that could powerfully be drawn upon by voters and candidates from established interests. This was not the natural or inevitable response to political oligarchy. The recourse to 'independence' was only possible within the context of a political culture suffused with 'Country' and neo-classical emphases, in which obligation was oppressive and an affront to masculine honour.

The culture of electoral independence, therefore, offered a comprehensive analysis of the voter's proper place in the electoral system, and the course of action that should be taken when this was not respected. In particular, independents opposed corruption or oligarchical ambition among the local political elite. The fact that their opponent was commonly a powerful patron, employer or landlord has led some historians to conclude that independence reflected a 'class' resentment at dependence upon the landed elite.[37] Independence, however, was not an egalitarian creed. It did not protest at the existence of traditional power, but at its perceived abuse. Indeed, when Sir Francis Burdett broke Middlesex's electoral monopoly in the 1800s, the independents contrasted his *true* nobility with that of his opponents. 'Of Sir Francis Burdett *personally*', they noted, 'we know that he is no mushroom Baronet, but of a stock very nearly as old as the creation of the Order'. Furthermore, the fact that 'his estate is very ample' ensures his disinterested attachment to their cause, since 'he is *no dependant*'.[38] The cause of electoral independence sometimes needed a champion to stand against the tools of oligarchy, whom voters could freely recognise with their independent suffrages, and a substantial gentleman usually fitted the bill.

The culture of electoral independence can also be regarded as being socially conservative in other respects. Independents sought the return of a past age when existing community relationships functioned properly, rather than the establishment of a new social order. The notion of a lost 'golden age' was a recurring theme in English culture in this period, and an enduring tradition of radicalism and reform sought to restore what was seen as a perfect ancient constitution that had been perverted by centuries of corruption. The independent candidate Mr S. Colleton Graves, for example, addressed the electors of Devon in 1812, evoking a time 'ere England's griefs began', when elections were conducted fairly and Englishmen were 'too honest to receive bribes'. He modelled his own political conduct on this mythical golden age, arriving at the nomination unannounced to force a contest by appealing to 'the Yeomanry of Devon'.[39] Candidates like Graves claimed to purge evil from the community and to re-establish a lost consensus. 'Independence' stood for the repudiation of corruption and historical decline, and the restoration of lost values: it was a backward-looking political creed. This serves to underline the indebtedness of Georgian politics to the classical-republican tradition, which characteristically views time in cyclical rather than progressive terms, a worldview in which masculinity is unstable and embattled.[40]

The 'independent' values of Georgian electors were offended by any attempt to violate the norms of local electoral life. In constituencies where a peer, employer or patron enjoyed a dominant electoral interest, he was in danger of incurring the wrath of independency. A patron who nurtured a borough in expectation of controlling its parliamentary representation had to tread very carefully when dealing with the voters, who were sensitive to patrician arrogance. Earl Grosvenor routinely nominated two candidates to the electors of Shaftesbury, whom they accepted after making a show of assessing their suitability. In 1820, however, he went too far: 'two strangers were again introduced, without any previous intimation or satisfactory explanation'. Independency was resorted to in Shaftesbury as the electors pledged 'to elect a man of their own choice', and an alternative candidate was sought to champion the independence of the town.[41]

There were many ways in which a patron or landlord could dominate a borough in order to control its parliamentary representation. Most constituencies returned two members, so if only two candidates stood they would be declared elected without the voters being polled. Powerful local families sought to avoid the need for an expensive contest by agreeing to share the two seats between them: this had the virtue of promoting consensus at the local level, but many voters were appalled that they were not consulted. Given that the seats were commonly split between a Whig and a Tory, voters believed that they effectively cancelled each other out, giving the constituency no weight in parliament. In some constituencies, like Shaftesbury, an independent 'third man' was sought to break the local monopoly. More generally, coalitions between local parties contravened electoral decorum, and 'backstairs' deals offended voters' normative sense of manly openness. Opposing such an alliance could be portrayed as an independent cause, such as at the Sussex context in 1820:

> Freeholders of the County of Sussex! hasten to the poll at Chichester! – Give plumpers for Mr. Compton Cavendish! – Destroy the Coalition which has been formed between Burrell and Curteis against your rights and liberties! – Let your cry be no Coalition – Cavendish and Independence for ever.[42]

Interference in the electorate, such as manipulating the creation of freemen, 'splitting' properties to create more voters, or importing

'foreigners' from outside the borough similarly offended voters, conscious of their corporate identity and the value of their franchises. More
seriously, there were examples of powerful figures exercising their local
social and economic power coercively against voters who defied their
wishes, by interfering in trade or evicting tenants.[43] In an electoral system
that relied so heavily on local social and economic relationships, electoral
independence's claim that freedom of election and community welfare
were intimately linked was comprehensible.

More than being a strategy or an ideology, however, electoral independence was primarily a lived role. Election contests provided the most
concrete opportunity for Georgian men to bring their 'independent' masculine identities to life, in a context where their actions could be seen as
having a direct bearing upon the nation's political destiny. It was a fundamental aspect of their *citizenship*, a category that enables us to understand
how self-identities were located within the larger collectivities of the
nation and the polity. In the electoral context, independence had several
connotations. Fundamentally, it was a question of liberty. The form of
liberty in question was of a classical kind, since it concerned freedom
from political obligation, or 'slavery'. Liberty was a manly condition,
voters were told, whereas political dependence was contemptible: 'MEN
in Independence bred ... Men who nought but slav'ry dread, On to
Victory'.[44] Independents presented the voters' choice in stark terms, to
make voting for their opponents inconceivable: 'An old Freeman anxious
for the *Independence* of the electors of the city of Durham, wishes to ask
them two questions, – Do you mean to be *Slaves*; or do you wish to be
Free? – If the former, vote for *Taylor*'.[45] The related vocabulary of 'yokes',
'bondage', 'thraldom' and 'vassalage' all recurred in electoral rhetoric, and
allowed electoral independents to identify their story with other struggles. Georgian voters identified themselves, not with contemporary negro
slaves in the Americas,[46] but with the Israelites of the Old Testament.
Linda Colley has noted how eighteenth-century Britons similarly saw
themselves as a chosen people, and Biblical tropes – especially relating to
the 'Israel in Egypt' romance – pervade the language of elections.[47]

Secondly, electoral independence involved manly self-assertion.
Georgian elections could be violent affairs, and even patrician candidates
were expected to get involved in the rough-and-tumble physicality.
Sugden described the violence of Weymouth's elections as if it were a
manly game, declaring 'I love to see a collision of the people, it evinces
that independence that is so dear to an Englishman'. The sporting
metaphor was commonly employed, since elections similarly involved a
disciplined struggle that celebrated manliness and abided by its own code

of honour, even to the extent of having 'team' colours.[48] Given that electoral street theatre was known to degenerate into pitched battles, military metaphors were also common. At Durham, Trevor looked forward to the victory of 'one who is now manfully fighting the battle of your real independence – for one who has dared to raise the banner of independence against one who has long – too long, ruled over its destinies'.[49]

Electoral independence prided conscientiousness. Shrewsbury's voters were instructed that 'Your Consciences demand of you the Free Unbiassed exercise of your judgement, in the important Choice of a Representative in Parliament'.[50] 'Reason', 'judgement' and 'reflection' were contrasted with the effects of demagoguery and of drink, one of the many forms of electoral treating.[51] Finally, models of male conduct were proposed with regard to the treatment of women and other dependants. 'Gallantry' was contrasted with implied sexual danger. Materials relating to the Liverpool election of 1796 particularly dwelt on this theme, as the more conservative candidates equated radicalism with the reported atrocities of the French Revolutionaries: 'If you have any regard for your Wives and your innocent and helpless Little Ones, Vote for Col. Gascoyne and John Tarleton, Esq'.[52] Such language was often explicitly melodramatic: in common with their theatrical heroes, voters were encouraged to prove their manliness by rushing to the defence of vulnerable and virtuous femininity. The constituency itself was also conceived of in the feminine, in order to motivate independent men to vindicate her (and their) honour.[53]

Electoral independence, therefore, was fundamentally a lived role: at election time, participants were instructed literally to 'act the part of Honest Independent Men'.[54] These sources often convey a sense that it was necessary to *prove* one's independence, to demonstrate it physically in some way. It is worth quoting at length from a Sussex handbill of 1820:

HONOR AND INDEPENDENCE!!
To the Worthy and Independent Freeholders of Chichester and its Vicinity.
GENTLEMEN,
You have now an opportunity of shewing to the world, whether your minds are guided by sordid interest and servile dependence, or loyal freedom, manly independence, and honor; that is, if you prefer wretched slavery, to liberty, despotic tyranny to noble Magna Charta, and the being deprived of your rights as Englishmen, to the blessings of a free, peaceful, and true old English constitution, then oppose Sir Godfrey, cry down virtue, and trample on independence: but if on the contrary, you wish to act like Britons, stand forward for your rights, forget

not that you are men, let truth, loyalty and freedom be your motto; and when the day of the contest shall arrive, prove to the world, by voting for Sir Godfrey Webster, that your principles are just, loyal, free, and uninterested.[55]

Voters are encouraged to 'shew', to 'act', to 'stand forward' and to 'prove to the world'. This passage constructs the act of voting for Sir Godfrey Webster as a way of publicly performing one's sense of honour and patriotism, in a context where the fate of the nation was at stake: an act of electoral independence to demonstrate one's personal independence.

Election contests provided many ritualised opportunities for men to manifest their manly independence. The canvass, for example, had many functions. For the voter, temporarily freed from the constraints of deference, it was an opportunity to assess the candidate. From the candidate's perspective, it was an opportunity to persuade, to extract promises, to exert implicit influence and – in smaller electorates – to gauge numerically their prospects of success.[56] The canvass purportedly enabled the candidate to pay his compliments to the elector and to acknowledge his independence: this was of such symbolic importance that canvasses took place even when there was no threat of a contest.[57] The voter's identity as an independent political subject could not be infringed, so the canvass was a delicately balanced performance. Both candidate and voter were placed in highly ritualised roles, which bore little relation to the actual relative extents of their political, social or economic power. David Stoker notes how candidates sought to maintain a 'genial and respectful, perhaps even deferential' air throughout, even with an uncooperative voter.[58] Candidates could not afford to offend their sensibilities by appearing to be overbearing, arrogant or inattentive. The ideal of behaviour in this situation may be gleaned from this glowing description of S. A. Bayntun at York in 1830:

> The principles he came forward to advocate contributed much to his popularity; and his gentlemanly manners, – the candour, urbanity, and manly frankness of his conduct, – won for him the 'golden opinions' from all classes . . . his canvass was conducted on the most honourable principles, that all the votes which were given him were given from the pure, unbiassed, independent will of the freemen, – A GREATER, A MORE GLORIOUS, TRIUMPH OF PRINCIPLE CANNOT BE IMAGINED.[59]

This account paints an idealised picture where both the candidate and the voter were playing the part of independent men, albeit in different moulds. The 'candour' and 'manly frankness' of the candidate suggest the straightforwardness and plain-dealing of the independent man; whereas the voter apparently reserved the right to conscientious self-determination in the exercise of his vote.

Voting itself could be a formidably confrontational event and was the primary opportunity for Georgian men to prove their manly independence. The practice of open voting demanded that voters declare their choice in public. This vote was recorded and the information was often made available – complete with name, address and occupation – in printed poll books. Should a voter choose to defy the wish of an employer, patron, or landlord, they would have to bear the consequences. Although actual reprisals were rare, voters were aware that they were accountable for their choice. It was regarded as actively desirable that men should openly perform their choice, and that it should be made known to their community. As if they needed reminding, electoral propaganda constantly reiterated the theme that voters were 'bound to perform that duty with boldness and openness'.[60]

Besides being a public act, the performance of declaring one's choice was further heightened by other aspects of polling. Firstly, the voter would have to get to the place of polling. At Weymouth elections in the 1820s, voters were required to display considerable fortitude in getting past a crowd that contained drunken partisans and hired thugs: there were numerous instances of respectable freeholders reaching the poll in ripped and sweat-soaked garments. Once they had reached the poll and endured a considerable wait, voters had to present themselves to the returning officer. This would either take place at the hustings itself or in a polling booth. The latter became more common in later years and afforded more protection from the crowd, but the voter still faced the candidates and an assortment of legal, civic and electoral personnel.[61] The voter would have to declare his name and – until prior registration was established in 1832 – the returning officer would demand his qualification. The parties' counsel would then have the opportunity to challenge the elector's right to vote, and to intimidate him further. If the voter's qualifications could not be dismissed, then the party lawyers could demand that one or more of a series of oaths be administered – relating to bribery, allegiance, supremacy, abjuration, transubstantiation and the veracity of his qualification. These oaths could be employed tactically to stall proceedings and intimidate voters, but were hugely significant in themselves. Oaths were performances with strict conventions and were an important aspect of Georgian political and legal culture. Besides the importance of personal honour, a declaration before God was a profoundly significant act in such a religious society. Only after fighting past crowds, defying lawyers and swearing before the Almighty could the elector declare how he wished to vote. This was the climax of his personal electoral performance and could well have been greeted by the acclamation of the surrounding crowds.

The ideal of 'the independent man', therefore, had important implications for the ways in which Georgian men conceived of themselves and the ways in which they should behave. The struggle for independence structured the stories that they told themselves about their own lives and – in particular – about the political contests in which their manly subjectivities were vividly brought to life. So far we have encountered some of the salient aspects of manly independence, a culture that was remarkably pervasive and enduring. 'Independence', however, was constantly subject to redefinition and debate, and the following chapters will chart the important shifts in the meaning of this key concept between the seventeenth and the nineteenth centuries. The questions of who was independent, what qualities they possessed, and what responsibilities they could be entrusted with, had profound implications for the nature of citizenship. Upon the definition of independence hinged the relationship between the worlds of gender and politics.

Notes

1 Sir John Carr, *Descriptive Travels in the Southern and Eastern Parts of Spain and the Balearic Isles, in the Year 1809* (London, 1811), pp. 19–20.

2 For example: L. Davidoff and C. Hall, *Family Fortunes: Men and Women of the English Middle Class, 1780–1850* (London: Routledge, 1987); V. Jones, 'The seductions of conduct: pleasure and conduct literature', in R. Porter and M. Roberts (eds), *Pleasure in the Eighteenth Century* (Basingstoke: Macmillan, 1996), pp. 77–107.

3 On male advice literature from the Victorian period, see John Tosh's *A Man's Place: Masculinity and the Middle-Class Home in Victorian England* (New Haven: Yale University Press, 1999), especially the bibliography pp. 231–3.

4 See Philip Carter, *Men and the Emergence of Polite Society 1660–1800* (Harlow: Longman, 2001), pp. 4–5.

5 George Ensor, *The Independent Man: Or, An Essay on the Formation and Development of those Principles and Faculties of the Human Mind which Constitute Moral and Intellectual Excellence*, 2 vols (London, 1806), vol. I, pp. 1, 11–12, 97–9, 211–12.

6 Ensor, *Independent Man*, vol. II, p. 343; pp. 290–2.

7 *Political Register* 8 (12 October 1805).

8 William Cobbett, *Advice to Young Men, and (Incidentally) to Young Women, in the Middle and Higher Ranks of Life* (1829), new edn (London, 1878), pp. 14, 12, 307, 37, 261, 259, 29.

9 William Cobbett, 'Boxing' in *Selections from Cobbett's Political Works*, ed. J. M. Cobbett and J. P. Cobbett, 6 vols (London 1835), vol. II, pp. 11–17.

10 Jones, 'Seductions of conduct'.

11 For example, William Green, *Plans of Economy; Or, a Guide to Riches . . . and Indepen-dence* (London, 1800); John Bone, *The Friend of the People . . . Recommending them to Adopt More Effectual Measures for Securing their Own Independence* (London, 1807); *The Political Primer; Or, Road to Public Honours* (London, 1826).

12 For example, the diaries of Edward Herford and Edwin Waugh: Tosh, *A Man's Place*, p. 111; P. Joyce, *Democratic Subjects: The Self and the Social in Nineteenth-Century England* (Cambridge: Cambridge University Press, 1994), Part 1.

13 For example, the memoirs of Henry Hunt and Thomas Holcroft: Henry Hunt, *Memoirs of Henry Hunt, Esq. Written by Himself, in His Majesty's Jail at Ilchester, in the County of Somerset*, 3 vols (London, 1822; reprinted Bath: Chivers, 1967); [Thomas Holcroft and William Hazlitt], *The Life of Thomas Holcroft*, ed. E. Colby, 2 vols (London: Constable, 1925).

14 *Political Primer*, p. iv.

15 John Walker, *The Academic Speaker . . . To Which is Prefixed, Elements of Gesture*, 3rd edn (London, 1797), pp. i, ix. I am grateful to Karen Harvey for this reference.

16 Quintessentially, E. Goffman, *The Presentation of Self in Everyday Life* (New York: Doubleday, 1959). For critiques of Goffman, see R. Schechner, *Between Theater and Anthropology* (Philadelphia: Pennsylvania University Press, 1985), p. 96; Hetherington, *Expressions of Identity: Space, Performance, Politics* (London: Sage, 1998), pp. 150–1.

17 Schechner, *Between Theater and Anthropology*, ch. 2.

18 J. Butler, *Excitable Speech: A Politics of the Performative* (London: Routledge, 1997), p. 10.

19 G. Cross, *Next Week – East Lynn: Domestic Drama in Performance 1820–1874* (Lewis-burg: Bucknell University Press, 1977); G. Taylor, *Players and Performances in Victorian Theatre* (Manchester: Manchester University Press, 1989).

20 P. Brooks, 'Melodrama, Body, Revolution', in *Melodrama: Stage, Picture, Screen* (London: British Film Institute, 1994), p. 19. See also T. Cassidy and C. Brunström, '"Playing is a Science": eighteenth-century actors' manuals and the proto-sociology of emotion', *British Journal for Eighteenth-Century Studies* 25:1 (2002), pp. 19–32.

21 Henry Siddons, *Practical Illustrations of Rhetorical Gesture and Action* (London, 1822), pp. 27, 97.

22 J. Fliegelman, *Declaring Independence: Jefferson, Natural Language, and the Culture of Performance* (Stanford: Stanford University Press, 1993).

23 J. Barish, *The Anti-Theatrical Prejudice* (Berkeley: California University Press, 1981), chs 8 and 10.

24 *The Norwich Election Budget* (Norwich, 1830), pp. 57, 18.

25 R. G. Thorne (ed.), *The House of Commons 1790–1820* (London: Secker and Warburg, 1986), vol. IV, pp. 324–7.

26 D. Donald, *The Age of Caricature: Satirical Prints in the Reign of George III* (New Haven: Yale University Press, 1996), p. 39.

27 Cross, *Next Week – East Lynn*, p. 121.

28 William Heath, 'Modern St. George Attacking the Monster of Despotism' (see cover) and Robert Cruikshank 'The Champion of Westminster defending the People' (figure 5).

29 John Gale Jones, *Sketch of a Political Tour Through Rochester, Chatham, Maidstone, Gravesend, &c.* (1796), ed. Philip MacDougal (Rochester: Baggins, 1997), p. 36.

30 Anne Hollander, *Seeing Through Clothes* (Berkeley: University of California Press, 1993), p. 227.

31 T. B. Macaulay, *The History of England from the Accession of James the Second* (1849–61) ed. C. Frith, 6 vols (London: Macmillan, 1913–15), vol. I, ch. 3.

32 G. Wickham, 'Gladstone, oratory, and the theatre', in P. Jagger (ed.), *Gladstone* (London: Hambledon, 1998), pp. 1–31.

33 Norma Landau, 'Independence, deference, and voter participation: the behaviour of the electorate in early eighteenth-century Kent', *Historical Journal* 22:3 (1979), pp. 561–83; W. Speck, *Tory and Whig: The Struggle in the Constituencies 1701–1715* (London: Macmillan, 1970); J. A. Phillips, *Electoral Behavior in Unreformed England: Plumpers, Splitters, and Straights* (Princeton: Princeton University Press, 1982).

34 N. Rogers, 'Aristocratic clientage, trade and independency: popular politics in pre-radical Westminster', *Past and Present* 61 (1973), pp. 70–106; John Belchem, *'Orator' Hunt: Henry Hunt and English working-class radicalism* (Oxford: Clarendon, 1985), p. 3; M. Philp, 'The fragmented ideology of reform', in his *The French Revolution and British Popular Politics* (Cambridge: Cambridge University Press, 1991), pp. 50–77 (pp. 54, 65).

35 Frank O'Gorman, *Voters, Patrons, and Parties: The Unreformed Electorate of Hanoverian England* (Oxford: Oxford University Press, 1989), pp. 259–85. See also R. Sweet, 'Freemen and independence in English borough politics, c.1770–1830', *Past and Present* 161 (1998), pp. 84–115.

36 For example: Rogers, 'Aristocratic clientage', pp. 78–84; O'Gorman, *Voters, Patrons, and Patrons*, pp. 281–4; G. Rudé, *Hanoverian London 1714–1808* (London: Secker and Warburg, 1971).

37 H. T. Dickinson, *The Politics of the People in Eighteenth-Century Britain* (Basingstoke: Macmillan, 1994), p. 221.

38 *A Full Account of the Proceedings at the Middlesex Election,* 2nd edn (London, 1804), p. 8.

39 *The Spirit of Election Wit* (Exeter, c. 1812), pp. 54–5, 43.

40 Stefan Dudink, 'Masculinity, effeminacy, time: conceptual change in the Dutch age of democratic revolutions', in S. Dudink, K. Hagemann and J. Tosh (eds), *Masculinities in Politics and War: Gendering Modern History* (Manchester: Manchester University Press, 2004), pp. 77–95.

41 J. Rutter, *Swyer versus Rutter: A Plain Narration* (Shaftesbury, 1826–27), p. 7.

42 *Account of the Sussex Election, Held at Chichester, March 13, 1820 . . .* (Chichester, 1820), p. 102.

43 The expulsion of James Shrimpton from the Red Lion (renamed the Grosvenor Arms) in 1824 was long a grievance of Shaftesbury's Independents. See Rutter, *Swyer versus Rutter*, p. 8.

44 'Beaumont and Liberty' handbill (Northumberland, 10 May 1826), John Rylands University Library of Manchester (hereafter JRULM) SC10183E, no. 281.

45 *The Contest Being a Complete Collection of the Controversial Papers, Including Poems and Songs during the Contested Election for the City of Durham, in March 1800* (Durham, 1800), p. 9.

46 Electoral independents identified more with the emancipator than the emancipated in this instance: 'Shall Men who have petitioned for, and obtained the Abolition of the Sale of the poor degraded African, now render *their* aid to perpetuate their own ignoble chains? God forbid! Nature recoils at the idea of so terrible a crime'. Handbill (Shrewsbury, 22 May 1819), JRULM SC12068F, no. 126.

47 L. Colley, *Britons: Forging the Nation 1707–1837* (New Haven: Yale University Press, 1992); *Full Account . . . Middlesex*, p. 23. See also 'Chronicles of the Second Manchester Election' handbill (Manchester, 1835), Manchester Central Library (hereafter MCL) f1835/1A.

48 *Dorset County Chronicle* (14 February 1828); 'Alnwick Races' handbill (Northumberland, 17 March 1826), JRULM SC10183E, no. 61.

49 *Proceedings and Poll at the Durham City Election* (Durham, 1837), p. 31.

50 Handbill (Shrewsbury, 22 May 1819), JRULM SC12068F, no. 126.

51 *Ibid.*

52 *The Poll for the Election of Members* (Liverpool, 1796), p. 26.

53 'Advertisement Extraordinary' handbill (Shrewsbury, 13 February 1796), JRULM SC12068F, no. 29.

54 Handbill (Shrewsbury, 22 June 1819), JRULM SC12068F, no. 126.

55 *Account of the Sussex Election*, pp. 83–4.

56 A canvasser's book survives from the 1832 contest in Lyme Regis. The canvasser notes down the stated voting inclinations for eligible inhabitants of the borough, and the projected tally was very close to the actual result. In some cases, however, we read the entry 'Will not vote', suggesting an element of evasion or defiance: Dorset Record Office PE/LRM:C1/3.

57 D. Stoker, 'Elections and Voting Behaviour: A Study of Elections in Northumberland, Durham, Cumberland, and Westmorland, 1760–1832' (unpublished doctoral thesis, University of Manchester, 1980), pp. 65–6.

58 Stoker, 'Elections and Voting Behaviour', p. 66.

59 *The Poll for Members in Parliament, to represent the City of York* (York, 1830), pp. vii, xi.

60 *Speeches and Addresses of the Candidates for the Representation of the County of York . . .* (Leeds, 1826), p. 133.

61 A plan of a Westmorland polling booth is given in Stoker, 'Elections and Voting Behaviour', Table 3, p. 159.

3

From the Civil War to the Seven Years War

I T IS PRODUCTIVE TO EXPLORE 'manly independence' in a chronological manner, in order to show how these ideas were used in different ways at different times by commentators from a variety of political and philosophical traditions. Over the next six chapters we will see how 'independence' was a highly contested notion, and how perspectives on manliness, virtue and liberty could be very personal, but this was not merely a matter of representation: much was at stake in the contest over 'the independent man'. In particular, 'independence' and 'dependence' were key terms when it came to negotiating the questions of who should legitimately participate in politics, and what qualities and behaviours political actors should exhibit. Through this long chronological perspective, it is possible to identify both broad traditions of usage and long-term shifts in meaning. We will see how conceptions of what sorts of people were capable of 'independence' gradually became more socially inclusive, as the emphasis shifted from forms of property and personal acquirements that were only accessible to persons of rank, to 'inner' qualities that were within the reach of all men, if emphatically not women. As such, there was a concomitant shift in the political location of what it meant to be 'independent', as this manly virtue that had once been exclusively identified with the political class of legislators was increasingly located in the electoral citizenry, and even the national repository of 'manhood' itself. Furthermore, whereas 'independence' had once been the boast of those who opposed the establishment from without, it would eventually be regarded as a desirable quality in persons who should be incorporated within the official political system as loyal citizens.

This chapter foregrounds the post-1760 period with which this study is largely concerned, and much of this is necessarily brief and selective. My focus will be the seventeenth- and eighteenth-century cultures of political opposition in which the idea of 'independence' had such a prominent role, and which provided much of the cultural heritage for its later Georgian and Victorian advocates. By 'opposition' I do not just mean the regular, organised 'Opposition' in parliament – which was not termed thus before the 1730s – but the stance of anybody who criticised, and situated themselves outside of, the political status quo. This included professed Whigs and Tories, persons within and outside parliament, republicans and monarchists, Hanoverians and Jacobites, Anglicans and dissenters – all of whom employed this idiom in comparable ways.

More specifically, what I seek to emphasise in this chapter is the prominence of a particular way of thinking about the political, social and moral world: the paradigm of virtue and corruption. It was from this essentially neo-classical worldview that the notion of 'independence' – the state of virtue as a manly freedom from obligation – acquired much of its power. As we will see, this ideology of political masculinity also took on meaning from other contemporary cultural currents, such as politeness, sociability, sensibility and commerce. These should not, however, be regarded as alternatives to or replacements for 'independence', a notion that historians of a 'polite and commercial' England commonly relegate to the (somewhat essentialised) category of 'traditional masculinity' alongside violence, courage and boorishness.[1] Where the questions of *political* virtue, action and entitlement were concerned, 'independence' was the dominant consideration and the one that endured well beyond the early Georgian debate on manners. Indeed, it is possible to take the 'neo-classical' thesis further than J. G. A. Pocock and Quentin Skinner, upon whose work I draw explicitly throughout this study. Rather than being replaced by liberal individualism or fundamentally altered after its encounter with commercial progress, the ideal of manly independence endured well into the Victorian period, suggesting that the paradigm of virtue and corruption was very difficult to displace. In particular, this preoccupation with obligation and virtue ensured that the political world was viewed in fundamentally gendered terms – a consideration that would become more rather than less important as we look beyond the mid-eighteenth century.

Before the seventeenth century, 'independence' would have been an improbable political creed. The political, social, biological, and spiritual universes were generally conceived of as a single hierarchical system in which authority descended from God. On earth, monarchs topped the Chain of Being, with all the gradations below exercising this divinely appointed power over their inferiors. Rather than being regarded as fundamentally different creatures, men and women were regarded as inhabiting essentially the same bodies. In a world of slippery gender difference, men's authority over women was not grounded in a fundamentally different biology: they merely possessed a superior balance of bodily elements and occupied a higher place on the sliding scale of authority.[2] There was, however, some emphasis upon the liberties, rights, and virtues of the individual within the English political tradition. Finance-hungry monarchs had to contend with an elected parliament with an ever-growing conception of its remit: the attempts by James I and Charles I to reassert royal prerogative on the grounds of Divine Right were famously controversial, and will not be explored here. Futhermore, commentators had long asserted that English yeomen possessed a sturdy libertarianism that made them indomitable in battle but difficult to govern and tax: we will see how this tradition was peculiarly adaptable to later modes of opposition argument.[3]

The English Civil War was crucial to the development of this idea. 'Independent' was a religious, parliamentary and military label, but it was not in this sense that the term would endure into the eighteenth century. What was more significant was a paradigm shift in contemporary conceptions of the constitution. The King's answer to the Nineteen Propositions of Both Houses of Parliament of June 1642, for example, portrayed England's government as consisting of three estates which must be held in balance:

> There being three kinds of government among men, absolute monarchy, aristocracy and democracy, and all these having their particular conveniences and inconveniences, the experience and wisdom of your ancestors hath so moulded this out of a mixture of these as to give this kingdom (as far as human prudence can provide) the conveniences of all three, without the inconveniences of any one, as long as the balance hangs even between the three estates . . .

This was one of the first texts in which the English constitution was conceptualised in terms analogous to classical republics.[4] Polybius had conceived of the perfect mixed constitution as comprising a balance between monarchy, aristocracy and democracy. In the early modern world, Venice was regarded as the exemplar of this theory, but Britain's King, Lords and Commons would increasingly be identified with neo-Roman conceptions of constitutional balance, and would even overtake the Italian republics in this respect.

Neo-classical schemes of constitutional balance were generally informed by an Aristotelean conception of the polity as consisting of independent persons. The aristocracy and democracy should consist only of independent men, because dependent people – their wives, children, servants and slaves – have neither the freedom nor the *virtus* to act for the common good. Educated Englishmen in the seventeenth century were well versed in the classics, and in the works of the Renaissance neo-classicists. Renaissance theorists agreed that republics crumbled when the people became corrupt, but their accounts of political virtue were by no means homogeneous. Whereas the civic humanists argued that the citizen should resemble Cicero's 'good man', Niccolò Machiavelli valued civic virtue for political reasons alone and emphasised armigerousness as the basis for the citizen's claim to power.[5] English commentators drew eclectically from all of these traditions, however, and classical and neo-classical vocabularies entered mainstream political discourse. By the 1640s, radical ideologues in the army were conceiving of themselves as citizen-soldiers, and the Roman terminology of 'patriot' and 'commonwealthman' was being applied to persons who argued that the monarchical branch of the constitution should be resisted by the other two.

The Civil War writer who did more than anybody to bring neo-classical arguments to the English political mainstream was James Harrington. Pocock, for one, puts Harrington at the centre of his analysis of anglophone thought in the seventeenth and eighteenth centuries. In his great work of 1656, *The Commonwealth of Oceana*, Harrington depicted a utopian polity in which he merged classical and civic human-ist concepts with an idealised – if instantly recognisable – vision of England. Harrington argued that wide ownership of property enabled Oceana to move away from its feudal past into an era where general free-dom and security were guaranteed by participatory military and consti-tutional procedures. An 'equal agrarian' distribution of land ensured that a population of substantial independent cultivators grew up, to whom the balance of power in the state shifted:

> By the statute of population, all lovers of husbandry that were used with twenty acres of ground and upwards were to be maintained and kept up for ever . . . and the proportion of land to be tilled being kept up, did of necessity enforce the dweller not to be a beggar or a cottager, but a man of some substance, that might keep his friends and servants and set the plough on going. This did mightily concern . . . the might and man-hood of the kingdom, and in effect amortize a great part of the lands into the hold and possession of the yeomanry, or middle people, who, living not in a servile or indigent fashion, were much unlinked from dependence upon their lords.[6]

The population of the state consists of 'freemen or citizens' who partici-pate in the military and democratic life of the Commonwealth, and 'ser-vants' who do not. Harrington does not question this exclusion in

Oceana, arguing that the maxim that servitude is 'inconsistent with free-dom or participation of government in a commonwealth' requires 'no proof'. Only Aristotle's householders are free from dependence upon the will of another: votes in a democracy should be given by individuals who 'can neither oblige . . . nor disoblige another'.[7] The independent political personality of the citizen was founded upon his (classical) position as a householder and his (Machiavellian) ability to bear arms in defence of himself and the state, but both of these were predicated upon the owner-ship of an 'estate', or freehold landed property – a recognisably English addition to these classical and neo-classical considerations. With this type of free personality, participating in a system where elections are free and officials are frequently 'rotated', liberty in Oceana is assured.

Harrington thereby introduced into English political theory the notion that freehold land confers independence, and that the distribution of property in the state – and thus the distribution of its armed inde-pendent citizens – should reflect the balance of political power. The clas-sical connections between virtue, liberty and power were given a material basis that was relevant to English conditions, an emphasis that was to per-vade English political culture and theory for the coming two centuries. This was entirely congruent with earlier Civil War arguments about the rights and responsibilities of individuals. Cromwell and Ireton main-tained that only men who 'live a freeman without dependence' should vote in parliamentary elections, so that they may not be 'given up to the will of others'. Sir William Petty justified the exclusion of certain groups from the franchise in these terms: 'I conceive the reason why we would exclude apprentices, or servants, or those that take alms, is because they depend upon the will of other men and should be afraid to displease'.[8] The Levellers opposed property qualifications for electors, but similarly excluded servants and paupers, and did not dismiss the consideration of property. They argued that men were independent by their own labour, and that political enfranchisement was necessary to preserve men's own-ership of themselves, in which freedom consisted: contrary to C. B. Macpherson's reading, empowerment was only a question of property insofar as it made men independent.[9] As we shall see, the Levellers' posi-tion concerning property and self-ownership anticipated late-Georgian radical arguments, and so did their handling of gender. Far from being sexually liberationist, Leveller men emphasised their *masculine* virtue as husbands and householders when making their case for broad male enfranchisement.[10]

Alongside its impact upon English political ideology, the years of the Civil War had a lasting influence upon political practice. In particular, as

Mark Kishlansky has argued, the business of parliamentary 'selection' began to resemble the modern procedure of 'election'.[11] The choice of Members of Parliament in early modern England was a consensual matter, as the community 'gave voices' for their nominees: the practice of sending two members from each constituency served to accommodate local rivalries and contests – necessitated by the appearance of more candidates than seats – were usually avoided. Over the course of the Revolution and after 1660, however, the number of contests increased, so that voters had to make choices, and choices that had a bearing on the heated political situation. This constituted a new political role for elector and elected. The elector now possessed a valuable political privilege rather than a periodic social obligation, and was expected to exercise it in an informed way, but it was the MP whose role changed most markedly. The representative was expected to embrace electoral competition and to view political office in a more responsible way: this was a long way from outright accountability, but he was required to have a dialogue with those to whom he owed his seat. Between the mid-seventeenth and the mid-eighteenth century, the MP was regarded as the fundamental element of political life: the common good depended upon the virtues and capacities of the men who comprised this political class.

In the years following the Restoration, writers such as Walter Moyle, Andrew Marvell, and Harrington's friend and populariser Henry Neville reiterated neo-classical dictums in order to critique the enhanced powers of prerogative and of the established Church. In the context of the Exclusion Crisis, Danby's attempt to build up a 'Court' party in the Commons, and the debates upon oaths for dissenters, opposition arguments took on a decidedly classical tinge.[12] The Whig 1st Earl of Shaftesbury was central to what Pocock terms this 'neo-Harringtonian' restatement.[13] In a speech in parliament on 20 October 1675 he argued that the powers of the Crown were being asserted in order to undermine the Lords, the Commons, 'and the Properties and Liberties of the People', thus unbalancing 'the Constitution of the *Government*'.[14] The famous *Letter From a Person of Quality, To His Friend in the Country* (1675), which issued from his camp, moved into recognisably eighteenth-century modes of opposition argument. It argued that '*a distinct Party*' is monopolising 'all the Power and Office of the Kingdom', and is upsetting the constitutional balance by asserting the prerogative, maintaining a 'standing Army', and by influencing parliament by means of 'Courtiers, Officers, Pensioners' in the lower house and 'Officers, Court Lords, and Bishops' in the upper.[15] The emphases upon standing armies and corruption through influence are absent in *Oceana* – raising the question of how far they are 'neo-Harringtonian' at all – but are undoubtedly neo-classical. The permanent army was feared less as a direct instrument of oppression than as a threat to the constitutional balance; and the 'corruption' of parliament (in the sense of a perverted balance rather than just bribery) undermined both the Polybian balance of estates and the individual virtues of parliamentarians. As such, the *Letter* dwelt upon the virtues of Shaftesbury and his allies, whose disinterestedness was evinced by their 'Quality, Parts, and Fortune', and who 'spoke plain like *Old English Lords*'.[16]

Fundamentally, opposition texts from the 1670s wedded Civil War neo-classicism with beliefs in national exceptionalism and a perfect ancient constitution. These were absent from both mid-century writings and their Mediterranean antecedents.[17] Whereas Harrington had argued that a balanced constitution would be established at the death of feudalism, Shaftesbury's supporters argued that England possessed a mixed government of ancient provenance, from which Charles and his ministers were deviating – a claim far more appealing to the backbenchers whose support they sought.[18] Commentators in this period argued that constitutional freedom was a nationally exclusive tradition ('the great Liberty we enjoy as *English Men*') to which Catholicism was the foreign antithesis. Whig writers conflated popery both with traditional instruments of oppression (monarchical absolutism justified through divine right) and its more modern manifestations: a pamphlet of 1677 informed its readers that their enemies were 'young beggarly Officers, Courtiers, over-hot Churchmen, and Papists', all persons whose dependence and compromised masculinity allegedly posed a threat to general liberty.[19]

The period of the Glorious Revolution was of tremendous importance for Georgian political life, and much of eighteenth-century political culture would consist of a debate about its implications for the power of parliament, contractual government, state religion, and the liberties of the subject. The question of manly 'independence' is of course related to these considerations. Algernon Sidney's *Discourses of Government* (1698), for example, rejected Filmer's monarchical absolutism in favour of contractual libertarianism, and asserted a classical truism that would be quoted by opposition thinkers throughout the following century:

> For as liberty solely consists in an independency upon the will of another, and by the name of slave we understand a man, who can neither dispose of his person nor goods, but enjoys all at the will of his master; there is no such thing in nature as a slave, if those men or nations are not slaves, who have no other title to what they enjoy, than the grace of a prince, which he may revoke whenever he pleaseth.[20]

Just as classical theorists denied slaves freedom and an independent personality because they were dependent upon their master, so did opposition writers affirm that an individual or nation that depended upon the will of an arbitrary ruler was absolutely unfree.

Political debate in the era of the Glorious Revolution has attracted the attention of gender historians and feminist political scientists, because the political discourse on monarchical power and legitimacy was fundamentally gendered. Sir John Filmer's *Patriarcha* presented the classic case for Divine Right monarchy by emphasising the analogy between the place of the king in the state and the father in the family. Opponents of the absolutist case had therefore to engage with the relations between men and women. John Locke denied the connection between states and families and insisted that both were contractual relationships.[21] His conviction that marriage was consensual and companionate influenced early feminist thought, although modern feminists have contended that his separation of the public and private spheres merely reworked patriarchy into its modern 'liberal' form. Carole Pateman has argued that Locke's separation of family and state merely rendered men's domestic domination of women invisible, a domination that was justified in relation to sexual 'nature' rather than political authority.[22]

The eighteenth-century notion of manly independence, however, had a republican rather than a liberal genealogy: it had a lot less to do with the deposition of James II than it did with subsequent developments in government and the military under William III. The new monarch's continental commitments required a permanent military establishment, which necessitated innovations in state finance in order to fund it. The 'standing army' hereafter became a permanent figure in the rhetoric of those who claimed to speak for the interests of the 'Country' in opposition to those of the 'Court': as we will see, it would endure in English political argument into the nineteenth century. Not only did the army itself threaten to unbalance the constitution in favour of the executive, but the multiplication of offices and contracts increased the power of the government to create 'dependants' who were obliged to support the executive, and could therefore not act conscientiously in the interests of principle and the general good. 'Country' politicians' suspicions of professional land armies were related to their stance on foreign policy. Opponents of the new regime alleged that Britain's international interests were being expensively and unpatriotically sacrificed to 'continental connections', namely the land wars of William III and his Hanoverian successors: for many 'Country' Tories, this was amplified by their hatred of Britain's new foreign monarchs. They argued that Britain's security and prosperity lay in a 'blue water' policy of European isolationism and imperial trade, based upon a strong navy rather than a standing army.[23] Domestic security should instead be entrusted to a voluntary militia of independent citizen-soldiers, which was held to be both more effective than dependent (but not necessarily dependable) mercenaries, and to be constitutionally superior. Many eighteenth-century commentators would draw upon Harringtonian and Saxon precedents for a militia, arguing that it represented an opportunity for citizens to demonstrate their manly *virtus*, and a return to the practice of the ancient constitution.

The financial institutions established from the 1690s also had a profound impact upon notions of what constituted an 'independent man'. Again, the multiplication of bureaucrats ensured that more men held their offices at the pleasure of the executive, and the government's reliance upon credit added the 'stockjobber' and the 'fundholder' to the 'Country' list of corrupted, dependent personalities. These self-interested individuals, 'Country' theorists argued, were not only parasites upon the wealth of the people, but threatened liberty by unbalancing parliament and corrupting the nation's morals: independent, disinterested and patriotic individuals should speak out against them. The debates about finance from the late seventeenth century crystallised notions of how political personalities were predicated upon the ownership of specific forms of property. 'Country' theorists argued that the moveable wealth generated by the speculators and contractors of the financial revolution not only lubricated the workings of executive influence, but was unstable and impermanent. Such paper wealth was believed fundamentally to consist in an expectation on government, whether or not it came in the form of patronage: it never fully belonged to the holder so was not a basis for virtuous liberty.[24] Those who lived off the income of their land, on the other hand, were beholden to nobody. 'Country' theorists argued that property in land was stable and permanent, and was owned by the nation's natural legislators: opposition Whig and Tory figures alike supported landed property qualifications for MPs, a socially exclusive measure that was felt to be conducive to liberty since it sought to keep out the corruptible newly moneyed. Viscount Bolingbroke, for example, later justified the Qualification Act in these terms:

> [The Act] requires that every Member for a Borough shall have 300 *l.* *per Annum*, and for a County, 600 *l. per Annum*; a Law, which was intended to confine the Election to such Persons as are *independent in their Circumstances*; have a valuable Stake in the *Land*; and must therefore be the most strongly engaged to consult the *publick Good*, and least liable to *Corruption*.[25]

Landed property connoted a 'Stake' in the nation, giving the owner an almost organic relationship with the countryside and the dependants that dwelt upon it. Land also connoted rural virtue, as celebrated by classical republicans and agrarians such as Harrington. 'Country' theorists – punning nation and countryside – made this a central plank of their critique,[26] and eighteenth-century popular culture maintained that the city was the seat of vice, luxury and death, whereas the countryside embodied the traditional Old English values of purity, benevolence and healthy vigour. Different political groups interpreted the Lord of the Soil in different ways, but they all assumed that the wealthy had superior claims to political virtue: Commonwealthmen praised the substantial freeholder-citizen; Great Whigs, the noble landowner; and Tories, the country gentleman. For 'independence' to become a more socially accessible idea, notions of what constituted propertied and rural virtue had substantially to be rethought.

'Old Whigs' accused the regime of betraying the principles of the Revolution, and contrasted themselves with the 'New' executive Whigs, who dominated the governments of William and the first two Georges. Whereas the New Whigs identified freedom with commerce, progress and the state, Old Whigs clung to a classical-patriot notion of liberty: they argued that virtue existed in the past and was in constant danger of corruption by those who wielded power, so faith should only be placed in the independent 'outs'.[27] Old Whigs believed that the events of 1688–89 reaffirmed the right to resist tyranny and the power of parliament over the monarchy, and reiterated opposition Whig beliefs in the independence of the representative and the dangers of executive influence.

Before we enter the Georgian period, it is worth noting the contemporary vogue for politeness, which had important implications for the gendering of political virtue and interaction. Its enthusiasts sought to promote a code of polite conduct that would enable easy conversation between individuals. Formerly the preserve of the court, civility was mobilised more widely in order to promote venues of association beyond its narrow confines: the clubs, coffee houses, and assemblies of 'the Town' were physical spaces in which gentlemen could conceive of themselves as constituting an independent, politicised public.[28] The culture of politeness thus had an oppositional potential, but one that was still socially exclusive. The 3rd Earl of Shaftesbury argued that this polite public represented a means by which gentlemen could exercise a cultural authority – a Whiggish alternative to the traditional forms of genteel power, the Church and the court. This was, however, emphatically a hegemony of the 'better sort' who, he claimed, naturally exercised a superior moral sensibility.[29] In this sense, cultivation was conducive to political freedom. Addison and Steele's opposition Whig periodicals the *Tatler* and *The Spectator* promoted this culture more widely, and achieved an avid middling-rank readership. As these 'polite Whigs' saw it, citizenship could be based upon urbanity, civility and commerce (in the sense of interaction rather than just trade). This model of political manliness was promoted as a progressive alternative to the more backward-looking prescriptions of Tories and patriots, who held these values in opprobrium. Recent historians of early eighteenth-century society and culture are certainly right to place 'politeness' at the centre of their narratives. Since this chapter is primarily concerned with the influences upon the post-1760 political world, however, it will give manners rather shorter shrift. As we will see, the 'patriot' ideal of a community of independent freeholders was paradoxically more appealing to late-Georgian political reformers than the – ostensibly more modern – polite varieties of Whiggery.

Although the advocates of politeness sought to achieve a synthesis between exterior refinement and inner virtue, many Georgians retained a suspicion of polish. A good example of this attitude is the 1737 stage play, *The Independent Patriot: Or, Musical Folly*. This comedy paints a comprehensive picture of the early Georgian cultural scene from the 'Country' perspective. The hero, Ned Medium, is 'Impartial in his Legislative capacity, Zealous in the genuine Interest of his Country, and a Despiser of the Covetous of all Party Denominations': he is 'an enemy of Corruption, and the False Taste of the Age'. His antithesis is the foppish Addle, who is obsessed with Italian opera, French witticisms and the niceties of politeness. Addle is 'a genuine Favourite with the Ladies', but the sensible Julia is resistant to his charms and it falls to her to pass judgement on the characters. When her companion notes that Medium 'may be a Man of Sense; but I swear he's an utter Stranger to Politeness', Julia makes a scornful aside: 'Mystery of Politeness! Ha, ha, bless us! What will this Creature be when she has grafted foreign Vanity on her Native Stock!' Needless to say, Julia recognises Medium's more substantial virtues and, at the conclusion of the play, makes her feelings known to her father: 'A truly virtuous Man will appear so in every Character of Life; he shines equally as a Lover, a Husband, a Son, a Father, a Friend, as a Patriot; he is slow in his Resolves, but steddy when he once determines . . . From these loose Hints, Guardian, you may guess at the sort of Man you're to choose for me'.[30] Julia rejects the polite man for the independent man who is straightforwardly virtuous in public and private life. In the world of virtue and corruption, refinement smacked of falsity, effeminacy, foreignness and obsequiousness. 'Independence' could be reconciled to politeness as a model of political manliness but, where constitutional action was concerned, it was certainly not replaced by it. Mid-Georgian England would have a 'Country' political culture, not a polite one, in which the independent man would take centre stage.

In the seventeenth century, 'independence' was not prominent in the English political vocabulary. By the eighteenth, it was ubiquitous. In particular, it was central to the ideological armoury of those who opposed the ruling oligarchy composed of the Hanoverian court and their favoured clique of executive Whigs, who employed the now-established system of clientage in order to dominate parliament. 'Country' opposition theorists argued that only 'independent men' – outside of and uncorrupted by Walpole's formidable network of patronage – had the freedom and manly virtue to speak out against the financially and morally corrupt ruling oligarchy. In this discursive context, 'independence' became a crucial element of a Georgian man's sense of political agency.

The 'Court' and 'Country' worldviews were by then well established, and had certain settled elements. 'Country' ideologues maintained that the branches of the constitution should retain their independence so that any threats to general weal could be checked. The Commons in particular was the bulwark of the balanced constitutional system, because it tapped the independence of 'the people' – specifically, the electorate composed of propertied male householders – in order to ensure that its own makeup was independent. MPs should guard their independence: free men acting virtuously, it was assumed, would always check any threats to liberty, property or security; whereas a person in a position of dependence was absolutely unfree to pursue these ends. The central conceptual binary in 'Country' thinking was classical: virtue versus corruption. The virtuous will oppose corruption, but virtue can be corrupted: in historical terms, 'corruption' is a story of decline from a past golden age, specifically the ancient constitution. Corruption connoted both moral degradation and a degeneration of order, and was identified with power and self-interest. Those who exercised power were inevitably driven to self-interest (the diametric opposite of 'the public good' and 'patriotism'), and so should constantly be monitored by those who do not. Self-interest manifested itself in many forms: ambition, venality, luxury (or unnecessary wants) and factious behaviour (including parties and preference for favourites). All of these undermined an individual's integrity, in the literal sense of a firm, bounded, independent personality. 'Faction' was the central political bugbear of an age when political parties were constitutionally suspect, and even a treasonable threat to the king's government. Thus

'Country' politicians undermined the instruments of the executive – patronage, standing armies and prerogative – and asserted their own superior moral rectitude, but also precluded any organisation, professionalisation, or even power-holding for themselves.

In England, 'Country' arguments were always counterbalanced by the 'Court' interpretation. Taking their strength both from Tory notions of monarchy and New Whig theories of executive government, 'Court' thinkers emphasised the fundamental *interdependence* of the branches of the constitution. The governing Whigs in particular argued that a strong executive was essential to the preservation of Protestantism, prosperity and progress. They reinterpreted 1688 in this light, playing down the right to resist and arguing that the Revolution established a new era of liberty: freedom was a modern phenomenon that their Whig forebears had wrested from tyrannical monarchs, rather than an ancient ideal that was being corrupted. Few New Whigs would dare openly to condemn independence, but an 'independent' protest from the floor of the House would doubtless have been considered disruptive: Walpole derided the professed patriotism of his critics as 'chimerical school-boy flights of classical learning'.[31] David Hume, on the Tory side of the 'Court' view, was more explicit. The use of parliamentary patronage, which the 'Country' theorists condemned outright, was necessary to keep the branches of the constitution in proper relation: 'We may, therefore, give to this influence what name we please; we may call it by the invidious appellations of *corruption* and *dependence*; but some degree and some kind of it are inseparable from the very nature of the constitution, and necessary to the preservation of our mixed government'. Far from being 'an infringement of BRITISH liberty', the interdependence within the constitution was fundamental to its survival.[32] Contrary to 'Country' convictions, virtue was a private business: a man could exercise probity in his private life and act for the general good without forgoing patronage or employment. Walpole himself cultivated a frank, unsophisticated masculine image that was somewhat at odds both with his vast wealth and with opposition portrayals of an arch-corruptor. As Chesterfield noted, he was 'good-natured, cheerful, social' in private life, 'whilst the impoliteness of his manner seemed to attest his sincerity'.[33]

A variety of groups who opposed the early Georgian Whig governments developed versions of the 'Country' model for this purpose. The opposition Whigs continued to condemn parliamentary influence, long parliaments and standing armies. The works of John Trenchard and Thomas Gordon, for example, achieved a wide readership in Britain and the American colonies. Their paper, the *Independent Whig*, claimed to 'have no manner of Attachment to any Party', and combined classical allusions with anticlerical and 'Country' tenets. An Independent Whig, they argued,

> scorns all implicit faith in the State, as well as the Church. The Author-
> ity of Names is nothing to him; he judges all Men by their Actions and
> Behaviour, and hates a Knave of his own Party, as much as he despises
> a Fool of another. He consents not that any Man or Body of Men, shall
> do what they please. He claims Right of examining all publick Measures
> and, if they deserve it, of censuring them. As he never saw much Power
> possessed without some Abuse, he takes it upon him to watch those that
> have it; and to acquit or expose them, according as they apply it to the
> Good of their Country, or their own crooked Purposes.[34]

Such was the early Georgian independent man: undeferential, forthright, suspicious of power, patriotic, and the monitor and repudiator of all political evil. Independent Whiggery was still, however, a genteel busi-ness: Trenchard was a wealthy countryman, and Gordon became one when he married Trenchard's widow (herself the daughter of a baronet). They appealed to 'the people', but the independent men whom they sought to address were also socially exclusive: 'by the people, I mean not the idle and indigent rabble under which name the people are often understood and traduced, but all who have property without the privi-leges of nobility'.[35] Thus we have one of the central paradoxes of early Georgian independence: on the one hand, 'the independent man' was free and refused to be spoken down to; on the other, he was himself a man of rank in a firmly hierarchical society. There was no sense that a claim to 'independence' entailed an end to 'dependence' for everybody else.

On this side of the Atlantic, however, the opposition Whigs were by no means the most popular or politically effective exponents of the 'Country' critique that their forebears had developed. In print, parlia-ment and the provinces, Tories expounded this Whiggish creed, however paradoxical this has seemed to historians: Robbins ignores them, and Skinner maintains that Bolingbroke's two decades as a 'Country' propa-gandist were entirely opportunistic.[36] It is doubtful that he stole the Whigs' clothes simply to demonstrate their apostasy, since the New Whigs had long distanced themselves from the Old. Rather, Bolingbroke appre-ciated the power of this idiom and became the leading proponent of the political culture of manly independence in the first half of the century. He was behind moves to create a 'Country party': something of a contradic-tion in terms, this was an anti-party that claimed to provide a focus for unambitious patriots, and a fulfilment of the pervasive desire for unity, loyalty and independence.[37] Moreover, Bolingbroke's writings were extremely effective, and figures as prominent as George III and Benjamin Disraeli were to cite him among their influences. In his contributions to the opposition paper the *Craftsman* (1726–34) he employed the 'Country' scheme in all its vividness, and reiterated how an individual should approach the world of politics.

Bolingbroke was concerned with both public and private virtue. In order to combat the 'corruption' that was corroding the constitution, representatives should demonstrate patriotism in public and selfless virtue as private men. In public life, MPs should possess landed property in order to guarantee their disinterestedness, and should exhibit 'the most hearty and disinterested Zeal' and 'a sedate and manly way of thinking' which 'apprehends all things'. In his personal life, an incorruptible man lives the life of 'great *Sobriety, Temperance, Oeconomy* and *Justice*'. He particularly commended a man who could speak 'with undaunted Courage the wise and generous sentiments of his Heart, whenever National affairs were under Deliberation, and thought it his greatest Glory to act the part of a *Briton*'.[38] For Bolingbroke, patriotic manly independence was a comprehensive model of being.

If the *Craftsman* envisaged independent men to be substantial squires, Bolingbroke's vision of personal independence had become even more socially elevated by the time of his famous writings on patriotism in the late 1730s. *On the Spirit of Patriotism* painted a vivid 'Country' picture of moral degeneration in Walpole's England, complaining of 'the general corruption, of the people, nursed up to a full maturity by his administration'. The 'prostitute' people cannot be trusted to save themselves, so should instead keep faith in a virtuous narrow elite:

> some men are in a particular manner designed to take care of that government on which the common happiness depends . . . it is the more incumbent on those who have this benevolence and this regard at heart, to employ all the means that the nature of government allows, and that rank, circumstances of situation, or superiority of talents, give them, to oppose evil, and promote good government.[39]

The message of his *Patriot King* (written in 1738) took independence to the very top of the political structure. Only a disinterested monarch, prepared to reject the practice of his predecessors and to govern 'independently of all parties', could rise above faction, unify the people, and govern for the good of all:

> It will be his aim to pursue true principles of government independently of all: and by a steddy adherence to this measure, his reign will become a undeniable and glorious proof, that a wise and good prince

may unite his subjects, and be himself the centre of their union, notwithstanding any of the divisions that have been hitherto mentioned.[40]

The political context for this plea was his attempt to forge an alliance with George II's successor, and there is more than a hint of the flattery that he professed to despise in this work.[41] Nevertheless, his appropriations of 'independence' and 'patriotism' were remarkable. These were ideas that had originated in efforts to *counter* executive power, by locating virtue and agency lower down the socio-political structure, but in all other respects the Patriot King was consistent with the early Georgian independent man. Beholden to nobody, and therefore uncorrupted, the independent man represented a fantasy of pure agency and selfless virtue, which could be employed to act decisively, to unite and to inspire.

While Bolingbroke tried to make the independent man more rarified, the Tories on the backbenches and in the constituencies employed this idiom in remarkably populist senses. They made a virtue of the fact that they were necessarily independent of the Whig oligarchy, and struck this pose in the boroughs in order to maintain their electoral base, patronising Independent Elector societies. Linda Colley argues that their commitment to Anglicanism and their ability to present themselves as co-victims of the Whigs were genuinely popular. Tories even developed the methods and critiques usually credited to radicals later in the century, such as constituency instructions, demands for the disfranchisement of pocket boroughs, and the link between taxation and representation (although they did not call for a wider franchise).[42] 'Country' patriotism and manly independence were therefore shared terrain rather than the product of a single political genealogy.

Indeed, as we enter the mid-century, political life was dominated by men who professed to disown party allegiances and traditions altogether. The independent country gentleman was a fixture of the mid-Georgian political scene, and came to be regarded as the Commons' traditional repository of basic manly virtue and the bulwark against overweening courts, self-seeking upstarts and aristocratic cliques. The country gentleman evinced a pointedly uncultivated gentility, in opposition to the personal style of the courtiers and professional politicians who supposedly posed threats to traditional rights and local autonomies. In theory all MPs fitted the description of 'independent country gentleman' – that is, non-noble landowners who sat on their own interest – but in practice many were not, and it came to connote a specific social and political type.[43] Namier brought to our attention the blunt, patriotic country gentleman whose boasted impartiality enabled him to support the king's government when he conscientiously could, but would also lead him fiercely to oppose anything that whiffed of party, centralisation, expense, or any of the usual 'Country' bugbears.[44] Derek Jarrett warns that Namier's picture has been taken too literally by historians, suggesting that their numbers were more limited and that many who struck an 'independent' pose were as financially dependent upon patrons and ministers as the career politicians that they condemned.[45] Again, we see that 'independence' was more a question of style and identity than the reflection of political or economic circumstances: the *idea* of the independent country gentleman was extremely powerful, and was a significant component of governance in a 'Country' culture that privileged property, rural virtue, straightforward manliness and personal autonomy.

In particular, the virtue that the country gentlemen claimed to epitomise was 'patriotism'. We have encountered this idea many times before but, by the mid-century, patriotism was associated as much with bellicose nationalism as with classical public spirit: even Bolingbroke's Patriot King of the 1730s would have been surprised at the antigallican, Protestant and imperial rhetoric of the 1740s and 1750s. We have seen how xenophobia was implicit in the 'patriot' stance regarding foreign policy, but opposition writers were increasingly employing a xenophobic rationale in their critiques of the domestic ruling elite. As Gerald Newman has argued, the traditional targets of 'Country' patriotism – courtiers, financiers and placemen – were condemned as being nationally alien, as well as morally corrupt. These accusations were widened to include the whole cosmopolitan *beau monde* and their rage for continental refinements and exotic luxuries.[46] The 'macaroni' and the 'nabob' – effeminised and degenerated by the Grand Tour and Indian wealth and exoticism, respectively – were added to the independent man's established 'others'. There was a reaction against the early Georgian project of politeness which, instead of enabling easy interaction, was widely perceived to have degenerated into studied, superficial, effeminate and *foreign* behaviour.[47] Mid-century patriots regarded all this as a threat to indigenous virtue and promoted a model of manliness that embodied the supposedly national traits of sincerity, straightforwardness, courage and independence. These qualities were increasingly identified with Saxon quasi-racial origins.[48] Manly independence was already regarded as eminently constitutional behaviour but, within this scheme, it was *nationally* appropriate to the ancient constitution, in contrast to the foreign traits of the governing class imposed by the Norman Yoke.

These developments paralleled contemporary efforts to create a national literary and artistic culture, in rejection of foreign influences. Much of the impetus behind early English Romanticism came from artists of middling social rank, excluded from elite patronage, aristocratic (often non-English) discourse, and the traditional cultural forum of the court: this was a 'Country' culture that was nationalist, anti-aristocratic and politically oppositional.[49] The works of the leading novelist of the day, Tobias Smollett, provide a good example of the pervasiveness of 'Country' concerns in mid-century imaginative culture. Literary critics, too committed to a Whig/Tory/Radical typology, have had difficulty locating Smollett politically because he was committed above all to 'independence'.[50] We will see in Chapter 5 how this idea is central to his novels and his poetry, but the works that epitomise both his own politics and mid-century 'Country' patriotism in general are his *Complete History of England* (1757–58) and its *Continuation* (1760–65).[51] Designed as a sequel to Hume's successful *History*, Smollett's work differs markedly from its 'Court' predecessor, telling instead a story of misguided monarchs, heroic oppositions and patronage-led national corruption. His description of England at the accession of George II evokes every 'Country' preoccupation:

> Dangerous encroachments had been made upon the constitution by the repeal of the act for triennial parliaments; by frequent suspensions of the Habeas corpus act upon frivolous occasions; by repealing clauses in the act of settlement; by votes of credit; by habituating the people to a standing army; and above all, by establishing a system of corruption, which at all times would secure a majority in parliament.

Crown influence was employed to create 'dependents' without conscience or manly individual will. This was both a symptom and a cause of national moral decay and the curtailment of cherished liberties:

> The vice, luxury, and prostitution of the age, the almost total extinction of sentiment, honour, and public spirit, had prepared the minds of men for slavery and corruption. The means were in the hands of the ministry: the public treasure was at their devotion: they manipulated places and pensions to increase the number of their dependents: they squandered away the money of the nation without taste, discernment, decency, or remorse.[52]

The dedicatee of the *History* was William Pitt, 1st Earl of Chatham, whom Smollett commended for 'his disinterested integrity, his incorruptible heart, his unconquerable spirit of independence, and his invariable attachment to the interest and liberty of his country'.[53] In many respects, Pitt was ideally suited to become the epitome of the mid-century independent man and the champion of the 'patriots' in parliament, the City and the nation at large. Of moderate birth and fortune, and lacking noble patrons, he had to rely upon his own determination and abilities in order to get on in politics. Pitt performed the required role to perfection, as Chesterfield noted by means of a theatrical metaphor:

> He came young into parliament, and upon that great theatre he soon equalled the oldest and ablest actor ... In that assembly, where the public good is so often talked of, and private interest singly pursued, he set out with acting the patriot, and performed that part so nobly, that he was adopted by the public as their chief, or rather their only uncorrupted champion.

In particular, Pitt epitomised the mid-century ideal of sincerity. He did not 'perform the part' in order to conceal his true self: rather, he faithfully externalised his 'inner' convictions. The other 'patriotic' and 'independent' qualities that Pitt's supporters identified in him were assertiveness, public spirit, love of his country and disinterestedness (although the latter was eventually sullied by his acceptance of two peerages and a £3,000 pension).[54] He succeeded in maintaining this image to such a degree that he even managed to overcome 'Country' suspicions of professional politicians and to carry this anti-ministerial posture into office, famously declaring that he would 'act as an independent minister or not at all'.[55] Pitt the Elder demonstrated the continuing cultural power of the idea of 'the independent man', and showed that it could be employed for both establishmentarian and anti-establishmentarian ends.

The period of political and military conflict that brought Pitt to prominence had a profound impact upon English political culture. In many respects, the Seven Years War (1756–63) set the stage for the subsequent political transformations in which the idea of 'the independent man' would have such a crucial role. Firstly, it was an important period for popular political participation. The struggle against France and her allies was regarded at the time as 'the People's War' and, as such, arguably represents an important moment in the history of citizenship. Not only did the invasion scares bring the war to the island nation more immediately than the usual colonial or continental conflicts, but this was a war whose conduct truly became a popular political issue. An article of August 1756 argued that 'the People' were actively involved in its conduct, as with no previous conflict: they had given assent to their MPs, sent applications to the throne and willingly granted funds: 'On the Whole, therefore, we may truly say that the People have behaved like Politicians and Heroes'.[56] It could be said that Pitt's premiership and the very war policy that he advocated were dependent upon the active involvement of the wider political nation. Marie Peters has shown how Pitt's rise involved courting 'popularity', in the eighteenth-century sense of pursuing 'patriot' causes in order to win the support of the 'Country' interest.[57]

The Seven Years War was not merely a political and military crisis, however. The early stages of the war did not go well and a succession of scandals and military reverses sent Georgian Britons into one of their periodic cultural panics. So much of English patriotic culture was 'other'-ed against the French that defeat at their hands threw an otherwise complacent worldview into crisis: if Englishmen were more free, prosperous, godly and manly than Frenchmen, how should they explain Minorca and Oswego? Critics of the government turned to a classical republican analysis: the nation was in danger because its people were corrupt. The Summer of 1756 witnessed jeremiads against gaming, luxury, theatregoing and political patronage. Possibly the most hysterical of these diagnoses came from the pen of John Brown, author of *An Estimate of the Manners and Principles of the Times* (1757). In this work he demonstrated systematically that the late 'public Miscarriages' stem from 'permanent and established Causes' in British social, moral and political life. In sum, 'the Character and Manners of our Times' are those of 'a *vain, luxurious,* and *selfish* EFFEMINACY'.[58] We have seen how gender was central to the Georgian critique of virtue. In the context of this cultural panic, military defeat was regarded as a failure of British manliness.

'Country' patriotism provided both a diagnosis and a cure. As they had done in the 1690s – a comparable period of crisis in gender and politics – the opposition turned to the militia as a cure-all for England's moral, political and military ills. The nation, they argued, should turn to the community of independent arms-bearing citizens for its defence. Citizen soldiers would be more effective than the German mercenaries that had been hired to defend the coasts, because they were virtuous, motivated and free. Seeking to harness the 'love of Liberty and Independence' that was inherent in Britons, militia reformers argued that a free man would fight more tenaciously for his liberty than the oppressed foreign soldier who was trying to wrest it from him.[59] Furthermore, militia service would restore manly virtue to Englishmen, facilitating a return to the conventional gender order.

True men, it was argued, would naturally want to defend their families. No Briton would rely upon 'Mercenaries and foreign Soldiers' to defend 'their Wives, their Children, their Properties, and every thing else that is dear to them as freeborn men'.[60] Militia reformers commonly drew upon this chivalric imagery in order to make a case for arming civilian men – which, in the context of mid-Georgian social values, was very difficult to argue against.

Between James Harrington and William Pitt, the independent man had come a long way. The 'independence' of the citizen of Oceana – predicated upon agrarian self-sufficiency, direct democracy, and the decay of feudal social distinctions – was a far cry from the allusive richness of concept in the 1750s. Nevertheless, the basic elements remained consistent. Within a chauvinist national culture and a neo-classical notion of liberty and virtue, 'independence' represented the epitome of manliness, martial valour, patriotism and political efficacy. Fundamentally, 'independence' was not accessible to all. Whether he was the freeholder-citizen of Oceana, Shaftesbury's polite gentleman, Bolingbroke's born ruler or Pitt's patriot minister, the independent man was a man of substantial property and station. 'Independence' may have connoted character traits but, without the requisite possessions and standing, these could not be realised through cultivation and leisure, or protected against corruption. Mid-Georgians did not believe that a virtuous man cast into indigence could stay virtuous for long. He would be driven to dependence, which absolutely corrupts and absolutely curtails personal freedom, absolutely preventing him from doing good. Constitutional action could be based only upon a political personality that was independent: the condition of non-obligation in which manly virtue was possible. The nation's key repository of 'independence' and personal virtue was the stratum of squires from whose ranks the members of the national parliament were drawn. In a sense, these were the citizens of the early Georgian quasi-republic.

The Seven Years War, on the other hand, demonstrates that the 'Country' inheritance had bequeathed to Georgian England a very rich notion of citizenship. Membership of the political nation entailed a model of conduct that was active, vigilant, patriotic and opposed to 'corruption' in all of its moral and structural forms. Up to the mid-century this 'independent' condition was indeed conceived of primarily in terms of landed property and rank, but the debate on the militia suggests that citizenship had the potential to be talked about in socially broader terms. Its proponents still conceived of the militiaman as an independent man of means,[61] but the emphasis upon gender in the debate suggested that independence and virtue could be conceived of in terms of maleness *per se*. As we will see, later political reformers would make a case for admitting more men to electoral citizenship in very similar terms to this case for military citizenship: the independent man would naturally want to protect and support those who depended upon him. In the following decades, citizenship would continue to be conceived of in terms of virtue and obligation, but it would move from a paradigm of rank to one of gender.

Notes

1 P. Carter, *Men and the Emergence of Polite Society, Britain 1660–1800* (Harlow: Longman, 2001), p. 70.

2 Thomas Laqueur, *Making Sex: Body and Gender from the Greeks to Freud* (Cambridge: Harvard University Press, 1982).

3 J. G. A. Pocock, *The Machiavellian Moment: Florentine Political Thought and the Atlantic Republican Tradition* (Princeton: Princeton University Press, 1975), p. 357.

4 J. P. Kenyon (ed.), *The Stuart Constitution: Documents and Commentary* (Cambridge: Cambridge University Press, 1966), p. 21.

5 Shelley Burtt, *Virtue Transformed: Political Argument in England, 1688–1740* (Cambridge: Cambridge University Press, 1992), p. 64.

6 James Harrington, *The Commonwealth of Oceana* (1656), in *The Commonwealth of Oceana and A System of Politics*, ed. J. G. A. Pocock (Cambridge: Cambridge University Press, 1992), p. 55.

7 Harrington, *Oceana*, p. 33.

8 A. S. P. Woodhouse (ed.), *Puritanism and Liberty: Being the Army Debates (1647–9) from the Clarke Manuscripts with Supplementary Documents* (London: Dent, 1938), pp. 58, 78, 83.

9 C. B. Macpherson, *The Political Theory of Possessive Individualism: Hobbes to Locke* (Oxford: Clarendon, 1962), pp. 107–59.

10 Ann Hughes, 'Gender and politics in Leveller literature', in S. D. Amussen and M. A. Kishlansky (eds) *Political Culture and Cultural Politics in Early Modern England* (Manchester: Manchester University Press, 1995), pp. 162–88.

11 Mark Kishlansky, *Parliamentary Selection: Social and Political Choice in Early Modern England* (Cambridge: Cambridge University Press, 1986).

12 For an example of a pamphlet seeking to popularise Harrington's ideas, see 'The Benefit of the Ballot' (n.d.), in *State Tracts: Being a Collection of Several Treatises Relating to Government* (London, 1689), pp. 443–4.

13 J. G. A. Pocock, 'Machiavelli, Harrington, and English political ideologies in the eighteenth century' (1965), in his *Politics, Language and Time* (London: Methuen, 1971), pp. 104–47.

14 'The Earl of Shaftesbury's Speech in the House of Lords' (1675), in *State Tracts*, pp. 57–64 (p. 59).

15 *A Letter from a Person of Quality, To His Friend in the Country* (1675), pp. 1, 2, 8.

16 *Letter from a Person of Quality*, pp. 28, 31.

17 Pocock, 'Machiavelli', p. 120.

18 See, for example, the arguments for frequent parliaments in 'The Debate or Arguments for Dissolving this Present Parliament' (1675), in *State Tracts*, pp. 65–8.

19 *Letter from a Person of Quality*, p. 27; 'An Appeal from the Country to the City', in *State Tracts*, p. 402.

20 Algernon Sidney, *Discourses Concerning Government*, ed. T. West (Indianapolis: Liberty, 1990), p. 17.

21 John Locke, 'Of Political or Civil Society', in *Two Treatises of Government*, ed. Peter Laslett (Cambridge: Cambridge University Press, 1960).

22 Carole Pateman, *The Sexual Contract: Aspects of Contractual Liberalism* (Stanford: Stanford University Press, 1988). For a critique of Pateman and an analysis of the gendering of political language in this period, see Rachel Weil, *Political Passions: Gender, the Family and Political Argument in England 1680–1714* (Manchester: Manchester University Press, 1999).

23 M. Peters, *Pitt and Popularity: The Patriot Minister and London Opinion during the Seven Years' War* (Oxford: Clarendon, 1980), p. 25.

24 J. G. A. Pocock, 'Authority and property: the question of liberal origins', in his *Virtue, Commerce, and History: Essays on Political Thought and History, Chiefly in the Eighteenth Century* (Cambridge, Cambridge University Press: 1985), pp. 51–71 (p. 66).

25 *Craftsman* 375 (8 September 1733).

26 M. Butler, 'Romanticism in England', in R. Porter and M. Teich (eds), *Romanticism in National Context* (Cambridge: Cambridge University Press, 1988), pp. 37–65 (p. 41); J. Sekora, *Luxury: The Concept in Western Thought, Eden to Smollett* (Baltimore: Johns Hopkins University Press, 1977).

27 Pocock, *Virtue, Commerce, and History*, p. 231.

28 Carter, *Men and the Emergence of Polite Society*.

29 L. Klein, *Shaftesbury and the Culture of Politeness: Moral Discourse and Cultural Politics in Early Eighteenth-century England* (Cambridge: Cambridge University Press, 1994); R. Markley, 'Sentimentality as Performance: Shaftesbury, Sterne, and the theatrics of virtue', in F. Nussbaum and L. Brown (eds), *The New Eighteenth Century: Theory, Politics, English Literature* (London: Methuen, 1987), pp. 210–30.

30 *The Independent Patriot: Or, Musical Folly. A Comedy. As it is Acted at the Theatre-Royal in Lincoln's Inn Fields* (London, 1737), pp. i, 43, 44, 65.

31 Philip Stanhope, 4th Earl of Chesterfield, *Characters* (1778), ed. A. McKenzie (Los Angeles, CA: William Andrews Clark Memorial Library, 1990), p. 32.

32 David Hume, 'On the independency of Parliament' (1741), in *Political Essays*, ed. K. Haakonssen (Cambridge: Cambridge University Press, 1994), pp. 24–7 (p. 26).

33 Chesterfield, *Characters*, pp. 31–2.

34 *The Independent Whig* 1 (20 January 1720); [Thomas Gordon], *The Character of an Independent Whig* (London, 1719), p. 3.

35 *The Works of Tacitus*, trans. Thomas Gordon, 2 vols (London, 1731), vol. II, p. 109.

36 C. Robbins, *The Eighteenth-Century Commonwealthman* (Cambridge: Harvard University Press, 1959); Q. Skinner, 'The principles and practice of opposition: the case of Bolingbroke versus Walpole', in N. McKendrick (ed.), *Historical Perspectives: Studies in English Thought and Society* (London: Europa, 1974), pp. 93–128.

37 A. S. Foord, *His Majesty's Opposition 1714–1830* (Oxford: Clarendon, 1964), pp. 37–41.

38 *Craftsman* 264 (24 July 1731), p. 132; 54 (15 July 1727), pp. 19–22.

39 Viscount Bolingbroke, 'On the Spirit of Patriotism' (written 1736, published 1749), in *Letters on the Spirit of Patriotism and on the Idea of a Patriot King*, ed. A. Hassall (Oxford: Clarendon, 1926), pp. 9–38 (pp. 10, 12).

40 Viscount Bolingbroke, 'The Idea of a Patriot King' (published 1749), in *Spirit of Patriotism*, pp. 39–141 (pp. 95, 101).

41 Foord, *His Majesty's Opposition*, p. 149.

42 L. Colley, *In Defiance of Oligarchy: The Tory Party 1714–60* (Cambridge: Cambridge University Press, 1982), pp. 160–70.

43 On parliamentary regulations concerning land ownership and independence from peers, see *The State of the Representation of England and Wales, Delivered to the Society, the Friends of the People . . .* (London, 1793), p. 10.

44 L. Namier, 'Country gentlemen in parliament, 1750–84' (1954), in his *Collected Essays, vol. II: Crossroads of Power* (London: Hamish Hamilton, 1962), pp. 30–45.

45 D. Jarrett, 'The myth of "patriotism" in eighteenth-century English politics', in J. Bromley and E. Kossman (eds), *Britain and the Netherlands, vol. V: Some Political Mythologies* (The Hague: Nijhoff, 1975), pp. 120–40.

46 G. Newman, *The Rise of English Nationalism: A Cultural History 1740–1830* (London: Weidenfeld and Nicolson, 1987).

47 This is epitomised by the figure of the 'fop' in early Georgian representations. Philip Carter maintains that the fop represented fears about the effect of the culture of politeness upon social interaction: *Men and the Emergence of Polite Society*, ch. 4.

48 Newman, *Rise of English Nationalism*, p. 118.

49 Butler, 'Romanticism in England'.

50 For example: R. Spector, 'Smollett's politics and *The Briton*, 9 October 1762', *Papers on Language and Literature* 26:2 (1976), pp. 280–4.

51 D. Greene, 'Smollett the historian: a reappraisal', in G. Rousseau and P.-G. Boucé (eds), *Tobias Smollett: Bicentennial Essays Presented to Lewis M. Knapp* (New York: Oxford University Press, 1971), pp. 25–56.

52 Tobias Smollett, *A Complete History of England*, 4 vols (London, 1757–58), vol. IV, p. 519.

53 Quoted in Chesterfield, *Characters*, p. 58.

54 Chesterfield, *Characters*, pp. 56, 56–8.

55 Quoted in Peters, *Pitt and Popularity*, p. 177.

56 *Harrop's Manchester Mercury* 231 (17 August 1756).

57 Peters, *Pitt and Popularity*, pp. 24–7.

58 John Brown, *An Estimate of the Manners and Principles of the Times* (London, 1757), pp. 11–12, 29, 51.

59 [Adam Ferguson], *Reflections Previous to the Establishment of a Militia* (London, 1756), p. 25.

60 *A Modest Address to the People of Great Britain* (London, 1756), p. 25.

61 Ferguson, *Reflections*, pp. 50–1.

4

Declarations of Independence, 1760–76

'Independence' was central to English conceptions of manliness, political virtue and constitutional legitimacy by the mid-eighteenth century. We will now examine the period 1760–1832 in more detail, and will focus upon the changing political and social meanings of manly independence. The 1760s and 1770s represented an important moment of transition in English political culture, when existing opposition styles and arguments became significantly more assertive in their critique of the establishment and began to empower persons beyond the traditional political classes. This had important implications for citizenship. As we have seen, 'Country' patriotism was fundamentally concerned with the manly virtues and capacities for free action (collectively, the 'independence') of parliamentary representatives. The radicals of the 1760s and 70s continued to assess political legitimacy primarily in terms of personal character and circumstance rather than rights, but located the balanced constitution's essential repository of virtuous 'independence' further down the socio-political scale: in the citizenry itself. As we will see, this drew upon the established tradition of electoral independence in the large open constituencies, and it was only when the government and their opponents got themselves embroiled in *electoral* set-pieces at the end of the decade that the notion of the independent citizen moved to the forefront of the radical critique. The manly, independent citizen-voter – such an important figure in Victorian politics – was a creation of the last third of the eighteenth century.

The reasons for this transition were primarily political. 'Independence' was the discursive meeting point for evaluations of political and masculine virtue, but – as so often in the history of this notion – an important shift of meaning occurred as a result of sea-changes in politics rather than gender relations. The accession of George III in October 1760 was followed by a reconfiguration of ministerial 'ins' and 'outs', and this had a significant effect in ideological terms. The Leicester House opposition clique reverted to defending the court, whereas prominent Whig groupings found themselves to be out in the political cold. So too were Pitt and his supporters, proponents of a 'patriot' foreign policy and 'Country' measures at home. Just as the Tories, when shorn of other avenues prior to 1760, had employed innovative methods and programmes to sustain their political presence, now supporters of Pitt and the Whigs used similar means to pursue an extra-parliamentary course. If oppositional Toryism had always been restrained by its fundamental monarchism and qualms about resistance, however, Whiggism was always concerned with curtailing prerogative power. Activists such as John Wilkes, the Beckfords and John Horne would rework 'Country' patriotism and its culture of manly independence in order to make oppositional politics more radical and bring it to a wider audience than ever before, changing the face of British politics in the process.

There are two parts to this chapter. The first is devoted to John Wilkes, who dominated the political scene in this period and is commonly regarded as being the first English radical. It would be worth examining Wilkes in detail for his multifaceted take upon manly independence alone, but his activities also contributed in a large part to the broader shift in the political significance of this idea. The second half of the chapter will explore the cultures of politics and gender in revolutionary America. As we will see, the colonists shared broadly the same 'Country' political culture as the English, and their rebellion against the Crown was conceived of within the historical conflict of virtue and corruption, in which the independent man was the central actor. The American interpretation of manly independence, however, also differed in several significant respects, and the transatlantic dialogue of the 1760s and 70s both reinforced and radicalised the place of this idea in English political life. It took both the Wilkite movement and the American Revolution to free masculine 'independence' from its mid-century 'Country' moorings.

John Wilkes as 'independent man'

John Wilkes and his followers approached political action in distinctive and innovative ways. The ideas that they employed included many that we have already encountered – including the 'Country' and neo-classical critiques, and ideas from popular and patriotic culture – as well as some elements that were less conventional in British political life. Common to these diverse sources was the idea of 'independence', which became increasingly important to his political critique and personal style. Already an emotive concept in British politics, 'independence' particularly suited Wilkes's cause because it explored questions of personal autonomy in terms of manliness, political virtue and national belonging. Wilkes is an especially interesting figure in this context because he demonstrates that questions of political action were fundamentally bound up with the gendered self. For a figure whose very sexuality had political overtones, the personal was indeed political.

Historians continue to find this much-studied figure to be elusive. Although cultural historians have begun to recognise that the more colourful aspects of his public image need to be taken seriously, the tenor of political studies is such that accounts of his political career remain frustratingly dry. Moreover, the paradoxes remain: was Wilkes a democrat or an elitist, idealist or hypocrite, virtuous enemy of corruption or rake on the make? I shall argue that only as a variety of apparently contradictory personae is Wilkes comprehensible. Recent studies of eighteenth-century gender have emphasised the *diversity* of masculinities on offer,[1] and Wilkes appears to have drawn from various sources in the construction of his political manhood. All of these identities related to the idea of 'independence' in fundamental ways, however, and it was this that gave his political image unity and logical consistency. It is worth focusing on Wilkes's personal interpretation of 'the independent man' under a series of distinct headings, in order to illustrate the allusive richness of the concept and the multifaceted nature of Wilkes's self-image and appeal. He was at once a classical citizen, a libertine, a gentleman and a political actor – but, first and probably foremost, he was a freeborn Englishman.

THE FREEBORN ENGLISHMAN

Englishness was central to Wilkes and his movement. Existing ideas about national character, national belonging, and its associated rights and responsibilities, were moulded into a powerful political identity that was both lived by Wilkes and prescribed to those who listened to him. The notion that England was an elect nation, whose people were uniquely virtuous, uniquely free, represented in parliament, and equal under the law, was by no means new, but the Wilkites were distinguished by their determination to take these platitudes seriously. Ideas that had often formerly functioned as no more than palliative myths were being acted upon.

In common with popular culture, 'Country' patriotism and electoral tradition, Wilkes celebrated a particular variety of 'English' manliness. As he declared in *The North Briton* of 2 April 1763, just days before Bute's resignation, 'the *English* are a people who will not suffer their rights to be trampled on'.[2] This vision of the 'independent man' emphasised the basic libertarianism of the freeborn Englishman who refused to be pushed around. This was a culture that posited directness, defiance and fearlessness as elements of national character, qualities that the Englishman reserves the right to assert against his governors:

> he will never tamely give up the glorious cause in which he is engaged; he will never be drawn away by arts of a subtle man, nor intimidated by the menaces of a wicked minister; he will always be ready to stand forth for his king and country; and, according to the old *English* plan of liberty, will praise or censure any minister, or any set of ministers, according to their behaviour.[3]

This brand of anglocentric patriotism was not a world away from the backbench belligerence that had recently reached its apogee during the Seven Years War.

The Wilkites, on the other hand, encouraged Englishmen to have a sense of their inherited liberties, and to take a protective attitude towards their supposed constitutional and legal rights. They insisted that the freeborn Englishman was entitled to due process under the law, in practice as well as in theory. As John Brewer argues, the Wilkites reverenced a particular vision of the English law. Politics and the law were inseparable in radical minds and in English notions of governance, for 'liberty' – the highest political value – was supposed to be sustained and protected by the traditional legal system.[4] In theory, English law in its purest form was perfect, and judges had simply to enact it properly. The use of discretion on their part was condemned as arbitrary and 'Scottish', connoting both the practice of civil law north of the border and popular prejudices that the Scots were tyrannically inclined. The site of discretion and independence in the English legal system, the Wilkites argued, lay in its representative element, the jury. Wilkes summed up his position in his famous set-piece speech at the Court of Common Pleas in 1763. Hoping that 'the genuine spirit of Magna Charta, that glorious inheritance, that distinguishing characteristic of Englishmen' was to be found in that court, he gladly committed his fate to 'an independent jury of free-born Englishmen … conscience bound, upon constitutional principles, by a verdict of *Guilty* or *Not Guilty*. I ask no more at the hands of *my Countrymen*'.[5] It is appropriate that the proper functioning of the English law in Wilkite eyes relied upon the 'independence' of that aspect of it that was supposedly reflective of the national character and the national will.

This vision of political and legal practice was situated in the context of a particularly chauvinistic view of England and its history. Linda Colley's *Britons* has done much to reinstate English patriotism and Scottophobia in historians' understanding of Wilkes and his cause.[6] George III famously opened his reign by declaring 'I glory in the name of Briton', but Wilkes wholeheartedly rejected this more inclusive national vocabulary.[7] He revelled in the international pre-eminence of 'England' and in Pitt's aggressive foreign policy, and the 'Introduction' to his projected history of England demonstrates that he was committed to an aggressively Whiggish view of the English past.[8] He commonly referred to the English libertarian and military pantheons – 'all the great patriots and heroes of *my* country, Alfred, king William the Third, Hampden, sir Walter Raleigh, &c'. – and incorporated this historical vision into his electoral addresses, encouraging his audience similarly to live its narrative:

> In this cause I will act under your auspices to the last moment of my life, fearless of danger in behalf of a nation, which knows the inestimable value of the fundamental rights and liberties of the body of the people, and has frequently cemented them with the blood of her heroic sons, of her truest patriots.[9]

The corollary of this cult of England was a virulent hatred of the Scots. Much of the power of Wilkes's campaign against Bute derived from his ability to turn the racism of 'Country' libertarian patriotism against the Scots, playing on popular prejudices that they were clannish, dependent, perpetrators (or easy victims) of tyranny, and poor. When the Scottish writer Tobias Smollett launched *The Briton* in support of Bute and a more inclusive notion of patriotism, Wilkes responded with pointed irony by titling his response *The North Briton*. In that paper, and throughout his writings, the Scot, the Jacobite, and the Tory are conflated into the treacherous villain of England's political drama:

> The restless and turbulent disposition of the *Scottish* nation before the union, their constant attachment to *France* and declared enmity to *England*, their repeated perfidies and rebellions since that period, with their servile behaviour in times of need, and overbearing insolence in power, have justly rendered the name *Scot* hateful to every true *Englishman*.[10]

The dependent Scot was the 'other' to Wilkes's independent, freeborn Englishman.

THE CLASSICAL CITIZEN

Wilkes prided himself on – and impressed his contemporaries with – the extent of his classical learning. He commonly compared the virtues and imperial accomplishments of the English with those of the Romans, usually to the advantage of the former. Furthermore, Wilkes actively identified his own struggles against tyranny with his classical heroes such as Brutus and Catullus, and his followers such as the printer John Almon endorsed the analogy:

> Catullus was indigent: so was Mr. Wilkes. Catullus had great patrons, but not liberal ones: so had Mr. Wilkes. Catullus excelled in a species of wit that was not very delicate: so did Mr. Wilkes. Catullus was the friend of liberty against Caesar: Mr. Wilkes gave ample proofs of his own attachment to liberty.[11]

Given Wilkes's familiarity with the classics, we should clearly consider his declarations of 'independence' and 'dependence' in terms of the highly gendered classical-republican conceptions of obligation, character and power that we explored in Chapter 1. His direct identification with Roman personages, indeed, suggests that his reading of the ancient world informed his entire notion of citizenship. As with many of his contemporaries, the pervasiveness of classical notions of 'independence' – from Roman and Renaissance sources, but also from 'Country' theory itself – enabled Wilkes to make sense of his political being in terms of his masculinity, and vice versa.

The martial element to Wilkes's masculinity should certainly be considered in classical terms. As we have seen, the Machiavellian brand of citizenship emphasised armigerousness as the basis both of a man's personal independence and of his right to participate in the state, and this had been an important theme in English political theory since at least James Harrington. Wilkes, for one, consciously cultivated the image of the patriotic warrior-citizen, his political addresses making much of his 'manly and intrepid' persona.[12] He famously participated in duels in order to prove his *virtus* and was proud of his rank of colonel in the Buckinghamshire militia. Like many of his contemporaries, Wilkes not only linked militia service to virtuous citizenship but was convinced of the constitutionality and military efficacy of such a force. In common with his 'Country' forebears earlier in the century, Wilkes believed that home defence should be entrusted to citizen amateurs rather than professional soldiers, who were less interested in the nation's welfare and could be employed by the executive to unbalance the political system. As he saw it, the militia was congruent both with classical citizenship and Saxon constitutional precedent. For two decades the militia had been a hot political issue, as a result of its sluggish response to the Jacobite invasion and the outcry raised by the hiring of German mercenaries to defend the southern counties during the Seven Years War. Wilkes was firmly on the pro-militia side in these debates, berating Hogarth for mocking the institution in 'The March to Finchley' (1749) and lauding the champion of the new Militia Bill:

> Mr. *Townshend* will still have the warm applause of his country, and the truest satisfaction, that of an honest heart, for his patriotic labours in establishing this great plan of internal defence, a *Militia*, which has delivered us from the ignominy of *foreign hirelings*, and the ridiculous fears of invasion, by a brave and well-disciplined body of *Englishmen*, at all times ready and zealous for the defence of their country, and of it's [*sic*] laws and constitution.[13]

Whereas Wilkes praised 'independent' conduct, he customarily accused his enemies of 'dependence', and this should be understood in terms of the classical-republican conception of power. As Anna Clark argues, Wilkes's homophobia should be regarded in this context. The Roman sexual system was based upon the male citizen's domination of others, so for a man to take a sexually passive role 'was to submit, to lose manhood, to show cowardice, even to lose citizenship'.[14] Wilkes portrayed the morality of the court in this light. Already conceived of as effeminate within the 'Country' scheme, the courtier was identified with homosexuality, to be countered by rampantly heterosexual independent citizens like himself. The figure of the sodomite recurs in Wilkite propaganda, as contrary both to 'nature' and to conventional authority. Bute in particular – and the Scots in general – came to be identified with this sexualised abuse of court power. *The North Briton* tells of how 'under the *Scotsman* a set of hungry, avaritious, dependants' perpetrate '*sordidness*, in public matters *profusion, corruption,* and *extravagance*'.[15] And neither the sexual innuendoes nor the intended target would have been lost on any reader in this supposedly abstract piece on royal 'favourites' in *The Monitor:*

> Such a man's, or if you will, such a minister's conduct is founded upon flattery, the most dangerous of all the vices in the body politic; forasmuch as the prince is undone under the appearance of a more faithful attachment to his person, family and interest; and, if it should happen, that the favourite has so insinuated himself into his heart, and got all his prejudices and passions on his side, there always follows a formation of that sort of fondness for him, which quickly produceth confidence in that person of a dangerous spirit, who will make the royal power subservient to his passions.

As such, the vocabulary of 'dependence', 'favourites', and of court patronage carried the connotations of domination/passivity, sexual immorality and the ignominious state of *obnoxius* – the converse of *virtus*, whereby an individual is dependent on the will of another. In classical theory, he who sexually submitted to another was in a position analogous to slavery, the opposite of manly citizenship.

A clear binary symbolic scheme emerges from these writings, pitting the classical manly virtues of the Wilkites against the moral depravity of the court. An article in *The Monitor* contrasts the 'candour, common sense, and integrity' of Wilkes with 'venality, court dependence, prostitution, and falsehood'.[16] A similar conflict is played out in this address 'To the Gentlemen, Clergy, and Freeholders of the County of Middlesex':

> I cannot, however, forbear congratulating you, as the most distinguished of Englishmen, on the honourable proof you have given, that the genuine spirit of independency, the true love of our country, for which the county of Middlesex has for ages been so eminently conspicuous, still glow in your hearts with unremitting ardour, still shine forth with undiminished lustre. Let the sons of venality bow the knee to the idol of sordid interest. Let them sacrifice every virtue at the shrine of corruption. Let them call their PUSILANIMITY prudence, while they ignominiously kiss the rod of power, and tamely stoop to the yoke, which artful ministers prepare, and arbitrarily impose.[17]

In the imagined polity of the Wilkites, the 'spirit of independency' inherent in true patriots and citizens is mobilised against dependency, passivity, slavery, and political and moral corruption.

THE LIBERTINE

Wilkes's own image and personality were inseparable from his cause. He became the very personification of liberty in the eyes of his followers, and probably believed it himself. Wilkes achieved the status of a martyr, and his personal trials took on the status of grand constitutional conflicts in which every Englishman's freedom was at stake. As he declared to the Middlesex freeholders following his expulsion from the Commons: 'The rights of this free kingdom, gentlemen, have often been violated in my person'.[18]

Wilkes's embodiment of 'liberty', however, was not confined to its political and legal senses. In the earlier stages of his career, in particular, Wilkes's pursuit of freedom extended to hedonism in his sexual, financial and convivial lives. John Sainsbury argues that Wilkes saw himself as heir to a libertine Whig tradition, a force for nature and enlightenment against the trammels of traditional society and politics: 'the symbol and agent of unruly (even diabolical) passions unleashed by defiance of the established order'.[19] In the mid-century, libertinism went hand-in-hand with philosophical deism, a common route to political radicalism and mockery of the confessional state. Erotic hedonism in particular was an important part of Wilkes's 'independent' personality, encompassing manly freedom, virility and domination over women. As it turned out, it was his obscene text *Essay on Woman* that gave the authorities the pretext to imprison him, and enabled Wilkes to turn private libertinism into a question of civil liberties. In terms of his public image, libertinism was almost physiognomically inherent, given the leering squint with which he had been associated since Hogarth's hostile 1763 caricature (a visual motif quickly appropriated by Wilkite cartoonists). In the early 1760s, Wilkes and his coterie flaunted their aspirant-aristocratic masculinity, conspicuously enjoying luxury and debauches while proving their superior bravery and wit in duelling and repartee, in cheerful defiance of authority. Sexuality and politics were fundamentally linked in the decade that Wilkes came to epitomise.

In the later sixties, however, societal mores were changing. When Wilkes returned to England and centre stage, many of the supporters he needed neither approved of his libertine morality nor accepted that his private life was separable from his public cause. When he stood, unsuccessfully, in the London election of 1768, his opponents commonly coupled the notions 'Liberty' and 'Licentiousness'.[20] A pamphlet from that contest summed up the views of his detractors, in the words of a speech from the hellish deity 'BLASPHEMY': Wilkes and his supporters are urged on 'in the same glorious cause of shaking off the shackles of religion and the laws, and being *free* from all possible *restraint*; the only *liberty* which is worthy of your animated intentions'.[21] A new image of political manhood was becoming popular and, as we will see, even 'that Devil Wilkes' had to change his public persona in order to maintain the adherence of his supporters in the 1770s and beyond.

THE GENTLEMAN OF PROPERTY AND RANK

The Wilkite phenomenon is often distinguished from its predecessors in terms of its demography.[22] Although Pitt the Elder had already demonstrated the populist potential of the 'Country' programme, in Wilkes's hands oppositional patriotism was brought to a broader social constituency than ever before. 'The independent man' and its associated conceptual paraphernalia, formerly elements of the critique of excluded elite factions, were linked to accessible and appealing values from traditional popular culture. The idea of the freeborn Englishman and the saturnalian licence of the crowd became elements of an anti-establishmentarian oppositional radicalism. In addition to plebeian street theatre, Wilkes specifically harnessed the support of middling-sort interests. Wilkes protested at the inequitable practice of credit and the law, and was eminently 'clubbable', appealing to the homosociality and boisterous patriotism of metropolitan clubs and trade associations.

Nevertheless, Wilkes was committed to a socially exclusive view of manly independence. Although he courted the crowd, his classical and Whiggish convictions restricted full political ability – and certainly political leadership – to men of standing and property. In a meeting with Earl Talbot in 1762, prior to duelling with him, he expressed his own standing in a sense that acknowledged both the Earl's social superiority and his own claims to gentility and manliness:

> I observed that I was a private English gentleman, perfectly free and independent, which I held to be a character of the highest dignity; that I obeyed with pleasure a gracious Sovereign, but would never submit to the arbitrary dictates of a fellow subject . . . my superior indeed in rank, fortune, and abilities, but my equal only in honour, courage, and liberty.[23]

There is an egalitarian, meritocratic twist at the end of this statement, but Wilkes's freedom and independence are here predicated upon the 'dignity' of his station, that of a 'private English gentleman'. Wilkes was no *country* gentleman, disdaining rural pursuits and setting himself up as a man-about-town at the earliest opportunity. He represents an advance from Namier's backbench squires insofar as he did not regard broad acres as the primary foundation of an independent political personality – but propertied gentility was still all-important.

The centrality of property to masculine independence in this period is highlighted by the inception of the Society of Supporters of the Bill of Rights, formed to clear Wilkes's debts. In the words of their founding circular letter: 'The public are, therefore, called upon by every tie of gratitude and humanity, so prevalent in British hearts, to raise an effectual barrier against such oppression, to rescue Mr. Wilkes from his present incumbrances, and to render him easy and independent'. In order to maintain Wilkes's political presence (a 'barrier against oppression') he had to be kept in the lifestyle to which, as a public gentleman and MP, he had become accustomed. The SSBR was no plebeian outfit, either. Wilkes's printer John Almon recalled that the organisation was composed of 'independent gentlemen, members of parliament, eminent merchants, considerable traders, and other persons of property'.[24] Some members of the SSBR, however, became dissatisfied with the organisation's activities and soon outstripped Wilkes in their political radicalism, conceiving of 'independence' in more socially accessible ways. In particular, Horne and his allies used the Society to promote electoral reform long before Wilkes himself took up the cause. Wilkes's professions of 'independence' in the 1760s, by contrast, revealed his Whiggish convictions that political representatives should be drawn from cultivated propertied gentleman amateurs like himself.

THE INDEPENDENT POLITICAL ACTOR

In terms of political theory, Wilkes's appropriation of 'independence' in the 1760s was squarely within the 'Country' critique. 'Independence' was the quality that pervaded good balanced government, with the various branches of the constitution in their proper relation. The task of independent men within this scheme was to counter any practice that threatened to upset the balance on which good government relied. He was the repudiator of corruption, standing armies, excessive expenditure and other forms of 'dependence' that posed threats to liberty. For the duration of Bute's ministry, patriots took on the age-old task of endeavouring 'to *undeceive* their Sovereign' from the influence of wicked ministers.[25]

In terms of a personal quality, the value of 'independence' occurs most frequently in Wilkite rhetoric in the context of elections: either as a role prescribed to electors in a Wilkite contest, or acted by Wilkes in his own capacity as an MP. We have already encountered the culture of electoral independence in Chapter 2, and Wilkes was one of its most effective exponents. Indeed, Wilkes's use of the 'independence' idiom became more systematic after his cause turned *electoral* in 1768. It was Wilkes's encounter with electoral culture in the large, open, metropolitan constituencies that brought the idea to the forefront of his critique: these were seats where the culture of electoral independency was already well established.[26] Much of Wilkes's achievement, as I have noted, lay in his ability to radicalise 'Country' patriotism and to bring it to a wider audience. When it came to electoral culture, he had only to underline what was already radically oppositional, playing on questions of representation, active citizenship, political freedom and the capacity for defying one's governors. It could be argued that Wilkes unbounded the electoral carnivalesque, licensing as an everyday political practice the misrule, inversion and libertarianism that Georgians were formerly prepared to accept only for the short duration of an election.

Wilkes's electoral propaganda was full of traditional appeals to the 'independence' of the electorate. He appealed to the heroic, motivational personae that Georgians adopted during election contests, giving his supporters a tangible task to perform in pursuit of a higher ideal. Voters were encouraged demonstratively to 'shew yourselves free and independent'; to be 'independent, unawed by power'; to maintain 'the rights and privileges of free-born subjects in a land of Liberty'; and to vindicate their corporate reputation for 'independence' as a constituency.[27] On his failure in the London election, Wilkite broadsides sought to shame supporters of his opponents with accusations of 'dependance' and its associated vocabulary of political ignominy:

> SACRED
> To the eternal Infamy of the city of ******,
> Whose Citizens, actuated by the meanest principles of
> Servility and dependance,
> Deaf to the voice of Liberty,
> Liberty acquired and defended by the death of so many
> Patriots and heroes
> To make room for placemen and ministerial tools,
> Rejected the only man,
> Capable of restoring, by his firmness,
> Authority to the laws,
> Independency to the councils,
> And security to the people of
> Great Britain.[28]

Wilkes also made much of his capacity as an independent member of the House of Commons. Indeed, between 1774 and 1789 it was the extent of his political – and certainly his oppositional – activity, avowedly monitoring expenditure and corruption (if speaking with a growing infrequency). Although he was effectively a ministerial (Pittite) candidate from 1784 he demonstratively sat on the opposition benches, a visible sign of his independence. His electoral propagandists portrayed him as a representative who disdained 'place, pension, or post', and Wilkes himself stated his patriotic credentials in similar terms in this published address to the electors of Middlesex, from prison in 1768: 'I am determined to remain entirely independent, uncorrupted, even unbiassed in an improper manner, and never to accept from the crown, either place, pension, gratuity, or emolument of any kind'.[29] Nevertheless, in the course of his cash-strapped career he sought a variety of posts and payoffs from ministers before finally landing the lucrative city chamberlainship in 1779. As he stated in a letter to the then chamberlain in 1775: 'After being harassed for so many years, I cannot but earnestly desire to arrive in a safe post, and acquire an honourable independence by a continuance of services in the best way I am able'.[30] This demanding post was far from being a sinecure, but the notion of acquiring a personal financial independence *through* a lucrative administrative position was a far cry from his anti-placemen rhetoric of the 1760s. As so often in this pre-professional politics, independence was loudly declared in public but was often a compromise in practice. Only a handful of aspiring politicians in Georgian England, however, had the acreage to fund a parliamentary career without recourse to the client economy. We should not blame Wilkes for failing to change this state of affairs single-handedly, and this does not change the fact that the *idea* of 'independence' was central both to his sense of self and to the political image that he sought to project.

In Jack Wilkes, therefore, we can see a man who both embraced manly independence and retained an ambivalence about its broader social and political implications. On the one hand, he championed the cause of the freeborn Englishman and revelled in the electoral traditions that celebrated the independence of the humble freeholder; on the other, his conception of personal independence can seem Whiggishly elitist. Of course, it would not have been out of character if the former appeals had been entirely pragmatic: Wilkes only relied upon popular causes and publicity when all other avenues to his advancement and protection were barred, a fact that was not lost on many of his more radical colleagues. The extent to which he conceived of his own political personality in terms of independence suggests that he believed at least some of this rhetoric, but he insisted that his own 'independence' was firmly that of a gentleman. Like all social climbers, Wilkes sought admittance to privilege and distinction rather than their overthrow.

Social and political mores were changing, however. As we will see in the next chapter, the later Wilkite movement attracted ideologues who were prepared to conceive of independence, property and personal virtue in more accessible terms. To a large extent, this was due to developments on the other side of the Atlantic. The North American colonies shared a 'Country' political culture, but one in which it was possible to conceive of manly independence in far less exclusive terms. The Revolution was, of course, profoundly concerned with the notion of 'independence' and it is necessary to explore this transatlantic dialogue in order to understand why English notions of political virtue and entitlement began to shift from the 1760s.

The American Revolution and manly independence

Modern historians are agreed that Britain and the American colonies shared a common political culture, at least up to the 1760s.[31] For most of the eighteenth century, the colonists saw themselves *as* British: they proudly exhibited an awareness of their ancestral heritage and had long expressed their grievances in terms of the rights of freeborn Britons. Even during the revolution, American commentators noted with approval that their national spirit was inherited from their British ancestors. In particular, there was an acute awareness that many seventeenth-century settlers had left Britain in search of political and religious liberty, and that America rather than Britain therefore constituted the more faithful incarnation of all that was good about the British political heritage. This perception was shared by English pro-Americans such as Baron Rokeby, who argued that the 'sacred flame' of patriotism and liberty burned brighter in America: it had providentially been exported from England 'at the time that it was in its greatest purity and perfection there' and had been preserved by 'a new and uncorrupted people'.[32]

The predominant emphasis in American political argument drew upon a specific British tradition: Old Whig republicanism, as conveyed to the eighteenth-century political mainstream via 'Country' patriotism. Since the publication of Bernard Bailyn's *Pamphlets of the American Revolution* in 1965, many American scholars have argued that revolutionary writers drew upon diverse sources – the classics, Enlightenment rationalism, common law, religious nonconformity – but that these were only brought together under the rubric of British 'Country' theory.[33] Bailyn and his successors have argued that 'Country' theory offered critiques of executive power and influence, social relations and empire that Americans had long found appropriate to their situation. 'Country' patriotism's peculiar blend of mixed balanced constitutionalism, agrarianism and individual libertarianism – cumulatively promoting the virtue of 'independence' – pervaded the rhetoric of the colonial assemblies and dominated American political theory up to the revolution and beyond. When Richard Price wrote in 1776 that the 'essence of our constitution consists in its independency', he could have been referring either to the British or to the American political tradition.[34]

The means by which Americans received this English political heritage, on the other hand, ensured that its simultaneous development in the colonies took a different course. Many seventeenth-century settlers had been on the losing side in British 'Country' conflicts and anti-Walpole opposition writings were devoured in the colonies.[35] As Pocock has suggested, the readership for such material was wider in America and the warnings about corruption, standing armies and wicked ministers were taken more literally there: the British characterisation of the client state was more rhetorical, and was often made by persons who actually aspired to benefit from it.[36] Furthermore, there was little by the way of a balancing

'Court' interpretation in America, and American radicals were more prone than their English counterparts to emphasise the contractual aspect to the 'Country' critique, particularly regarding the right to consent to the imposition of taxes via direct representation. Given their distance from the centre of power and the difficulty with which American interests could be promoted within Westminster, virtual representation was a less compelling defence of the electoral status quo in Massachusetts than it was in Manchester. When colonial grievances were re-aggravated around 1773, therefore, commentators on both sides of the Atlantic were employing the same political idiom but with different connotations, contributing both to the ease with which analogies between the two countries were drawn and to the mutual miscomprehension that ensued.

The terms 'independence' and 'dependence' pervade sources relating to the revolutionary period. 'Independence' became a revolutionary shibboleth, the personal and national value to which all true patriots subscribed. This glorification of independence is most obvious in relation to the Declaration of Independence, but historians rarely place this profession of 'independence' in its appropriate discursive context. In particular, it is necessary to recognise that the *national* independence symbolised by the Declaration and the *personal* independence lauded by the revolutionaries were comprehended in the same way: both were highly gendered, and drew their conception of virtue from Old Whig neo-classicism and 'Country' patriotism.

In international terms, the American Revolution was a family affair. The relationship between Great Britain and the colonies was construed in terms of the familial model of independence and dependence: most writers, both revolutionary and loyalist, resorted to this patriarchal metaphor at some stage to describe the relative statuses, power relationships, responsibilities, and histories of parts of the Empire.[37] Within this model, Great Britain was the adult, parent country. It was commonly conceived of in tandem, consisting of a 'mother country' (the nation) and the 'father of his people' (the king): as the adult of the imperial household, Britain was independent and therefore sovereign and fully in control of itself and its dependants. Imperial possessions were children in a position of familial dependence, whom the parents guided and protected (militarily if necessary) in exchange for their obedience, for they lacked the maturity to govern themselves: in a position of obligation, they were not full national beings. The loyalist account of this family history maintained that this reciprocal yet unequal relationship still subsisted, but critics disagreed. The parents had failed in their responsibilities, they argued, and had become unreasonable in their demands. The 'mother country' had become 'proud, luxurious' and 'vicious'; seduced by 'the sordid acts of intriguing men'; and had attempted to 'devour [her] young' or 'sink them into slaves'.[38] If the female parent was conceived of in terms of depravity and neglect, the male was increasingly identified with aggression. As Paine reiterated in *Common Sense*, George III was an oppressive patriarch and not a benevolent father. *Common Sense* enabled many ordinary Americans to throw off their innate loyalty to the King, characterising him as a 'brute' – thus outside of normal human relationships – and even effecting his symbolic death.[39] The Declaration of Independence was largely concerned with a list of his villainies, by which the 'Tyrant' has cast America 'out of his Protection'.[40]

According to the revolutionaries, the son in the imperial family not only deserved not to be abused, but was no longer a child. The English radical John Cartwright employed the familial metaphor at length to demonstrate that America had come of age, and therefore should not be taxed:

> the power of a parent doth not extend to any act of tyranny or injustice; and totally ceases when the child arrives at the years of maturity. Then, as to the *property* of the child, a parent cannot take it from him even *with* his consent; and as soon as his independency puts it in his power to give it to his parent, he hath also the power of withholding it if he thinks proper. In short, during infancy, he must be protected agreeable to the laws of equity; when arrived at manhood, he is free, and becomes his own protector.

America was no longer a dependant, lacking property, a full personality, sovereignty, manliness and self-will. It was now a (male) adult: independent, sovereign, self-governing, and free. Cartwright hoped that the son would not become estranged from his parent, and that degrading dependence would be superseded by 'a manly and independent friendship'.[41] The revolutionaries, on the other hand, were more concerned with the implications of autonomy. The Declaration of Independence was a statement about America's manly virtue and adulthood, constituting itself as a sovereign being within the gendered contemporary understanding of 'independence'. The 'Political Bands' that it sought to 'dissolve' were the equivalent of apron strings, implying immaturity, helplessness, passivity and subordination. 'Independence' was far from being merely a question of separation from Britain.

When American writers expressed their horror at 'dependence' upon Britain, they did so within this discursive context. At the national, institutional, and personal level 'dependence' implied a degrading lack of manly virtue and liberty. Like British 'Country' writers, Americans employed the vocabulary of slavery in the neo-classical sense, as the ultimate condition of degrading unfreedom. Americans were in a condition of slavery when they were subject to the will of another government, irrespective of whether coercion was exercised. Specifically, this view informed the colonists' vehement response to the questions of taxation and representation from the 1760s. Burke recognised that the Americans did not see political liberty primarily in an abstract sense, but 'on English principles': it consisted of having a say in the election of those who govern and tax.[42] As John Dickinson put it:

> We are taxed without our consent, expressed by ourselves or our representatives. We are therefore – – – – – –
> SLAVES.
> Miserabile vulgus.
> A miserable tribe.[43]

Fliegelman suggests that this political language of slavery 'had the rhetorical consequence of trivialising the literal reality of chattel slavery', which the revolution never sought to question.[44] As with English political culture, Americans primarily employed the concept of 'slavery' in biblical and classical senses, which elided analogies between their own emancipation and that denied to their negro slaves.

Within the revolutionaries' 'Country' conception of mixed balanced constitutionalism, 'dependence' connoted the dangerous and illegitimate use of political influence. As Bushman makes clear, for most of the century the colonists' quarrel was not with the king but with the Crown – the bureaucracy and patronage network that administered in his name.[45] Anti-Walpole 'Country' writings had taught the colonists to perceive an unaccountable bureaucracy, Crown-appointed judges, and Treasury patronage collectively as both expensive and a fundamental threat to liberty. As such, the Declaration of Independence railed against dependent judges, while William Gordon and John Dickinson argued that the current system of appointed colonial governors and Crown patronage created networks of 'tools' and 'creatures', 'dependent' upon the will of wicked British ministers.[46]

Like their English opposition counterparts, Americans maintained that only 'independent men' could repudiate this state of affairs. The figure of the 'independent man' repeatedly appears in American writings and was unquestionably the social and political ideal of the revolutionaries. As with the English 'independent man', the American version was free from compromising obligations, manly, patriotic, conscientious, libertarian and self-supporting – in opposition eyes, the markers of virtue and the conditions for full political subjectivity. There were also significant differences in emphasis between the English and American versions. Firstly, the revolutionaries employed 'independence' in a more socially inclusive sense than most of their British contemporaries. The Virginia Bill of Rights (1776) stated boldly that 'all men are by nature equally free and independent', but even the American revolutionaries had not yet reached the point where independence was fully associated with all biological males.[47] The term 'man' was employed qualitatively. When the revolutionaries claimed the rights of 'men' and the sovereignty of 'the people', both were employed in an exclusive sense to denote the collectivity of white independent male adults. Slaves and Indians did not qualify, nor – as we will see when we examine electoral qualifications – did any white male who was in a position of dependence. The Virginia document was, though, consistent with the ideal that all white adult males had the *potential* for citizenship.

Secondly, 'manly independence' as a personal virtue had very different connotations in the colonies, where the social ideal was the armed freeholding cultivator. Independence in this vision concerned not the showy patrician refinements of a Wilkes, but simple virtues accessible to all – the 'moderation, temperance, frugality, and virtue' celebrated in the Virginia Bill of Rights.[48] Abstemiousness and rural self-sufficiency were the routes to independence. Thomas Jefferson praised his nation's husbandmen as constituting the 'healthy part' of the citizenry:

> Those who labour in the earth are the chosen people of God, if he ever had a chosen people, whose breasts he has made his peculiar deposit for substantial and genuine virtue . . . Corruption of morals in the mass of cultivators is a phenomenon of which no age nor nation has furnished an example. It is the mark set on those, who not looking up to heaven, to their own soil and industry, as does the husbandman, for their subsistence, depend for it on the casualties and caprice of customers. Dependence begets subservience and venality, suffocates the germ of virtue, and prepares fit tools for the designs of ambition.[49]

It should be stressed that these were not merely vague ideals or goals, but were generally held to be the current state of American society. In comparison with Britain, the New World's relatively wide distribution of freehold property, relative lack of social hierarchy, and promise of unlimited natural resources were felt by Britons and Americans alike to provide conditions conducive to personal independence. Commentators on both sides of the Atlantic believed that ordinary Americans were hardy independent yeomen. In turn, this was interpreted as a source of

America's strength, providing a virtuous citizenry that would check any vicious tendencies in government: as Gordon put it, 'while every farmer is a freeholder, the spirit of liberty will prevail'.[50] This idea was commonly expressed in explicitly neo-classical terms and many contemporaries believed that the colonists had realised Harrington's vision of a dispersed rural polity of independent propertied citizens. Indeed, there was a proposal in 1780 that Massachusetts be renamed 'Oceana'. America's social, religious, and institutional conditions – once seen as characteristics of underdevelopment – were construed as being ideal for political liberty.

Britons and Americans therefore believed that the American social structure was inherently suited to republicanism and resistant to monarchism. As Bushman has argued, monarchy was understood as an entire social system of hierarchical dependencies, with the monarch as the highest patron atop a structure of sub-patrons and landlords reaching down throughout society.[51] This social ethos was established in *ancien régime* Britain – partly explaining why positions of independence were so highly prized – but British governors were frustrated by their inability to replicate this in the North American colonies, a failure that was accounted for in terms of America's supposedly flat social structure. As Gordon put it, when the British 'gain over a gentleman of note and eminence in the colonies they make no considerable acquisition. He takes few or none with him; he is rather despised, than adhered to by his former friends. He has not, as in Britain, dependants who must act in conformity to his nod'.[52] Whether all this is sociologically true is another matter, although recent socio-economic studies suggest that there were objectively fewer persons in positions of dependence in the colonies than in Britain.[53] What is significant is that contemporaries comprehended their society in terms of relations of dependence and independence; and that monarchy was identified with the former, and republicanism the latter. What Gordon was arguing was that there was some economic inequality in America but that it did not imply the ethos of dependence. William Knox, undersecretary of state for the colonies, agreed. He noted that the relationship between landlord and tenant did not subsist in a land where 'every Male Inhabitant became a Freeholder': 'This mode excluded all ideas of subordination and dependence'.[54]

Appropriately, there was wide political participation in America. Electorates were large, even before the revolution, but it was the high proportion of freeholders and not the absence of qualifications that made them inclusive. Even the colonists were socially – not to say racially and sexually – selective in order to ensure the independence of its voters. James Wilson, a signer of the Declaration of Independence, condemned the English electoral system, not for the bribery of the elite, but for the large number of poor dependent people who were admitted to the vote: English electoral qualifications admitted 'the most dependent and the least respectable part of the commons' to the franchise. He drew the contrast with America:

> With us, every freeman who possesses an attachment to the community, and a common interest with his fellow citizens, and is not in a situation necessarily dependent, is entitled to a vote for members . . . With us, therefore, it may be expected, that a voice of the representatives will be the faithful echo of the voice of the people.[55]

Wilson thus outlined the political rationale of the new state: political legitimacy rested upon the consent of its independent men. If sovereignty rested in 'the people' – in the eighteenth-century sense of certain adult males – then representative assemblies should 'be the faithful echo' of their voice, and the legitimacy of politicians lay in obtaining their mandate. The electoral system tapped the repository of manly independence in American society, which lay in the mass of freeholder citizens.

As Fliegelman has shown, this recasting of political legitimacy took place in the context of an 'elocutionary revolution', whereby the consent of the governed was obtained through the emotional credibility of the written and spoken word. Writers and speakers had to win over their audiences by demonstrating a sincere sensibility.[56] In this period the culture of sensibility was at its height on both sides of the Atlantic. Whereas sensual psychology had first focused upon women and the socially elevated, by the 1760s the 'man of feeling' offered an alternative to a culture of politeness that had apparently degenerated into stilted vanity and duplicity. Sincere expressiveness and moral self-consciousness were increasingly given pride of place in political manhood and – fundamentally – were accessible to all, since all men experienced the world in the same way. This had a profound impact upon the political style of the revolutionary era. Politicians felt the need to act the part of the true patriot, who did not need to flatter and deceive like an English courtier, because the people recognised his plain honesty. In the early republic, newspapers became simpler in style and content and political language became more emotional and direct.[57] Even British supporters such as Paine and Cartwright – not normally identified with the culture of sensibility – appealed to the 'feeling' of their readers, encouraging them to consult their 'own hearts'.[58] Male sensibility was here being emphasised in order to suggest that all men had the inherent capacity to participate in political life, and should thus demand a place in it.

Indeed, revolutionaries maintained that republicanism required not just a different social ethos to monarchism but a different type of personality: the real revolution had to take place in American minds and many believed that it had done so prior to 1776.[59] The personal values of 'independent' sincerity, egalitarianism, patriotism and simple virtue were prescribed; and 'dependent' deference, obsequiousness and luxury were condemned. Parallel with the English reformation of manners movement, American writers urged their readers to undertake 'a reformation of manners and customs' of their own, promoting the 'independent' personality type that was believed to be fundamental to the success of the new republic.[60] Commentators such as Dickinson reiterated the classical dictum that liberty was a fragile and passive – indeed, feminine – entity, requiring constant attention, protection, and personal virtue from active manly citizens: they should breathe a 'fervent spirit, animating them to actions of prudence, justice, modesty, bravery, humanity and magnanimity'.[61] Republics, the argument went, were historically fragile forms of government and required considerable vigilance on the part of their independent citizens. Within the paradigm of virtue and corruption, the survival of the republic relied upon the existence of an active, independent and manly citizenry.

The political culture of 1770s America had a profound effect upon British political life. The next chapter will show how conceptions of political virtue and legitimacy had substantially to be rethought after the encounter with American republicanism: a political culture that was sufficiently similar to enable analogies to be drawn, but one in which it was possible to conceive of manly independence and citizenship in more socially accessible terms. From this point onwards, citizenship would be identified primarily with the electorate rather than with those it chose to be their representatives. The independence that enabled citizenship was therefore thought about in new ways: a condition that could be based upon smaller freehold property, a receptive sensibility and simple virtues such as rurality, industry and abstemiousness. As such, independence began to be equated less with property and rank, and more with masculinity itself. John Wilkes and his coadjutors may have started the process of reinventing the 'independent man' in England, but it was the dialogue with rebels on the other side of the Atlantic that gave the notion genuine democratic potential. It fell to Wilkes's successors to work out the implications of this important cultural shift.

Notes

1 See, for example, the essays collected in Tim Hitchcock and Michèle Cohen (eds), *English Masculinities 1660–1800* (London: Longman, 1999).

2 *The North Briton*, 3 vols (London, 1763): no. 26 (2 April 1763), vol. II, p. 223.

3 *North Briton* 26 (27 November 1762), vol. II, p. 25.

4 John Brewer, 'The Wilkites and the law, 1763–74: a study in radical notions of governance', in J. Brewer and J. Styles (eds), *An Ungovernable People: The English and their Law in the Seventeenth and Eighteenth Centuries* (London: Hutchinson, 1980), pp. 128–71 (p. 132).

5 *English Liberty. Being a Collection of Interesting Tracts, From the Year 1762 to 1769, Containing the Private Correspondence, Public Letters, Speeches, and Addresses, of John Wilkes, Esq.* (London, n.d.), p. 88.

6 Linda Colley, *Britons: Forging the Nation 1707–1837* (New Haven: Yale University Press, 1992), pp. 105–17.

7 At the opening of his first parliament on 18 November 1760: *The History, Debates, and Proceeding of both Houses of Parliament of Great Britain*, 7 vols (London 1792) vol. III, p. 445.

8 The 'Introduction' was posthumously printed in *The Correspondence of the Late John Wilkes with his Friends*, ed. John Almon, 5 vols (London, 1805), vol. V, pp. 161–205.

9 *Correspondence of John Wilkes*, vol. III, p. 56; *English Liberty*, p. 320.

10 *North Briton* 43 (26 March 1763), vol. II, p. 213.

11 *Correspondence of John Wilkes*, vol. IV, p. 219; see also vol. V, p. 204.

12 'To the worthy Freeholders and Independent Gentlemen Farmers of the county of Middlesex', in *The Battle of the Quills: Or, Wilkes Attacked and Defended* (London, 1768), p. 69.

13 *North Briton* 17 (21 May 1762), vol. I, pp. 164–5.

14 Anna Clark, 'The Chevalier D'Eon and Wilkes: masculinity and politics in the eighteenth century', *Eighteenth-Century Studies* 32:1 (1998), pp. 19–48 (p. 25).

15 *North Briton* 42 (19 March 1763), vol. II, p. 205.

16 *The Monitor, Or British Freeholder* 357 (22 May 1762); 358 (29 May 1762).

17 *English Liberty*, p. 162.

18 *English Liberty*, p. 291.

19 John Sainsbury, 'Wilkes and libertinism', *Studies in Eighteenth-Century Culture* 26 (1998), pp. 151–74 (p. 156).

20 For example, the speech by the Lord Mayor at the nomination ceremony of 16 March: *Battle of the Quills*, p. 41.

21 'WILKES and BLASPHEMY for ever!' (n.d. – 1768?), in *Battle of the Quills*, pp. 26–9 (p. 26). See also: 'To the Gentlemen of No Property and Free-Booters of the County of Middlesex' (25 March 1768), *Battle of the Quills*, pp. 61–2.

22 For example, George Rudé, *Wilkes and Liberty: A Social Study of 1763 to 1774* (Oxford: Clarendon, 1962).

23 *English Liberty*, p. 55.

24 *Correspondence of John Wilkes*, vol. IV, pp. 8, 7.

25 'Letter to the Worthy Electors of the Borough of Aylesbury' (1764) reprinted in *English Liberty*, pp. 125–35 (p. 129).

26 Nicholas Rogers, 'Aristocratic clientage, trade and independency: popular politics in pre-radical Westminster', *Past and Present* 61 (1973), pp. 70–106.
27 *Battle of the Quills*, pp. 55, 45, 61, 69.
28 'INSCRIPTION for a Pillar to be erected in Dorsetshire' (handbill [n.d. – 1768?]), *Battle of the Quills*, p. 60.
29 *Battle of the Quills*, p. 55; 'To the Gentlemen, Clergy, and Freeholders of the County of Middlesex', in *English Liberty*, pp. 192–4 (p. 94).
30 Wilkes to Sir Steven Janssen (18 November 1775): quoted in P. D. G. Thomas, *John Wilkes: A Friend to Liberty* (Oxford: Oxford University Press, 1996), p. 156.
31 B. Bailyn, *The Ideological Origins of the American Revolution* (Cambridge: Harvard University Press, 1967); G. S. Wood, *The Creation of the American Republic, 1776–1787* (Chapel Hill; North Carolina University Press, 1969); J. Derry, *English Politics and the American Revolution* (London: Dent, 1976); L. Banning, *The Jeffersonian Persuasion: Evolution of a Party Ideology* (Ithaca: Cornell University Press, 1978); R. Bushman, *King and People in Provincial Massachusetts* (Chapel Hill: North Carolina University Press, 1985).
32 Matthew Robinson-Morris, Baron Rokeby, *Considerations on the Measures Carrying on With Respect to the British Colonies in North America* (1774), in P. Smith (ed.), *English Defenders of American Freedoms* (Washington: Library of Congress, 1972), pp. 45–105 (pp. 94–5).
33 B. Bailyn, *Pamphlets of the American Revolution, 1750–1776*, 4 vols (Cambridge: Harvard University Press, 1965).
34 Richard Price, *Observations on the Nature of Civil Liberty, the Principles of Government, and the Justice and Policy of the War with America* (1776), in *Richard Price: Political Writings*, ed. D. Thomas (Cambridge: Cambridge University Press, 1991), pp. 20–75 (p. 45).
35 Bailyn, *Ideological Origins*, p. 48.
36 J. G. A. Pocock, *Virtue, Commerce, and History: Essays on Political Thought and History, Chiefly in the Eighteenth Century* (Cambridge: Cambridge University Press, 1985), pp. 273–4.
37 E. G. Burrows and M. Wallace, 'The American Revolution: the ideology and psychology of national liberation', *Perspectives in American History* 6 (1972), pp. 165–307.
38 Cartwright, *American Independence, the Interest and Glory of Great Britain* (1774), in Smith (ed.), *English Defenders*, pp. 131–92 (pp. 148, 142); [John Dickinson], *Letters from a Farmer in Pennsylvania* (Philadelphia, 1768), p. 26; Thomas Paine, *Common Sense*, in *Political Writings*, ed. B. Kuklick (Cambridge: Cambridge University Press, 1989), pp. 1–38 (p. 18); Dickinson, *Letters*, p. 27.
39 W. D. Jordan, 'Familial politics: Thomas Paine and the killing of the King, 1776', *Journal of American History* 60 (1973), pp. 294–308.
40 'The Dunlap Broadside of the Declaration of Independence', in E. Dumbauld, *The Declaration of Independence and What it Means Today* (Norman: Oklahoma University Press, 1950), pp. 157–61 (p. 160).
41 Cartwright, *American Independence*, pp. 139, 142. For the language of 'independence' in this context, see Paine, *Common Sense*, pp. 23, 24, 34; Price, *Observations*, p. 39.
42 Edmund Burke, *Pre-Revolutionary Writings*, ed. I. Harris (Cambridge: Cambridge University Press, 1993), p. 222.
43 Dickinson, *Letters*, p. 38.

44 J. Fliegelman, *Declaring Independence: Jefferson, Natural Language, and the Culture of Performance* (Stanford: Stanford University Press, 1993), p. 141.

45 Bushman, *King and People*, p. 88.

46 'Declaration of Independence', p. 159; Dickinson, *Letters*, pp. 50, 68.

47 'Virginia Bill of Rights' in Dumbauld, *Declaration of Independence*, pp. 168–70 (p. 168).

48 *Ibid.*, p. 170.

49 Thomas Jefferson, *Notes on the State of Virginia* (1787), ed. W. Peden (Chapel Hill: North Carolina University Press, 1955), pp. 164–5.

50 William Gordon, *History of the Rise, Progress and Establishment, of the Independence of the United States of America*, 4 vols (London, 1788), vol. I, p. 269.

51 Bushman, *King and People*, p. 25.

52 Gordon, *History*, p. 143.

53 J. Greene, *The Intellectual Construction of America: Exceptionalism and Identity from 1492 to 1800* (Chapel Hill: North Carolina University Press, 1993), p. 204.

54 J. Greene, 'William Knox's explanation for the American Revolution', *William and Mary Quarterly*, 3rd series, 30 (1973), pp. 293–306 (p. 299).

55 James Wilson, 'Lectures on Law', in *The Works of James Wilson*, ed. R. G. McCloskey, 2 vols (Cambridge: Harvard University Press, 1967), vol. I, pp. 312–13.

56 Fliegelman, *Declaring Independence*, pp. 1–2.

57 G. Wood, 'The democratization of mind in the American Revolution', in R. Horwitz (ed.), *The Moral Foundations of the American Republic* (Charlottesville, VA: Virginia University Press, 1986), pp. 108–35.

58 Paine, *Common Sense*, p. 2; Cartwright, *American Independence*, p. 188.

59 Bailyn, *Ideological Origins*, p. 60; Wood, 'Democratization'.

60 'Letter from a Gentleman in Wilmington, Delaware', *Columbia Magazine* (November 1790).

61 Dickinson, *Letters*, p. 15.

5

Rethinking the independent
Englishman, 1770–97

I N THE PREVIOUS CHAPTER we saw how conceptions of 'independence' began significantly to change in the 1760s, and explored the political masculinity of the man who did much to stimulate this shift, John Wilkes. British politics, however, would never have another 'independent man' in the Wilkes mould: political life in the 1770s and 1780s was pointedly very different. Not only were different political issues pursued in the later period, but the style of 1780s extra-parliamentary politics contrasted sharply with that of the Wilkites. This was not so much in reaction to Wilkes himself – who was commonly remembered with gratitude and affection – but to aspects of his time that he had wholeheartedly epitomised. His earlier libertinism (sexual, convivial and philosophical), aspirant-aristocratic refinements and uncomplicated patriotism were repellent to the cultural climate in which his radical successors had to work.

The question remains why this should have happened. The current historiography, more concerned with the content than with the form of opposition politics, is vague on this point. The American Revolution is – appropriately – at the heart of existing accounts of the 1770s in England, but how this gets us from 'that devil Wilkes' in the 1760s to respectable clerics such as Wyvill and Price in the 1780s is unclear. Political historians have focused upon changes in political theory, while ignoring important shifts in the ways that gender and personal virtue were evaluated. Transformations in the idea of 'the independent man' offer a productive perspective on this important period of change in opposition politics, and should be central to our understanding of the period. We have seen how the American Revolution was crucially concerned with the question of 'independence': this chapter will show how the transatlantic political and cultural interplay profoundly affected conceptions of manliness, patriotism and virtue in England, prompting a period of intense self-criticism and reinvention. Indeed, the 1780s may be characterised as a decade of national soul-searching, not limited to radicalism or even politics *per se*, but in which persons outside of the traditional political nation joined in an exercise in 'public opinion' in an unprecedentedly broad sense, placing England's manners, morality and character under scrutiny.

If English political ideologies informed Americans' perception of their dispute with the mother country, the American Revolution also had a profound and lasting impact upon English politics. News from across the Atlantic was closely followed in England from the 1760s: every new crisis, victory, or setback informed the course and complexion of domestic politics, affecting the purported legitimacy of successive governments and their critics. The effect on English radical argument has been widely acknowledged: as we will see, the American Revolution broke old shibboleths and introduced new themes. Historians have had less to say, however, about the resulting shift in the style and psychology of English politics. In particular, notions of political virtue and manhood were substantially rethought in an atmosphere of intense self-scrutiny, and the promotion of new versions of 'the independent man' was central to this project.

From (at least) the Stamp Act crisis, English radicals perceived that their fate was intimately linked with that of the colonists. Just as Americans identified the victimisation of Wilkes with their own dealings with government, critics of the establishment in England regarded interference in the taxation, judiciary and assemblies of the colonies as a blueprint for planned oppression at home. Both groups perceived actions against the other to be part of the same conspiracy against liberty and corresponded offering solidarity and support. As John Sainsbury has argued, radical support for the American cause was far from opportunistic but was based on a common ideological commitment, to the extent that support for America became the 'touchstone of patriot integrity'.[1]

The course of events made this position more difficult and revealed the extent of ideological divergence between English and American radicals. From 1775 the patriots opposed the government's policy of coercion as a civil war that was symptomatic of domestic corruption. Supporting America was consistent with Wilkite radicalism and its urban commercial base: the war was opposed as an unpatriotic 'Scotch quarrel' that was damaging trade.[2] The adverse reaction to the Boston Tea Party and the effectiveness of the government's loyalist appeals, however, weakened radical support. By October loyal petitions were outnumbering pro-American ones by two to one. The Wilkites attributed loyalist signatures to 'Jews, Papists, Contractors, Justices, and the whole ministerial group of creatures and runners of the Ministry, who, to gratify their Lordlings in place, would endeavour even to extend discord, faction, and civil war, to still greater lengths'.[3] Radicals alleged that the war was deliberately calculated to corrupt independent citizens: wartime enabled the client state to extend the tentacles of corruption even further, enveloping more dependants into its conspiracy.

The Declaration of Independence and *Common Sense* were received with hostility in England. Wilkes claimed that the ministry deliberately 'drove the Americans into the present state of independency' and Price saw the Declaration as punishment for Britain's moral guilt.[4] The radical pro-Americans – still hoping for a reconciliation and, in many cases, committed to British sovereignty – were compromised. The 'civil war' myth was exploded: radicals now courted treason by supporting an external enemy and claims to 'patriotism' became more problematic. America's alliance with France and Spain in 1778 arguably put the final nail in English radical patriotism's coffin. Some radicals abandoned the tradition of anti-French patriotism altogether; others maintained anti-gallicanism while incongruously seeking peace with America.[5] The Gordon riots – in which opposition figures like Alderman Bull were embarrassingly prominent – only hastened radical efforts to dissociate themselves from anti-popery and the prejudices of the urban mob.

The American Revolution and war therefore changed both the content and the form of English radicalism. The colonial dispute altered the reformers' critique of sovereignty and the representative system. As we have seen, the question of colonial taxation focused English minds on the relationship between taxation and electoral consent. The early eighteenth-century 'Country' programme – even up to the early Wilkite agitations – was concerned with the purity of MPs, focusing upon parliamentary influence and the frequency of elections. This was consistent with the notion of 'virtual representation', since the country gentlemen claimed to speak for the nation, disdaining instructions from their constituents. It was only from the mid-1760s that the widespread lack of direct representation was seen as problematic. In defending the Crown's right to collect taxation in unrepresented America, the government implicitly acknowledged the inadequacy of the domestic electoral system. In so many ways, the dispute with America created a space for English radicals and reformers to critique current practices of electoral entitlement and to explore the qualities that citizen-voters should possess.

As such, the first calls for structural electoral reform date from this period. Horne and his allies sought to use the Society of Supporters of the Bill of Rights to champion electoral reform and Wilkes holds the distinction of tabling the first reform motion in the Commons, in March 1776. It was a remarkably sweeping measure, disfranchising 'dependent paltry boroughs', enfranchising the unrepresented trading towns and bolstering the populous counties. When it came to the question of who should be admitted to the franchise, however, Wilkes echoed the ambiguities of the Americans. Wilkes talked in terms of restoring 'the people' to their ancient share in the legislature, and asserted that the 'meanest mechanic, the poorest peasant and day labourer, has important rights respecting his personal liberty [and] that of his wife and children' that should be defended by a share in 'the power of making those laws, which deeply interest them'. The familial emphasis in his argument is significant, and is one that he reiterated later in his speech: 'Each law relative to marriage, to the protection of a wife, sister, or daughter, against violence and brutal lust, to every contract with a rapacious or unjust master, is of importance to the manufacturer, the cottager, the servant, as well as to the rich subjects of a state'. As in electoral culture, this melodramatic scenario pervaded parliamentary rhetoric, justifying male action by proposing that women and children faced sexual danger. Wilkes was here associating electoral entitlement with the male stations of husband and father, in order to claim wider enfranchisement for men: independent men would naturally want to protect and represent those who depended upon them. In so doing, Wilkes sought to shift the basis of 'independence' from property and rank to gender, and established a tradition of argument that would be followed by reformers for decades to come. This did not yet, however, entail universal male suffrage. His statement that 'every free agent in this kingdom' should be 'represented in Parliament' was revealing, implicitly restricting the franchise to independent men.[6] Wilkes's 1776 reform proposal did not quite take his earlier championing of the freeborn Englishman to its logical conclusion in terms of democratic citizenship, but it required the American issue for him to take enfranchisement as far as he did.

As we will see, the American use of the concept of inalienable natural rights encouraged many of Wilkes's contemporaries to conceive of political entitlement in even more inclusive terms. This shift of attention from the rights of Englishmen and the sovereignty of the English parliament to more universal conceptions was related to the enforced radical abandonment of national chauvinism. This had a profound effect on English radicalism, requiring it to seek a new *raison d'être*, a different conception of virtue and a viable aesthetic. This radical soul-searching coincided with a mood of national malaise and self-criticism. Defeat in war and disillusionment with ineffective and inconsistent politicians contributed to a general sense that England was morally degenerate: as in the 1750s, the nation was subject to a comprehensive cultural panic, whereby national morals, manners, political values and gender relations were placed under scrutiny. Dissenters such as Richard Price had long bemoaned the immorality of their countrymen but, after the defeat at Yorktown in 1781, conservatives and radicals alike agreed with his diagnosis of England's ills:

> In this hour of tremendous danger it would become us to turn our thoughts to Heaven. This is what our brethren in the Colonies are doing. From one end of North-America to the other they are fasting and praying. But what are we doing? We are ridiculing them as fanatics, and scoffing at religion. We are running wild after pleasure and forgetting every thing serious at masquerades. We are trafficking for boroughs, perjuring ourselves at elections, and selling ourselves for places. Which side then is providence likely to favour?[7]

Contemporaries commonly merged classical and religious evaluations of personal behaviour in this way, arguing that moral standards constituted both the temporal strength of a state and the extent to which it could hope for divine favour. The paradigm of virtue and corruption, therefore, remained central to English worldviews in the 1780s. It was not replaced by the preoccupation with manners: on the contrary, public virtue was linked to manners in the eighteenth-century mind and the revival of the reformation of manners movement in the 1780s should be regarded in this context of national moral and political self-censure.[8]

Significantly, Price's list of national sins included the state of the representative system. The huge parliamentary reform movement of the eighties was similarly based upon the premise that the political world needed purifying – perhaps explaining the paradoxical political conservatism of the time, the consequent failure to reform (despite prime ministerial sponsorship) and the striking seriousness of the reformers' moral tone. The Reverend Christopher Wyvill, for example, argued that his Association Movement sought 'the restoration of national morals, then sinking under the debasing influence of our Government'.[9] Political reformers like Wyvill and Price still worked within broadly 'Country' parameters, evaluating the virtue and efficacy of the political system in terms of the Commons' ability to resist the pernicious influence of the executive. Price painted a dystopian picture of an England where the sapping of the people's morality and independence both accelerated and resulted from the Crown's all-pervasive corrupting design:

> When the influence of the crown, strengthened by luxury and an universal profligacy of manners, will have tainted every breast, broken

down every fence of liberty, and rendered us a nation of tame and contented vassals: when a general election will be nothing but a general
auction of boroughs; and when Parliament, the Grand Council of the
nation and the once faithful guardian of the state and a terror to evil
ministers, will be degenerated into a body of sycophants, dependent
and venal . . .

Faithful to their classical predecessors, 'Country' theorists maintained
that you had to be virtuous to be free: if England was 'in a sink', it boded
ill for her liberties.[10]

In the wake of the American War, therefore, notions of personal and
national virtue were hotly debated, and the idea of 'the independent man'
– the repudiator of corruption – came to be discussed in important new
senses. In particular, the value of 'independence' was reworked in relation
to three idealised figures of masculinity: the man of simplicity, the man of
gentility and the man of rights.

The man of simplicity

We have seen how the American revolutionaries elevated the ideal of the
plain man. The ordinary American male was held to be a small freeholder
who achieved self-sufficiency through his own industry, was proudly
independent in all his dealings and, in particular, pleased and expressed
himself in a virtuously simple way. John Dickinson's Pennsylvanian
farmer explains that he has 'a contented grateful mind', is 'happy without
bustle' and 'was taught to love *humanity* and *liberty*'.[11] And Benjamin
Franklin, in one of his many letters to the British press, objected to John
Bull's convoluted defences of virtual representation and – with provoca-
tive irony – encouraged him to speak 'much *plainer English*': he signed the
letter 'HOMESPUN'.[12] Partly as a result of America's well-publicised
grievances, this ideal was also tremendously influential in England, a fact
often overlooked by British historians. As Gordon Wood has noted, the
1770s saw a transatlantic 'sentimentalization of the common man and
of natural and spontaneous speech':[13] the English conception of the
independent man was profoundly affected by this phenomenon.

Manly simplicity informed the newfound anti-aristocratic edge to
political radicalism. In the Wilkite 1760s, noble 'outs' had been courted to
oppose noble 'ins', but in the 1770s aristocracy *per se* was politically suspect and only 'the people' were true patriots. Gerald Newman argues that
– in common with the rest of the century – this was because radicals identified the ruling elite as foreign and conceived of them in racist terms.[14] I
would argue instead that radicalism was losing its xenophobic rationale

by this stage, but that they still sought to replace the elite with something more indigenous – of 'the people' – and presented their own claims in those terms. Wilkes, for example, found the need to reinvent himself along these lines from the late 1760s in tune with the new model of political manhood (and in order to win the support of the merchants and dissenters upon whom his career in metropolitan politics relied). He was still a freeborn Englishman, but had to modify his libertine, freethinking, proto-aristocratic persona into something simpler, more restrained and humbly virtuous. He published a third-person defence of his conduct in the *Political Register* where he presented himself as a reformed rake, now virtuous in his private life but no less committed to constitutional liberty in public:

> Mr. Wilkes has irreproachably the merit of a good subject, for he has always paid a due respect to the laws, a reverence to the constitution, an obedience to the cause of the magistrate, and to all just authority . . . After the sharpest provocations, the conduct of Mr. Wilkes has been cool, temperate, and prudent . . . I hope he will atone for the dissipation of too gay a youth, and that the rest of his life will be usefully employed for this nation, whether in the gloom of a prison, or at large among cheerful and genial friends, of sense and honour, with a steady, disinterested, and inviolable attachment to the cause of liberty.[15]

Hereafter, Wilkes emphasised humanitarian, charitable and civic causes, and his longstanding attachment to religious toleration, and he condemned the aristocratic politicians whom he had formerly aped and courted. His tenure as Mayor was marked by the utmost respectability and, with his daughter Polly, he paraded a familial image that won the affection of 1770s Londoners. Wilkes's private correspondence shows that he had always doted upon his daughter, but he consciously presented himself in this mould during his period of civic office: as in his reform motion, *fatherhood* was central to his newfound political masculinity. Wilkes's personification of liberty had shifted from unrestraint to self-restraint, from rakish defiance to paternal respectability. In so doing, his career embodied an important shift that was to occur in the definition of 'the independent man' – and in the tenor of British political society – over the coming century.

In a sense, this shift built upon longstanding foundations. 'Country' patriotism had long praised simple virtues such as plain dealing, directness and – in particular – rurality. Wilkes, as we have seen, very much presented himself as a gentleman of the town rather than of the country,[16] but in so doing he disqualified himself from an important legitimising theme in opposition thought. The existing emphasis on rural virtue was revitalised by writings from America, which further encouraged radicals to change the basis for 'independence' from substantial landholding to simple rural virtues accessible to all.

This change was particularly notable in imaginative literature. The novelist, historian and journalist Tobias Smollett was no radical but, over the course of the 1760s, came to appreciate the value of manly simplicity. As we have seen, Smollett had long been preoccupied with the notion of 'independence', but in his earlier work he had identified this quality with the traditional country gentry. The eponymous heroes of *Roderick Random* (1748) and *Peregrine Pickle* (1751) strive from straitened circumstances to render themselves independent. Roderick endures humiliating and fruitless dependencies upon effeminate patrons ('a servile dependence on that rascal Cringer') until he finally succeeds in his ambition to 'live by my own talents independant of treacherous friends, and supercilious scorn'.[17] Peregrine too is financially redeemed and becomes the archetypal independent country gentleman: 'a man of vast consequence among his country neighbours' who 'bore his prosperity with surprising temperance . . . affability and moderation'.[18] These works' reiterated condemnations of clientage, urban vice, court politicians and 'dependence' suggest that Smollett saw 'independence' in political terms, in line with the 'Country' politics of his *Complete History of England*: the substantial country gentleman was presented as the only bulwark against the encroaching national corruption.

Smollett scholars have generally missed this political meaning to 'independence'[19] and have neglected the work that bears most directly upon the subject, the 'Ode to Independence' written around 1766 and published posthumously in 1773.[20] In many respects it may be read as a reflection upon his experiences in the early 1760s when he endured widespread vilification for attacking Wilkes in his journal *The Briton* while in the pay of the Buteite court. He remained very defensive about his 'Country' credentials and had qualms about requesting a place for his services: given the emphases of the 'Country' scheme regarding patronage, and the tenor of British opinion in the 1760s, the onus was on Smollett to deny his own dependence and corruption. As such, the 'Ode to Independence' seeks to convey that he retains his own integrity and idealism, condemning 'venal bards' and 'hireling minstrels' (lines 98–9) and employing the Pindaric form to lofty effect. Indeed, this declaration of 'independence' may have been in conscious contradistinction to the 'independence' of the Wilkites.[21] In particular, Smollett deployed 'Country' patriotism's contempt for luxury, sensuality and the urban – a recourse not open to Wilkes and his City acolytes. The 'Ode to Independence' condemns luxury and the moral squalor of the metropolis, which Wilkes's libertinism, hedonism and financial imprudence apparently epitomised. Smollett speaks in general terms in the 'Ode', but can barely contain his disgust, possibly implicating even his own work at court:

> Those sculptured halls my feet shall never tread,
> Where varnished Vice and Vanity combin'd,
> To dazzle and seduce, their banners spread;
> And forge vile shackles for the free-born mind . . .
> Where ever-dimpling Falshood pert and vain,
> Presents her cup of stale Profession's froth;
> And pale Disease, with all his bloated train,
> Torments the sons of Gluttony and Sloth.
>
> (lines 81–4, 89–92)

In opposition to this he presents a picture of rural virtue in the final antistrophe of the poem, which must rank as one of the earliest statements of the independent man of simplicity:

> Nature I'll court in her sequester'd haunts,
> By mountain, meadow, streamlet, grove, or cell,
> Where the pois'd lark his evening ditty chaunts,
> And Health, and Peace, and Contemplation dwell.
> There Study shall with Solitude recline;
> And Friendship pledge me to his fellow-swains;
> And Toil and Temperance sedately twine
> The slender cord that fluttering Life sustains;
> And fearless Poverty shall guard the door;
> And Taste unspoil'd the frugal table spread;
> And Industry supply the humble store;
> And Sleep unbrib'd his dews refreshing shed:
> White-mantled Innocence, ethereal spright,
> Shall chase far off the goblins of the night;
> And Independence o'er the day preside,
> Propitious power! my patron and my pride.
>
> (lines 95–120)

The gentle intimacy and nature-worship of this passage contrast with the rest of the work, resulting in a striking shift of tone. The aggressive national and sexual chauvinism of mid-century patriotism is rejected in favour of – possibly even feminine – feeling, a selflessness based on self-denial rather than bombastic shows of public virtue. Smollett seems to imply that struggles on behalf of Liberty are only supportable – and the distracting vices and corruptions of lines 81–104 only avoidable – by the kind of private virtue typified by bracing frugality, unworldliness, industry and a sense of self-sufficiency.

This shift in Smollett's conception of 'independent' virtue – from country gentleman to manly simplicity – was highly prescient. Smollett's privileging of the 'true' individual self over external refinements and social pretensions looked forward to Romanticism and the Victorian cults of 'character', self-help and manly plainness. 'Independence' itself was to take this course over the eighteenth and nineteenth centuries: the 'Ode' should be seen as a transitional work, between the early Georgian association of 'independence' with the social, intellectual, and political elite, and its Victorian association with manhood *per se*. Nor was Smollett alone in this respect. A number of poets chose to celebrate 'independence' over the coming decades, constituting something of a late-Georgian sub-genre. Some were squarely within the 'Country' idiom, rallying the Whig pantheon against independence's usual foes,[22] whereas others engaged more fully with the questions raised in the last antistrophe of Smollett's 'Ode'. Hugh Downman and Mary Russell Mitford reject the false values and temptations of modern life, arguing that true freedom is to be found in the basic virtues accessible to all, self-sufficiency and self-respect;[23] and Wordsworth romanticises this same argument in 'Resolution and Independence' – probably the best-known of all these works – which suggests that the rural poor possess an other-worldly power.[24] This glut of comparable verse between 1780 and 1830 suggests that the idea of 'independence' appealed to the temperament of the Romantic period. As well as addressing political ideals, 'independence' negotiated the dilemma faced by artists reluctant to subsist under patronage but unable to support themselves by their own artistic labours: with art as with politics, patronage was regarded as a threat to conscientiousness, freedom and self-respect. Moreover, an ode or sonnet to 'independence' allowed the author to celebrate the autonomy of the self, the imaginative freedom of principled interiority or fearless intrepidity, as well as the ideal of general (or national) liberty. What better outlet for the zeal of the literary patriot or the idealistic outsider?

Paradoxically, these values were also aped by the fashionable elite, in some incongruously stylised ways. Rural simplicity fitted the vogue for Romanticism and sensibility. Amanda Vickery notes 'a cult of ostentatious solitude', manifested in the construction of grottoes and hermitages in country estates and pleasure gardens. This was in part built upon classical prescriptions: the Roman ideal of intellectualised leisure (*otium*) fuelled by the revival of Horace and the Stoics. In particular, the home came to be regarded as the venue for virtue and refined feeling.[25] The virtue that Christopher Wyvill claimed to exemplify was specifically of a rural and domestic kind, suggesting that domesticity should not simply be regarded as the feminine and apolitical side to the public independence / private dependence dichotomy. Wyvill explored these issues at length in an open letter to William Pitt in 1796. Eulogising himself in the third person, he states his wish to spend his life in 'domestic peace and happiness' in the 'privacy of a country retreat':

> Privacy he has preferred, because privacy was more agreeable to his taste. He was pleased with the blameless occupations of a country life; he loved the contemplation of nature . . . But retirement was his choice for reasons of greater weight and gravity. He valued his independence; he felt the honest pride of a freeman; and independence and freedom he knew were best preserved at a distance from the prodigality and ensnaring allurements of the capital.[26]

As we saw in Smollett's 'Ode to Independence', a 'retreat' of idyllic rurality and simple domestic security is posited as necessary to preserve one's 'independence', so essential to a virtuous public political persona. For Wyvill, 'retirement' is also a space for 'the cultivation of virtue, and the pursuits of literature'. This conscious separation from the capital's moral and political corruption keeps his virtue unsullied so that – like his 'Country' forebears – he is able to respond in times of national danger. Whatever his inclinations towards the 'sequestered life', 'on various public occasions, he has not been slow to stand forth, nor afraid to act his part in the busy scene of politics'.[27] When called upon, he can take on the role of the courageous, direct, sincere champion of political virtue. The hurly burly of public politics, though, is not his natural sphere: he intervenes out of a sense of duty and principle rather than a desire for self-aggrandisement: a common defence in an age that viewed professional politicians with distaste. Whether this is entirely to be believed is another matter. Christie suggests that 'the pursuits of a country gentleman and politician' – enabled by a financially advantageous marriage – were more congenial to Wyvill than those of a country parson.[28] It is nevertheless a telling insight into how opposition political activity was justified at the end of the eighteenth century.

When Wyvill was writing in 1796, the culture of sensibility was already in trouble. In the context of loyalist representations of the French Revolution, inherent virtue was delusive and socially levelling, and unfettered feminine feeling was dangerous.[29] The independent man of simplicity, however, lived on: we will see how domestic virtue was fundamental to the premises of the 1832 Reform Act, and manly simplicity showed the way to muscular Christianity, neo-stoicism and the Victorian paterfamilias.[30]

The man of gentility

In the last three decades of the century, questions of virtue and refinement were also being rethought in the world of parliamentary politics. From the 1770s a discourse of political corruption predominated that was qualitatively different from the highly personalised conflicts of the Wilkite 1760s, questioning the structure and personnel of the political world in a comprehensive way. This necessarily involved a focus upon the high rather than the humble: in particular, the roles of the gentleman and the aristocrat in politics were placed under scrutiny. As we have seen, radicals in the 1770s questioned the aristocracy's natural right to rule: radical critics focused upon the perceived personal failings of the elite, suggesting that humbler people of demonstrable private virtue were more fit to exercise public responsibility. In reality, however, government and political leadership by the social elite remained enduring in practice and compelling in theory, and new justifications for the political role of gentlemen and aristocrats were proposed to meet the needs of the times.

The English notion of 'the gentleman' had a long heritage. It drew upon diverse sources, from classical notions of a guardian class and the medieval courtly value of *gentilesse*, to the early modern styles of the Italian courtier and the French *honête homme*, as codified in courtesy literature. Eighteenth-century England witnessed a reaction against the superficiality of courtly gentility, as witnessed by the controversy surrounding the publication of Chesterfield's *Letters to His Son* in 1774.[31] Indeed, the term 'gentleman' was losing its exclusive connotations and was coming to be applied to anyone who claimed to be worthy of respect: by the Victorian period 'gentleman' was nearly all-embracing, and was more identified with personal character than with rank. In eighteenth-century England, however, gentility's emphasis on social stature and the fulfilment of responsibilities had a very real application since power in parliament and the localities was generally wielded by gentlemen, from the great nobles to the landed gentry of the counties.[32]

As we saw in Chapter 3, the mid-century House of Commons was dominated by a particular kind of gentleman: the independent country gentleman MP. The *English Chronicle*, for example, described the proprietorial incumbent of Bodmin between 1753 and 1784:

> George Hunt Esq. is a gentleman of independent fortune . . . He is
> attached to no set of political tenets in particular, but following the dic-
> tates of an independent and upright mind has uniformly voted for or
> against such a system as he thought any way advantageous or inimical
> to the real interests of his country . . . He can neither be said to possess
> the shining qualities necessary for constituting a public orator, nor the
> systematic solidity requisite in a great statesman, but is nevertheless
> eminently qualified for the important trust he holds, *viz.* the honest
> representative of a free people.[33]

Such men had long been regarded as natural legislators: lords of the soil
who, being free and rurally virtuous citizens themselves, were best qualified to preserve freedom and virtue for everybody else. This commentator from 1780, however, was fully apprised of their limitations. Although
they held the balance in the Commons, their boasted individualism made
them ineffective as a bloc: they only associated in times of emergency and
even then on expressly anti-party terms, such as the St Albans Tavern
group of 1784 that sought an unlikely government of 'best men' comprising both Pitt *and* Fox. Furthermore, as Quentin Skinner notes, 'the virtues
of the independent country gentleman began to look irrelevant and
even inimical to a polite and commercial age'.[34] As we saw in Chapter 2,
Gillray's 1799 caricature of Thomas Tyrwitt Jones suggests that the bucolic
and bloody-minded country gent was an amusing anachronism by the
end of the century. The independent gentleman MP was a dying breed in
a world of bureaucratic, political and financial professionalisation and
centralisation.

The most comprehensive critique of the independent gentleman MP
was Edmund Burke's *Thoughts on the Causes of the Present Discontents* of
April 1770.[35] In what came to be regarded as the manifesto of the Rock-
inghamites, Burke reflected upon the increased power of Crown and
court since 1760, and argued that men of virtue should associate in a party
in order to present an effective opposition and a potential government.
This scheme of party opposition was in implicit rejection of the anti-
party patriotism of Chatham, 'broadbottom' and the radicals. In making
a case for the virtue of 'connexion', however, Burke had also to reason
against the prejudices of the independent MPs whose support Rocking-
ham courted. The *Thoughts* were originally penned in the form of an
open letter to John White, an old-fashioned 'Country Whig' who sat for
East Retford between 1733 and 1768. Burke joins in the 'Country' lament
that a 'spirit of independence' and a 'strenuous resistance to every appearance of lawless power' are no longer considered assets in the 'new modelled' Commons. He paints a dismal picture of the independent MP's lot,

resigned to electoral expense in the boroughs and futile rectitude in the Commons, and argues that they owe it to themselves and to the country to be more effective:

> It is not enough, in a situation of trust in the commonwealth, that a man means well to his country; it is not enough that in his single person he never did an evil act, but always voted according to his conscience . . . This innoxious and ineffectual character, that seems formed upon a plan of apology and disculpation, falls miserably short on the mark of public duty.

Instead, Burke proposes, virtuous gentlemen should act in concert with the nation's natural aristocratic leaders and constitute a government in *'connexion with the sentiments and opinions of the people'.*[36] This is still very much within the bounds of virtual representation, however. Only disinterested substantial gentlemen – 'the natural strength of the kingdom, the great peers, the leading landed gentlemen, the opulent merchants and manufacturers, the substantial yeomanry' – can fulfil this role of trusteeship, offering the gentleman MP an effectual outlet for his patriotic independence.[37]

Burke's new vision of the gentleman politician should be placed in the context of a widespread reassertion of the value of gentility in politics. Christopher Wyvill and his colleagues in the Yorkshire Association judged that the persons with the 'independent' virtue required to rescue Britain from moral and political disaster in the 1780s were substantial country gentlemen like themselves. Unlike the independent gentlemen MPs, these were gentlemen who claimed for themselves an extra-parliamentary political role, and their proposals for structural parliamentary reform went beyond the mid-century 'Country' programme. To Wyvill, only 'independent men' were able to resist 'Parliamentary Seduction':[38] political virtue and vice were polarised in tellingly gendered terms, so we need to turn our attention to Wyvill's professions of manliness to understand the man and his movement. Wyvill's conception of independent manliness was specifically of a genteel, rural and propertied kind. The Committee of the Yorkshire Association referred to themselves as the 'sixty-one gentlemen', 'The Yorkshire Gentlemen', or 'those independent gentlemen, who wish to secure their country from a renewal of that corrupt system of government'.[39] The Association built upon the existing structures of county politics – county meetings, elections for knights of the shire, petitions, addresses in the press – in which substantial country gentlemen predominated. Wyvill held a Harringtonian belief that a state should reflect the will of its propertied countrymen and, as such, sought to increase the number of county voters and members.

Wyvill hoped that this would result in the return of more men like Sir George Savile, who had the private means and public standing that he so revered. Savile served for many years as a county member for Yorkshire and was widely regarded as 'the very embodiment of independent Whiggism' and the epitome of the gentleman MP.[40] His memorial statue in York Minster emphasises the gentlemanly qualities that he supposedly brought to the political world. His statue blends classical citizenship with contemporary values: he is depicted in an easy pose, resting upon a column in 1780s dress. The inscription extols his many qualities, demonstrating that public and private virtue were inseparable in Georgian political masculinities:

> In private life, he was benevolent, and sincere;
> His charities were extensive and secret;
> His whole heart was founded on principles
> Of generosity, mildness, justice, and universal candour.
> In public, the patron of every national improvement;
> In the senate, incorrupt;
> In his commerce with the world, disinterested.

Members like Savile had a claim to natural leadership in the supposedly organic social order of county society, and possessed weight and independence on the floor of the House. The Association sought to place their electoral weight behind candidates in this mould, backing 'a gentleman of independent character and fortune' for Yorkshire, and commending Surrey's county members for their 'steady, upright, and independent conduct in Parliament'.[41]

The Association's celebration of gentlemanliness, however, was not uncritical towards the social elite. Frank O'Gorman highlights the anti-aristocratic character of the movement, describing how they outmanoeuvred the Rockinghams and asserted their independence from Westminster's elite factions: Wyvill considered the influence of the aristocracy to be 'just as great a threat to the country as that of the Crown'.[42] Wyvill's condemnations of irreligion, luxury and vice were aimed at the very high as well as the very low, privileging instead the virtue of the 'independent' social middle in which the gentry had a position of leadership. Wyvill would not have considered the influence of rank, learning and prestige to be an improper recourse. This distinction between influence and nomination (the *abuse* of influence) would become a central tenet of Whig reform; but Wyvill believed that influence should be exerted by a virtuous gentry rather than by a corrupt, monopolising, absentee aristocracy:

> While independent men, supported by large bodies of their fellow citi-
> zens, have the virtue thus to resist corruption, the antient English
> vigour has not abandoned this nation; the hope of a radical reforma-
> tion cannot be ill-founded; their honest example cannot fail to animate
> the timorous, to awe the corrupt, and gradually to restore the genuine
> love of liberty and the English constitution.[43]

The Association was the means by which the voice of independent
gentlemen could be heard in the cause of reform.

Wyvill's pitting of virtuous gentlemen against corrupt aristocrats typified attitudes towards political virtue in the 1780s. Charles James Fox
experienced difficulty maintaining his status as disinterested statesman
and 'Man of the People' on the one hand, and gambler, socialite and Whig
aristocrat on the other. At the notorious Westminster election of 1784 his
supporters still maintained that Fox – 'your own noble Champion' – was a
truly independent man, but his opponents were able to draw upon a wide
range of symbolic resources to argue that he was anything but. As Phyllis
Deutsch argues, the reputation of Fox and his allies for gambling was politically damaging at a time when private and public responsibility were
becoming conflated. Gaming implied instability and dependence upon the
arbitrary will of (feminine) Fortune: 'the drama, exclusivity, and emotion-
ality of aristocratic play had come to exemplify the private vice and public
irresponsibility of the ruling class'.[44] Fox became 'Renard', 'Shufflecard' or
'the high priest of drunkenness, gaming, and every species of debauchery'.[45] Attacks on his colleague the Duchess of Devonshire were also framed
in terms of a highly gendered notion of virtue. Anti-Whig propagandists
focused upon her womanhood, portraying her as lascivious, vain, wild and
neglectful of her domestic responsibilities.[46] This was arguably not a comment on the inappropriateness of female electioneering *per se*, which was
in itself not unusual.[47] Rather, her reputation as leader of fashion, faro
gamer and adulterer – all perceived vices of the nobility – made her
vulnerable to the morally puritan, anti-aristocratic polemic of the times.

One politician who turned this ethos to his advantage was the
Younger Pitt. To many of his contemporaries he was the epitome of the
independent man: in contrast to Fox, they argued, Pitt was sincere, disinterested and patriotic, a Chatham and not a Holland.[48] In the House, Pitt
styled himself as an 'independent Whig' who abhorred party and rested
on the uncultivated support of the independent members (although
Treasury patronage and the favour of the King were, in reality, essential to
the survival of his long-lived administration). In addition, many reformers abandoned Fox for Pitt, impressed both with his desire for efficiency
and independence, and his personal style:

> In his public demeanour, and in debate with his antagonists, Mr. Pitt may be lofty and daring; but in his deportment in private society there is much ease and affability . . . Mr. Wyvill loved the man, and looked up to the minister with reverence and veneration, as a truly Patriot Statesmen, devoted to combat and destroy the monstrous system of corruption, and destined to the high honour to be the political saviour of his country.[49]

The man of gentility in 1780s politics evinced independence in both his public and private personae: the one was the guarantee of the other.

By the 1790s, however, the opposition politicians and ideologues grouped around Charles James Fox had again made a case for the role of the aristocrat and fine gentleman in politics. Fox, for one, modified the image of his private life that had compromised his public role in the crises of 1782–84: he paid his debts, gave up gaming, got married, and – though still an indefatigable presence in the Commons until the 1797 secession – traded his conspicuous public life for study and domesticity.[50] But the Foxite Whigs had no doubt that they *were* aristocrats (or, in a few cases, little short of it) and that their statuses as the guardians of popular liberties, the opposition in parliament and the leaders of initiatives outside of it were not only compatible with their rank but were fundamentally predicated upon the 'independence' that it conferred.

Fox took the theory of party further than Burke had done in his *Present Discontents*. The Foxites conceived of party and organised opposition as permanent institutions necessary to protect popular liberties against the executive. This was informed by their horror of Chathamite politics (a non-noble leader relying on non-party support), the monarch's prerogative power and the influence of the Crown – all of which they had suffered under. Principled 'connexion' in party did not preclude individual independence. On the contrary, the Great Whig families were sufficiently substantial that their disinterestedness and personal honour were guaranteed; and, as heirs to the tradition of Whig constitutionalism, they were the historic trustees of the people's liberties.[51] The Foxites were insistently aristocratic: politics was the appropriate and expected vocation for men of their rank, whose property conferred leisure, cultivation and independent public virtue. A Foxite polemicist of 1794 made a virtue of the fact that opposition figures had greater fortunes than the administration, suggesting that the latter were self-seeking as a result. He continued: 'Men of property are not only more intelligent, but more interested in the government of this country, than men of no property, and therefore are more likely to interfere in its conduct, and thwart its favourite measures'.[52] This made them the natural leaders of the people and the means by which the people's grievances could be articulated. Furthermore, the aristocrat's personal independence supposedly ensured that his attachment to a popular cause was disinterested.[53]

The most explicit indication that the Foxite Whigs regarded themselves as the nation's genteel leaders was the title of the association that sprang from their ranks,[54] 'The Friends of the People': they were advocates, but were not themselves *of* the commonality. From the 150 or so recorded members, there were a handful of professors, clergymen, dissenters, lawyers and literary men – many of whom were prominent society figures – but the prime movers in the association were largely drawn from aristocrats and substantial squires. The Friends boasted at least two earls, three lords, four knights, several heirs (such as Grey and Howard), and many others from well-to-do families. The character of the society was pointedly aristocratic – stringent membership regulations and a steep subscription fee sought to preserve its exclusivity – and those who recognised them as leaders of the extra-parliamentary reform movement did so on these terms. The Sheffield Society for Constitutional Information was suitably deferential, acknowledging the 'superior judgement' of 'respectable and worthy characters': 'Looking up to the Friends of the People as our leaders in this great and necessary business, we shall be happy, and esteem it a great favour, to receive any communication which they may vouchsafe to favour us with'.[55] Members of the society shared Fox's opinion of the political role of the true aristocrat.[56] Erskine explained to the House that he believed in a 'natural aristocracy'. His problem was with *false* aristocrats: 'during this administration, so many peers had been made, not for any of those merits which properly claimed the honour, but for possessing parliamentary influence, that this part of the constitution would be ruined by its own corruption'.[57] Only genuine aristocrats like the Friends were independent gentlemen.

The strategy of the Friends of the People was to respond to the crisis with moderate reform in order 'to do away with every cause of complaint': this, they judged, would avert threats to property, liberty and social order.[58] Daniel Stuart argued that the lesson of the French Revolution was not that reform was dangerous, but that failure to reform drove the people to extremities.[59] As such, the Friends were part ally, part rival to the existing radical societies, hoping to temper or supersede them. In reality, their advocacy of moderation in polarised times was doomed, and the reform motions in the House that they initiated were disastrous for the Whigs. Nevertheless, Grey's motions of 1793 and 1797 sparked the biggest parliamentary debates on reform of the century and shed much light on the arguments that many of the same men would employ in 1830–32. The reform critique that emerged – and the very fact that they were able to steer a moderate course with ideological consistency at a time when debate was driven to philosophical absolutes – owed a great deal to the notion of manly 'independence'.

Iain Hampsher-Monk and Harold Ellis have offered compelling analyses of the Friends' reform ideology, emphasising civic humanism and a critique of electoral influence, respectively.[60] The notion of 'the independent man', however, drew upon both of these traditions: the Friends' critique should be understood in terms of this multifaceted conception of manly political virtue. Republicanism does indeed offer a productive perspective upon the Friends' conception of the electoral system. Voters were considered as 'citizens' and were conceptualised in terms of their virtue: great emphasis was placed upon both their independence – their ability to act as a virtuous check in a balanced constitution – and their stake in the general weal. Where all men were virtuous, independent and attached to the community, all should have the vote. Several Friends revered the American social and political system where – they believed – this ideal was almost realised in practice and Fox commended the 'vigour' of classical democracies.[61] This was not the case in 'the present corrupt state' of British society, however, so universal suffrage was inadvisable.[62]

This is where civic humanism coincides with electoral influence. Universal suffrage was dangerous precisely because it would enfranchise dependent people upon whom coercion could be brought to bear. Thomas Erskine provided a detailed justification of this point of view in the 1797 debate: 'The system of universal suffrage would throw into the hands of some individuals a dangerous preponderance – One man employing a great number of persons might, by influencing their conduct, unite in himself, perhaps, a thousand votes, and thus destroy freedom of election'. This was 'inconsistent with the true spirit of independent elections'.[63] On purely pragmatic grounds, therefore, certain persons should be excluded from the franchise. The test for inclusion was 'independence'. As Fox famously argued: 'My opinion is, that the best plan of representation is that which shall bring into activity the greatest number of independent voters, and that is defective which would bring forth the greatest number of those whose situation and condition take from them the power of deliberation'.[64] To a certain extent 'independence' was measured in terms of property, which implied self-sufficiency and a stake in the country, combined with a Machiavellian conviction that the polity should reflect its distribution. But Grey's plan was vague on this point, suggesting only that 'a certain annual rent a certain number of

years' should be fixed for the counties (where a uniform property qualification subsisted anyway).[65] The primary test of independence was one
of gender and obligation: voters should be male householders. Fox
continued with a telling *reductio ad absurdum*:

> I hope gentlemen will not smile if I endeavour to illustrate my position
> by referring to the example of the other sex. In all the theories and pro-
> jects of the most absurd speculation, it has never been suggested that it
> would be advisable to extend the elective franchise to the female sex . . .
> Why! but because by the law of nations, and perhaps also by the law of
> nature, that sex is dependent upon ours; and because, therefore, their
> voices would be governed by the relation in which they stand in society.

By drawing a sharp distinction between female dependence and male
independence, Fox sought to realign the criteria for citizenship along the
lines of gender, so as to justify wider enfranchisement for men. His appeal
to 'nature' (biological sex difference) rather than tradition was typical of
the Enlightenment. The Whigs were not calling for universal male suffrage: only certain sorts of men should be entrusted with the vote, but this
too was evaluated qualitatively in terms of gender. Less manly men
should, like women, be excluded: 'The desideratum to be obtained, is
independent voters, and that, I say, would be a defective system that
should bring regiments of soldiers, of servants, and of persons whose low
condition necessarily curbed the independence of their minds'.[66]

It is not as if the Whigs envisaged that dependent people would be
unrepresented. The doctrine of virtual representation – once applied to
continents and still applied to cities – could be applied to families. As
Erskine reasoned:

> All the people in their various degrees, not included personally in such
> a representation, are members of some house or another; they are
> therefore represented in the persons of their fathers, or their nearest
> kindred, and bound in every feeling, as well as every interest, which
> grows out of social existence, to support an assembly proceeding from
> such a universal rational will . . .[67]

Furthermore, the householder was in the 'respectable situation' of father
and master, attained 'by honest industry and fair exertions'.[68] As Wilkes
had done, the Whig reformers valorised the (masculine) station of fatherhood. They propose that a father and husband would make a responsible
voter because of his supposedly natural regard for their welfare. Erskine
even evoked a romantic family scene – 'a little circle round his fireside' –
challenging anybody to deny that the humble father has a 'stake in the
public fate'.[69] He assumes that paternal affection subsists within the

late-Georgian sentimental family, but he makes the statement to political effect, to claim wider enfranchisement for men.

The Foxites also offered a novel critique of electoral influence. Ellis places much emphasis on the Friends' *State of the Representation* of 1793.[70] The report draws the distinction between '*Nomination*' – boroughs where most voters are 'immediate dependents' of one individual, who thus has 'undoubted control' over elections – and '*Influence*'. Nomination boroughs should be eradicated, they argue, but influence was more complex. Where property and rank 'obtain a degree of weight beyond what is natural' and exert the influence of fear or bribery, it should be opposed. On the other hand, property and rank also involve an 'honourable attachment' that should be encouraged: 'Where fortune enables, and disposition induces a man to discharge the friendly offices of neighbourhood and connexion with zeal and liberality'.[71] This is the crux of Foxite thinking, where the world of parliamentary reform (the independent elector) meets that of privilege (the independent gentleman). Voters should be independent so that they can freely recognise their natural leaders. Thus independent voters should return independent members – in the sense of disinterested public virtue rather than non-party – restoring balance to the constitution. Grey's speeches in the 1793 and 1797 reform debates are pervaded with the language of 'independence', arguing that the electoral system should be changed specifically to ensure that both voters and members possessed this quality: 'no government could be lasting or free which was not founded on virtue, and on that independence of mind and conduct among the people which created energy, and led to every thing that was noble and generous, and that alone could conduce to the strength and safety of a state . . .'.[72] The men who would be excluded from the Commons by independent voting would be men 'without property, without industry, and without talents':[73] the low-born self-seeking mediocrities who, the Foxites alleged, kept Pitt in office. If more great men (like themselves) were returned to the Commons, a proper counterweight could be posed to the prerogative and the people's liberties restored.

In so many ways, Charles James Fox and the Society of the Friends of the People look forward to the Reform Act. Following the defeat of Grey's motion in 1797 the Foxites seceded from parliament and did not pursue parliamentary reform when they returned. The next generation of Whig gentlemen reformers, however, would employ remarkably similar arguments and Grey himself would reiterate his creed of 'independence' as an old man in 1830–32. Although radicals would continue to employ the tradition of 'independence' against the aristocracy, the ideal of the independent gentleman and his independent electors would endure well into the Victorian period.

The man of rights

The Foxites, however, were only one of many groups calling for reform in the 1790s. The question of English 'radicalism' in the period of the French Revolution has been much explored and debated.[74] The narrative is familiar: events in France provided a backdrop for domestic reform campaigns, and a two-way 'debate' about the Revolution's implications for British institutions took place, as the reformist initiative passed from gentlemen to 'radical' artisans and labourers. Such accounts, however, often lack definitional clarity. As Mark Philp argues, reformism in this period was 'protean stuff', and political and ideological division preclude any sense of a unified movement.[75] Furthermore, historians – even those who claim to be critiquing the concept – employ the nouns 'radical' and 'radicalism' even though these were *not* contemporary terms of identification.[76] 'Reformer' was current, as were vaguer formulations (such as 'a friend to moral and political improvement') that suggest that senses of identity in this area were experimental and provisional.[77] In this chapter I have followed the present convention of distinguishing between 'radicals' and 'reformers', because they are useful terms of art: 'radical' connotes something about the temperament and critical scope of a political actor that the more moderate term 'reformer' lacks. Nevertheless, to devote a section to 'radicalism in the 1790s' would be wholly anachronistic. I am offering a different focus, which enables me to emphasise an area of agreement among various critics of the establishment, rather than just the differences. In this section I will explore how persons of diverse reformist and radical hues proposed a common model of manly 'independence', based upon the notion of the individual as the bearer of rights.

The question of how far radicals were influenced by the tradition of 'independence' is a vexed one. J. G. A. Pocock and Gregory Claeys have emphasised the influence of 'Country' and neo-classical traditions upon the radicals of the 1790s, but Philp has taken exception to this: 'It is one thing to recognise the continued force of the language of "independence", but quite another to think that this necessarily dominates the new universalist and national forms of political language which are an increasing presence in British political life from the 1760s onward'. He dismisses 'independence' as 'rhetoric', from which we should not 'read off' an ideological position.[78] I would agree that a profession of 'independence' should not be regarded as a *reflection* of an individual's position, either socially or politically; but we should not ignore a culture that they clearly found to be meaningful. On the contrary, the culture of manly 'independence' was central to 1790s radicalism. Radicals conceived of political entitlement in unprecedentedly inclusive ways, so it was necessary to redefine this central marker of political empowerment. Contrary to their 'Country' predecessors and their Whig contemporaries, radicals argued that 'independence' was not a matter of rank, property or even nationality, but was within the reach of every male adult, if only political, legal and social conditions would permit it. In political terms, 'independence' became both the chicken and the egg: independence was an important reason why all men should qualify for the vote, but they could only guarantee their independence if they were enfranchised and thus not subject to the arbitrary will of their governors. This emphasis upon the entitlements of humble men reached its logical conclusion in the Paineite conceptions of popular sovereignty and natural rights. To a large extent, Thomas Paine succeeded in freeing conceptions of citizenship and rights from their traditional 'Country' parameters but even he was indebted to the neo-classical conception of 'independence'.

We have seen how support for radical reform in England collapsed by the mid-1780s, but it had revived again before the outbreak of the French Revolution. The campaigns for the abolition of the slave trade and the repeal of the Test and Corporation Acts, and the centenary of 1688 served to focus attention upon the rights of the individual, and to stimulate calls for a reform of the political system. The significance of the Glorious Revolution had been contested throughout the century but, in the light of the American Revolution, radicals were inclined to view the changes of 1688–89 as incomplete. Richard Price famously stated the principles of the Revolution to be 'the right to chuse our governors, or cashier them for misconduct, and to frame a government for ourselves', and therefore argue that the promise of 1688 had not been realised.[79] Price's invocation of the right to resist and to form governments was based upon the assumption – reinforced by the American experience – that sovereignty resided in the people and that governments rested upon their consent.

This theory of popular sovereignty and consent placed a renewed emphasis upon the political power held in the present by the independent individual. Although some radicals such as John Thelwall continued to argue in terms of historical entitlements, others powerfully employed the theory of popular sovereignty to argue that prescriptive rights were null and void. Paine's justification for this was original and highly influential, and centred on the rights of the individual. He argued that rights are not inherited but come directly from God and inhere in every person. The collectivity of individuals – the people – constitute the sovereignty in a state. Government is an artificial contrivance ('a necessary evil') created by the people at the beginning of society for their benefit, and only perpetuated thereafter with their consent.[80] Each generation reserves the right to reconstitute its institutions of government as it sees fit, because to deny the people the right to alter their inherited institutions is to alienate them from the rights that they hold in the present: 'The vanity and presumption of governing beyond the grave is the most ridiculous and insolent of all tyrannies. Man has no property in man; neither has any generation a property in the generations which are to follow'.[81] The notion that no man should have property in another was central to Paine's thought: in a free society, men would be independent.

Radicals insisted that man should no longer be subject to the arbitrary will of another, and that only equal legal and electoral rights could guarantee this. When a man lacks the vote he cannot check his governors and so is dependent upon their will (or 'enslaved'), whereas with the vote he is politically independent. As Cartwright argued in 1795: '*John, Thomas*, and *Harry*, merely by having *a right to vote*, for a representative of that elective *body* of which they are severally *members*, do enjoy *political freedom*; because the *body* of which they are *members*, and in which . . . they enjoy *equal active citizenship*, is, in the full sense of the words, politically free'. Since it is 'POLITICAL LIBERTY . . . that makes a man in political society a *person* and not a *thing*', to deny him the vote is to deny his personhood.[82] The liberty that radicals sought was thus of a classical republican kind: freedom from dominion rather than freedom from constraint. Gregory Claeys and Karen Ford have shown that classical republicanism was an important element of Paine's thought, and which enabled him to develop his own brand of 'democratic republicanism'.[83] Individuals are dependent – and thus denied human dignity and self-determination – when they are alienated from rights that should be recognised as inherent. Again, this is particularly true of electoral citizenship, for it is that which enables individuals to check or to consent to their governors: 'The right of voting for representatives is the primary right by which other rights are protected. To take away this right is to reduce a man to slavery, for slavery consists in being subject to the will of another, and he that has not a vote in the election of representatives is in this case'.[84]

Radicals in the 1790s also employed the language of 'independence' and 'dependence' to conceptualise political virtue and vice. Paine, for one, clearly employs a republican understanding of obligation throughout his work. In *The Rights of Man*, for example, he declares his authorial position: 'Independence is my happiness, and I view things as they are, without regard to place or person'.[85] The contrast was often drawn with his opponent Burke, who was widely castigated for his supposed dependence upon aristocrats.[86] Similarly, the London Corresponding Society (LCS) dismissed their critics as 'dependants of the Ministry', and branded Reeves's 'slavish and malevolent' Association for Protecting Liberty and Property as 'The PLACE and PENSION SOCIETY of the Crown and Anchor'.[87] Like the old 'Country' opposition, the radicals of the 1790s denied that their opponents had a legitimate voice, by arguing that persons in a position of dependence lacked an autonomous, conscientious personality.

The radicals' and reformers' conceptions of the types of persons that *were* capable and deserving of independence were unprecedentedly broad. Given their substantial factional and ideological diversity, there were inevitable disagreements – but it is nevertheless significant that all subscribed to the notion of 'the independent man', and conceptualised it in comparable ways. It is worth exploring the ways in which radicals conceived of personal independence with respect to nationality, property, arms-bearing, individualism and (most importantly) gender.

The first aspect of 'independence' that radicals sought to address was the conviction that it was an exclusively English virtue. In the eighteenth century, 'independence' was associated with the English national character, and thus with a nationally exclusive libertarian tradition: 'independence' was the personal quality required of citizens who enjoyed the liberties enshrined in the ancient constitution. We have seen how political radicals had been forced to move away from anglocentric patriotism from the 1770s, but they continued to admire the English radical-Whig pantheon,[88] and some even subscribed to the notion that the English national character was inherently libertarian. The veteran reformer John Cartwright, despite the universalist tenor of his American writings, retained his belief in a shared national character, boasting 'an English Nature, that hates despotism even in its mildest and most polished forms'. Although he gradually appreciated republicanism, he revered King Alfred and the Saxon constitution, believing that the ancient English constitution ('the title deed to our political estate') embodied the laws of nature and God.[89] Others similarly argued that natural and historical rights were not inconsistent in this way, and that the English had unique claims to the manly independence that their political system required.[90] Nevertheless, the Paineite conviction that liberty was not dependent upon nationality or ancient constitutions was extremely influential in plebeian radicalism. Price encouraged his audience to love their country but 'to carry our views beyond it': 'we ought to consider ourselves as citizens of the world, and take care to maintain a just regard to the rights of other countries'.[91] As we will see in the next chapter, however, this stance became difficult to maintain in the context of war and the anti-libertarian turn of events in France; and, ironically, conservatives were able to occupy the patriotic space that radicals had vacated to great popular effect.

'Country' and neo-classical theorists had maintained that the personal independence required for citizenship was predicated upon the ownership of property, and *landed* property in particular. There was a move away from these propertied understandings of independence – and thus from the reform schemes of Wyvill and the Foxite Whigs – in 1790s plebeian radicalism. Metropolitan radicals had long emphasised non-landed forms of wealth, including the property inherent in one's labour, as bases for political entitlement. The rational dissenter David Williams argued that 'All men, at the age of eighteen, who are not vagabonds or in the hands of a justice, have a right to vote; because they contribute by their industry to the support of the state'.[92] Paine departed from classical republicanism in arguing unequivocally that rights should be attached to persons and not to property: 'If property is to be made the criterion, it is a total departure from every moral principle of liberty, because it is attaching rights to mere matter, and making man the agent of that matter'. Paine still retained the concept of property insofar as he conceptualised rights as 'a species of property' inherent to the individual that cannot be sold or given away (but, perversely, can be alienated).[93] Political rights were not reliant upon propertied independence, but became the indefeasible property of the independent personality.

Another criterion for independent manliness and citizenship in classical and Harringtonian writings had been the bearing of arms in the defence of the state, but very few radicals espoused this in the 1790s. The Society for Constitutional Information (SCI) had discussed citizen militias during the Gordon Riots but, by and large, radicals who talked of arming in the 1790s did so with a view to overthrowing the state rather than defending it.[94] The exception was Major Cartwright. In *The Commonwealth in Danger* (1795) he – paradoxically – both expressed sympathy for the French Revolution and argued that Britons should demonstrate their citizenship by repelling the expected invasion. He cited Saxon precedents and Harrington's *Oceana* at length in order to justify an 'armed nation': 'I know of no line so unexceptionable, so constitutional, and so easily drawn, as that of arming every taxed householder'.[95] This would not only provide a cheap and effective military force, but would restore 'republican energy' to the constitution: 'the generous, manly openness of free men [would] again become our characteristic'. Furthermore, arming the nation would be its political salvation:

> A million of armed men supporting the state with their purse, and defending it with their lives, will know that none have so great a stake as themselves in the government; nor more right to have a voice in the direction of affairs. The circle of representation will consequently be at least co-extensive with the circle of arms. Hence arming the people, and reforming parliaments, are inseparable.[96]

As we will see in the next chapter, his arguments were highly prescient: many men *did* volunteer to defend Britain in the coming decade and, although radical reform was not their motive, it did become more difficult to deny them citizenship thereafter.

To a large degree, radicals paid less attention to the traditional marks of independence – nationality, property and martial capability – and instead underlined more accessible aspects of manly individualism. Radicals advocated the humble virtue of the simple man, emphasising inner 'truth' and straightforwardness, and confidently offered up their theories to the sincere judgement of their audience.[97] In the context of Romanticism and Revolution, radicals were able to emphasise the egalitarian aspects of the culture of feeling: every man experiences the world in the same way, so has an equal right to human dignity and entitlements. As Smollett had done in the 1760s, Romantic radicals like the playwright Thomas Holcroft argued that true independence lay in fortitude and abstemiousness:

> That man is independent whose mind is prepared to meet all fortunes, and be happy under the worst; who is conscious that industry in any country will supply the very few wants of his species; and who, while he can enjoy the delicacies of taste as exquisitely as a glutton, can transfer that luxury by the activity of his mind and body to the simplest viands. Every other man is a slave though he were more wealthy than Midas.[98]

Besides rejecting patronage, radical independent men also reiterated the Georgian conviction that faction was a threat to conscientious self-determination. William Hazlitt described Holcroft as 'a man of too honest, too independent a turn of mind to be a time-server, to lend himself as a tool to the violence of any party'.[99] An important aspect of this independence was the ability to act politically independent of patricians. Thomas Hardy's LCS was a significant departure from the gentry-led societies of the eighties: they '*demonstrated* that the *people* could act for themselves – that they did not want the *assistance* of great men, or popular leaders'.[100] Many radicals sought the ballot as an integral part of their parliamentary reform schemes, so that humble voters could resist the very patrician influence that Whig reformers sought to preserve. For Cartwright secret voting was the necessary accompaniment to universal suffrage: 'very few indeed will be truly independent votes without the friendly shield of the ballot'.[101]

The radicals of the 1790s espoused a culture of assertive libertarianism that encouraged men to cherish their rights: 'The love of freedom is as inseparable from our nature, as the life-blood which flows from the heart. – It is that imperishable spark in the bosom of man, which time may smother, but which eternity cannot extinguish'.[102] Two important components of this libertarianism were radical nonconformity and intellectual individualism. Nonconformist Protestantism emphasises that God's truth is accessible to all, independent of traditional orthodoxies and hierarchies, and this commonly fostered a critical attitude towards existing political beliefs and institutions. Besides seeking an end to their own civil disabilities, dissenters had long been prominent participants in metropolitan radicalism, and societies such as the SCI were modelled upon the nonconformist debating clubs in which Priestley, Price and Burgh had developed their ideas.[103] Certainly, religion should be central to our understanding of Paine. Claeys remarks upon Paine's 'puritan rage', and Quakerism informed both his humanitarianism and his conception of individual worth: his belief in inherent rights of divine origin was arguably influenced by the concept of 'inner light'. The nonconformist emphasis on learning God's will by studying creation – prominent in Paine's later deism – reinforced the radical sense of intellectual self-determination. The ability of the (male) individual to think for himself, and to disdain dependence upon political or intellectual authority, was central to radical independence. Paine's *Rights of Man* in particular encouraged its readers to shake off the mentality of subservience and intellectually to recreate themselves,[104] and political education was fundamental to the 1790s radical project. The SCI, for example, sought to convert men to radicalism through education and argued that the French revolutionaries 'dispersed the mists of ignorance, and taught man to reason for himself'.[105] In historical terms, manly independence was more usually associated with the resistance of decline rather than with progress: in the 'Country' scheme, virtue degenerates from a past ideal state, and 'independence' is the boast of those who oppose corruption and seek a return to the golden age. In the 1790s, however, 'independence' was revitalised by forward-looking Enlightenment rationalism and optimism.

Plebeian radicals in the 1790s thus proposed an unprecedentedly accessible model of personal independence as the basis for political entitlement, but important exclusions remained. Doubts remained about the 'independence' of domestic servants.[106] By the 1790s Paine was arguing against all electoral qualifications, but in 1770s America he had argued against enfranchising 'dependent' state officials and also persons who had forfeited their franchise such as criminals and those who refused to recognise the state (namely American Tories).[107] Paine was entirely conventional in denying some functions to persons under twenty-one. Minors had rights but they were 'preserved inviolate' by 'the sacred guardianship of the aged' – who could not dispossess them – until they came of age.[108]

Only a small minority of radicals, however, would have argued against women's exclusion from civil and political entitlement.[109] Indeed, it is difficult to reconstruct how radicals viewed women because femininity was largely effaced from their discourse: throughout this section, it has been difficult to avoid employing terms like 'mankind', 'humanity', 'the people' and 'the individual' in the *male* sense that contemporary radicals employed them. Hilda Smith has demonstrated how these supposedly universal terms had been employed in a masculine sense since at least the seventeenth century, excluding women both from citizenship and even from the use of universalising arguments for female empowerment.[110] The doctrine of the 'Rights of Man', however, further masculinised the realm of political citizenship, and the attempt to shore up the 'natural' boundaries between male 'independence' and female 'dependence' was central to this project. As far as English radicals were concerned, the criteria for empowering 'independence' – rationality, martial capability, self-ownership, assertiveness, even natural rights – were all aspects of a *manly* subjectivity.

One commentator who famously protested against this state of affairs in the 1790s was Mary Wollstonecraft. In *A Vindication of the Rights of Women* she did not take issue with the masculinism of the radicals (in whose circles she moved) but with the willing dependence of women of her own class. She too drew upon Lockean sensationalist psychology and argued that women were artificially conditioned as creatures of sensibility and luxury who were incapable of reason or self-sufficiency, and were thus excessively dependent upon their menfolk. Wollstonecraft recommended changes in women's education and an increase in opportunities for 'women of a superior cast . . . by which they can pursue more extensive plans of usefulness and independence'. Significantly, the *Vindication* even hinted that 'women ought to have representatives, instead of being arbitrarily governed without having a direct share allowed them in the deliberations of government'.[111] Her critique of oppression and corruption, however, is only comprehensible within a dissenting radical context, a tradition that drew upon the neo-classical preoccupation with the manly health of the citizenry.[112] The qualities that she admires – independence, rationality, strength, dignity, virtue – are all associated with manliness in her text, and she frequently expresses her contempt for her female contemporaries who do not aspire to these public-spirited ideals. Instead, she encourages women 'to become more masculine and respectable': her ideal was the independent man 'from the middle rank of life'.[113] Even the century's most thoroughgoing critic of female exclusion could not resist the lure of manly independence.

Nevertheless, 'independence' had shifted significantly since the early 1770s. The English experience of revolution-from-afar in America and France had helped to free this central libertarian and anti-establishmentarian idea from its traditional exclusive reference points. The American Revolution in particular – which employed the same critical idiom, and which offered analogies with English institutions, national characteristics and political traditions – had a profound effect upon English conceptions of 'the independent man'. In place of its early Georgian association with high rank, substantial landed property and anglocentric patriotism, radicals and reformers could now conceive of 'independence' in more accessible terms. If 'independence' could be viewed in terms of sincere sensibility, rationality, humble virtues and inherent rights, then political entitlement could be conceived of far more broadly. The period 1770–97 played a pivotal role in the shifting meaning of 'independence', from the exterior acquirements of patricians to 'inner' qualities accessible to all men. As we have seen, however, this reformist project of reconceptualising citizenship along the lines of masculinity necessarily had exclusive implications where women were concerned: indeed, it was often explicitly misogynistic.

In the event, many of the ideas of the 1790s radicals did not endure. In terms of popular reformist politics, constitutionalism proved to be a far more accessible and appealing political culture than the 'rights of every generation' principle. Reform, when it came, would commonly be justified in relation to more traditional points of reference. More immediately, radicalism could not compete with the popularity of loyalism and the heavy hand of the state in the context of war and threatened invasions. The next chapter will explore how the culture of manly independence was at first problematic for loyalist conservatives, until they too learned to harness its motivating power.

Notes

1 John Sainsbury, *Disaffected Patriots: London Supporters of Revolutionary America 1769–1782* (Kingston: McGill-Queen's University Press, 1987), pp. ix, 31.

2 Linda Colley, 'Radical patriotism in eighteenth-century England' (1983), in R. Samuel (ed.), *Patriotism: The Making and Unmaking of British National Identity*, vol. I: *History and Politics* (London, Routledge, 1989), pp. 167–87 (p. 176).

3 *London Evening Post* (5–7 October 1775): quoted in Sainsbury, *Disaffected Patriots*, p. 115.

4 Commons (31 October 1776): *The Parliamentary Register*, 17 vols (London, 1802), vol. V, p. 14.

5 For example, in support of the pro-American Admiral Keppel: Sainsbury, *Disaffected Patriots*, pp. 144–8.

6 21 March 1776: *The Parliamentary Register*, vol. III, pp. 178–88 (pp. 180, 182, 186, 185).

7 Richard Price, *Observations on the Nature of Civil Liberty* (1776), in *Political Writings*, ed. D. Thomas (Cambridge: Cambridge University Press, 1991), p. 69.

8 J. Innes, 'Politics and morals: the reformation of manners movement in later eighteenth-century England', in E. Hellmuth (ed.), *The Transformation of Political Culture* (Oxford: Oxford University Press, 1990), pp. 57–118.

9 Christopher Wyvill, *The Correspondence of the Rev. C. Wyvill with the Right Honourable William Pitt*, 2 vols (Newcastle, 1796–97), vol. I, p. 52.

10 Price, *Observations*, pp. 42, 41.

11 John Dickinson, *Letters from a Farmer in Pennsylvania* (Philadelphia, 1768), p. 3.

12 Letter to the *Gazetteer* (15 January 1766): *Benjamin Franklin's Letters to the Press, 1758–1775*, ed. V. Crane (Chapel Hill: North Carolina University Press, 1950), pp. 49–52 (p. 52).

13 Gordon Wood, 'The democratization of mind in the American Revolution', in R. Horwitz (ed.), *The Moral Foundations of the American Republic*, 3rd edn (Charlottesville: Virginia University Press, 1986), pp. 108–35 (p. 124).

14 G. Newman, *The Rise of English Nationalism: A Cultural History 1740–1830* (London: Weidenfeld and Nicolson, 1987), pp. 183–205.

15 'A Letter on the Public Conduct of Mr. Wilkes' (n.d.), reprinted in *The Correspondence of the Late John Wilkes with his Friends*, ed. John Almon, 5 vols (London, 1805), vol. I, pp. 244–71 (pp. 262, 270).

16 P. D. G. Thomas, *John Wilkes: A Friend to Liberty* (Oxford: Oxford University Press, 1996), pp. 155, 216.

17 Tobias Smollett, *The Adventures of Roderick Random* (1748), ed. P.-G. Boucé (Oxford: Oxford University Press, 1979), pp. 77, 243. The language of 'dependence' recurs in the novel in its degrading sense: pp. 19, 28, 67, 73–5, 98, 214, 257, 306–7.

18 Tobias Smollett, *The Adventures of Peregrine Pickle, in which are included Memoirs of a Lady of Quality* (1751), ed. J. Clifford (Oxford: Oxford University Press, 1969), p. 770.

19 Iain Campbell Ross alone acknowledges that 'independence' is 'one of the most powerful and persistent ideas of eighteenth-century Britain' and analyses *Peregrine Pickle* in these terms: 'With dignity and importance: Peregrine Pickle as country gentleman', in A. Bold (ed.), *Smollett: Author of the First Distinction* (London: Vision Press, 1982), pp. 148–69.

20 Tobias Smollett, 'Ode to Independence', in *Poems, Plays, and* The Briton, ed. O. Brack and L. Chilton with introductions by B. Gassman (Athens: Georgia University Press, 1993), pp. 57–61. On the authenticity and dating of the work, see L. Norwood, 'The authenticity of Smollett's *Ode to Independence*', *Review of English Studies* 65 (1941), pp. 55–64.

21 I explore this in greater detail in 'Tobias Smollett's "Ode to Independence" and Georgian political culture', *British Journal for Eighteenth-Century Studies* 26:1 (2003), pp. 27–39.

22 William Mason, 'Ode to Independency', in *The Works of William Mason, M.A.*, 4 vols (London, 1811), vol. I, pp. 38–41; George Alexander Stevens, 'Independency', in *Songs, Comic and Satyrical*, 2nd edn (London, 1788), pp. 22–3; George Dyer, 'Ode V. Independence', in *Poetics*, 2 vols (London, 1812), vol. I, pp. 30–3; Mary Robinson, 'Sonnet. To Independence', in *The Poetical Works*, ed. M. E. Robinson, 3 vols (London, 1806), vol. III, p. 109.

23 Hugh Downman 'To Independence', in *Infancy, a poem*, 6th edn (Exeter, 1803), pp. 219–23; Mary Russell Mitford, in 'Independence', in *Dramatic Scenes, Sonnets, and Other Poems* (London, 1827), pp. 339–43.

24 William Wordsworth, 'Resolution and Independence' (1802), in *Wordsworth: Poetical Works*, ed. T. Hutchinson and E. De Selincourt, new edn (London: Oxford University Press, 1971), pp. 155–7. See G. Harrison, 'Wordsworth's leech gatherer: liminal power and the "Spirit of Independence"', *Journal of English Literary History* 56 (1989), pp. 327–50.

25 Amanda Vickery, *The Gentleman's Daughter: Women's Lives in Georgian England* (New Haven: Yale University Press, 1998), p. 283; Philip Carter, *Men and the Emergence of Polite Society, Britain 1660–1800* (Harlow: Longman, 2001), pp. 70, 93–8.

26 *Correspondence of the Rev. C. Wyvill*, vol. I, pp. 50–1.

27 Christopher Wyvill, 'The Case of the Rev. C. Wyvill Respecting the Right Honourable William Pitt', in *Correspondence of the Rev. C. Wyvill*, vol. I, pp. 50–89 (p. 51).

28 I. R. Christie, 'The Yorkshire Association, 1780–4: a study in political organisation', *Historical Journal* 3:2 (1960), pp. 144–61 (p. 146).

29 John Brewer, *The Pleasures of the Imagination: English Culture in the Eighteenth Century* (London: Harper Collins, 1997), pp. 121–2.

30 J. G. Barker-Benfield, *The Culture of Sensibility: Sex and Society in Eighteenth-Century Britain* (Chicago: Chicago University Press, 1992), p. 77; Carter, *Men and the Emergence of Polite Society*, p. 214; David Alderson, *Mansex Fine: Religion, Manliness, and Imperialism in Nineteenth-Century British Culture* (Manchester: Manchester University Press, 1998); John Tosh, 'Gentlemanly politeness and manly simplicity in Victorian England', *Transactions of the Royal Historical Society* 12 (2002), pp. 455–72.

31 P. Mason, *The English Gentleman: The Rise and Fall of an Ideal* (London: Deutsch, 1982), pp. 21–66; Carter, *Men and the Emergence of Polite Society*, pp. 5–6, 76–87.

32 D. Jarrett, *England in the Age of Hogarth* (London: Hart-Davies, 1974), pp. 12–13.

33 Quoted in *The House of Commons 1754–1790*, eds L. Namier and J. Brooke, 5 vols (London: Secker and Warburg, 1964), vol. I, p. 149.

34 Q. Skinner, *Liberty before Liberalism* (Cambridge: Cambridge University Press, 1998), p. 97.

35 Edmund Burke, *Thoughts on the Causes of the Present Discontents* (1770), in *The Writings and Speeches of Edmund Burke*, vol. II: *Party, Parliament, and the American Crisis 1766–1774*, ed. P. Langford (Oxford: Clarendon Press, 1981), pp. 251–323.

36 Burke, *Thoughts*, pp. 258, 296, 299, 315, 280. Frank O'Gorman emphasises the impor-
    tance of aristocratic leadership in Burke's model: *The Rise of Party in England: The
    Rockingham Whigs 1760–82* (London: Allen and Unwin, 1975), pp. 263–5.
37 Burke, *Thoughts*, p. 282.
38 Christopher Wyvill, *Political Papers, Chiefly Respecting the Attempt of the County of
    York, and other Considerable Districts, Commenced in 1779, and Continued during sev-
    eral subsequent years, to effect a Reformation of the Parliament of Great Britain*, 3 vols
    (York, 1794), vol. II, p. 260.
39 Wyvill, *Political Papers*, vol. I, pp. 4, 113, 412.
40 Paul Langford, *A Polite and Commercial People: England 1727–1783* (Oxford: Oxford
    University Press, 1989), p. 376.
41 Wyvill, *Political Papers*, vol. I, pp. 274, 88.
42 O'Gorman, *Rise of Party*, p. 408. Eugene Black similarly argues that the Association
    sought to work 'beyond the traditional aristocratic lines of national political connec-
    tion': *The Association: British Extraparliamentary Political Organisation, 1769–1793*
    (Cambridge: Harvard University Press, 1963), p. 16.
43 'Report of the General Meeting of Deputies from Associated Counties' (9 May 1781) in
    Wyvill, *Political Papers*, vol. I, pp. 332–42 (pp. 340–1).
44 P. Deutsch, 'Moral trespass in Georgian London: gaming, gender, and electoral politics
    in the age of George III', *Historical Journal* 39:3 (1996), pp. 637–55 (p. 637).
45 *History of the Westminster Election* (London, 1785), pp. 91, 99.
46 Anne Stott, '"Female Patriotism": Georgiana, Duchess of Devonshire, and the West-
    minster Election of 1784', *Eighteenth-Century Life* 17 (1993), pp. 60–84.
47 Elaine Chalus, '"That Epidemical Madness": Women and electoral politics in the late
    eighteenth century', in H. Barker and E. Chalus (eds), *Gender in Eighteenth-Century Eng-
    land: Roles, Representations, and Responsibilities* (London: Longman, 1997), pp. 151–78.
48 'But *Chatham*, thank Heaven! Has left us a *son*; / When he takes the helm, we are sure
    not undone; / The glory his father reviv'd of the land, / And *Britannia* has taken *Pitt*
    by the hand'. Election broadside, Westminster 1784: *History of the Westminster Election*,
    p. 427.
49 *Correspondence of the Rev. C. Wyvill*, vol. I, p. 85.
50 Deutsch, 'Moral trespass', p. 655; L. Mitchell, *Charles James Fox*, 2nd edn (London:
    Penguin, 1997), ch. 9.
51 Peter Mandler, *Aristocratic Government in the Age of Reform: Whigs and Liberals,
    1830–1852* (Oxford: Clarendon Press, 1990), p. 19.
52 [Daniel Stuart], *Peace and Reform, against War and Corruption* (London, 1794),
    pp. 52–60, 100.
53 John Belchem and James Epstein, 'The nineteenth-century gentleman leader revisited',
    Social History 22:2 (1997), pp. 174–93 (pp. 179–81).
54 Many of the radicals and rising stars within the party joined, but Fox – seeking to
    reunite a Whig party split by events in France – had tactical reasons not to.
55 Samuel Ashton – Friends of the People (Sheffield, 14 May 1792): 'Proceedings of the
    Society of the Friends of the People' in Wyvill, *Political Papers*, vol. III, pp. 128–292 of
    Appendix (pp. 161–4).
56 Their inaugural address appealed to 'the avowed opinions of men of established rep-
    utation, or of distinguished rank in their country': W. Cobbett (ed.), *The Parliamen-
    tary History of England*, 36 vols (London, 1806–20), vol. XXIX, p. 1305.

57 Thomas Erskine (Commons, 30 April 1792): *Parliamentary History*, vol. XXIX, p. 1330.

58 Charles Grey (Commons, 30 April, 1792): *Parliamentary History*, vol. XXIX, p. 1301.

59 [Stuart], *Peace and Reform*, pp. 46–7, 160.

60 Iain Hampsher-Monk, 'Civic humanism and parliamentary reform: the case of the Society of the Friends of the People', *Journal of British Studies* 18:2 (1978), pp. 70–89; Harold Ellis, 'Aristocratic influence and electoral independence: the Whig model of parliamentary reform 1792–1832', *Journal of Modern History* 51:4 (1979) On Demand Supplement, pp. D1251–76.

61 For example, Christopher Wyvill, quoted in Hampsher-Monk, 'Civic humanism', pp. 82–3; Charles James Fox (Commons, 7 May 1793): *Parliamentary History*, vol. XXX, pp. 915–16; (Commons, 26 May 1797): *Parliamentary History*, vol. XXXIII, p. 714.

62 Wyvill characteristically conflated poverty, sin and social disorder: 'Universal suffrage seems to be inadvisable in the present corrupt state of society: extremely numerous assemblies of people always have some tendency to disorder and tumult; and in any state of society, disorder and tumult ought to be checked and repressed', *Correspondence*, vol. I, p. 70.

63 Thomas Erskine (Commons, 26 May 1797): *Parliamentary History*, vol. XXXIII, pp. 663, 665.

64 Charles James Fox (Commons, 26 May 1797): *ibid.*, p. 726.

65 Charles Grey (Commons, 26 May 1797): *ibid.*, p. 649.

66 Charles James Fox (Commons, 26 May 1797): *ibid.*, pp. 726, 727.

67 Thomas Erskine (Commons, 26 May 1797): *ibid.*, p. 665.

68 Charles Grey (Commons, 26 May 1797): *ibid.*, p. 660.

69 Thomas Erskine (Commons, 26 May 1797): *ibid.*, p. 650.

70 Ellis, 'Aristocratic influence', p. 1259. Hampsher-Monk, by contrast, dismisses it as an 'ambiguous' document of 'studied imprecision': 'Civic humanism', pp. 78, 79.

71 *The State of the Representation of England and Wales, Delivered to the Society, the Friends of the People, associated for the purpose of obtaining a Parliamentary Reform, on Saturday the 9th of February 1793* (London, 1793), pp. 26–7.

72 Charles Grey (Commons, 6 May 1793): *Parliamentary History*, vol. XXX, p. 807.

73 Charles Grey (Commons, 26 May 1797): *Parliamentary History*, vol. XXXIII, p. 650.

74 For example: Olivia Smith, *The Politics of Language 1791–1819* (Oxford: Oxford University Press, 1984); Mark Philp (ed.), *The French Revolution and British Popular Politics* (Cambridge: Cambridge University Press, 1991); and numerous works by H. T. Dickinson, including *British Radicalism and the French Revolution* (London: Blackwell, 1985).

75 Mark Philp, 'The fragmented ideology of reform', in *The French Revolution*, pp. 50–77 (p. 56).

76 As noted by J. C. D. Clark, who himself employs the terms: *English Society, 1688–1832* (Cambridge: Cambridge University Press, 1995), p. 348.

77 Henry Yorke, *A Letter to the Reformers* (1798); Thomas Holcroft [and William Hazlitt], *The Life of Thomas Holcroft*, ed. E. Colby, 2 vols (London: Constable, 1925), vol. II, p. 12.

78 J. G, A. Pocock, *Virtue, Commerce, and History: Essays on Political Thought and History, Chiefly in the Eighteenth Century* (Cambridge: Cambridge University Press, 1985), pp. 279–94; G. Claeys, *Thomas Paine: Social and Political Thought* (Boston: Unwin Hyman, 1989); Philp, 'Fragmented ideology', pp. 54, 65.

79 Richard Price, *A Discourse on the Love of our Country, delivered on Nov. 4, 1789, at the Meeting-House in the Old Jewry, to the Society for Commemorating the Revolution in Great Britain* (1789), in *Political Writings*, pp. 176–96 (pp. 189–90).

80 Thomas Paine, *Common Sense*, in *Political Writings*, ed. B. Kuklick (Cambridge: Cambridge University Press, 1989), pp. 1–38 (pp. 3–5).

81 Thomas Paine, *The Rights of Man* (1791–2), ed. T. Benn and C. Bigsby (London: Dent, 1993), p. 9.

82 John Cartwright, *The Commonwealth in Danger* (London, 1795), pp. lxiv, 89.

83 Claeys, *Thomas Paine*, p. 6; Karen Ford, 'The Political Theory of Thomas Paine (1737–1809): Is there a conflict between liberty and democracy?' (unpublished PhD thesis, University of Manchester, 1995).

84 Thomas Paine, *Dissertation on First Principles of Government* (1795), in *The Writings of Thomas Paine*, ed. M. Conway, 4 vols (New York: AMS, 1967), vol. III, pp. 256–77 (p. 267).

85 Paine, *Rights of Man* (1791–92), p. 178. On his professed disinterestedness, see pp. 171–2.

86 Claeys, *Thomas Paine*, p. 72. For the language of 'dependence' in *Rights of Man*, see pp. 20, 87, 98, 153, 158–9, 178, 211–12.

87 *Address of the London Corresponding Society* (29 November 1793) and *Address to the Nation, from the London Corresponding Society* (8 July 1793), in G. Claeys (ed.) *Political Writings of the 1970s*, 4 vols (London: William Pickering, 1995), vol. IV, pp. 57–65 (pp. 62, 58, 60).

88 Richard Price eulogised 'Milton, Locke, Sidney, Hoadly, etc. in this country', but was quick to balance this with 'Montesquieu, Fenelon, Turgot, etc. in France': *Discourse on the Love of our Country*, p. 182.

89 John Cartwright, *A Letter to the Electors of Nottingham* (London, 1803), p. 17.

90 J. Epstein, *Radical Expression: Political Language, Ritual, and Symbol in England, 1790–1850* (Oxford: Oxford University Press, 1994), p. 23.

91 Price, *Discourse on the Love of our Country*, p. 181.

92 Quoted in H. T. Dickinson, *Liberty and Property: Political Ideology in Eighteenth-Century Britain* (London: Weidenfeld and Nicolson, 1977), p. 228.

93 Paine, *First Principles*, pp. 273, 265.

94 William Jones's *On the Legal Mode of Suppressing Riots* (London, 1781) argued that a 'free militia in which every adult male citizen participated went hand in hand with political liberty': Black, *The Association*, p. 183.

95 Cartwright, *Commonwealth in Danger*, p. 83; see also pp. 109–27 on Harrington; pp. 25, 141 on the Saxon militia.

96 Cartwright, *Commonwealth in Danger*, pp. 43, 17.

97 [Joseph Gerrald], *The Address of the British Convention, Assembled at Edinburgh, November 19, 1793, to the People of Great Britain* (London, 1793), in Claeys (ed.) *Political Writings of the 1790s*, vol. IV, pp. 85–93 (p. 85).

98 Holcroft to William Dunlap (10 December 1796), in *Life of Thomas Holcroft*, vol. II, p. 91.

99 *Life of Thomas Holcroft*, vol. II, p. 2.

100 *The Black Dwarf* 2:35 (2 September 1818), p. 551. See also the letters from the SCI and the United Irishmen in Wyvill, *Political Papers*, vol. III, pp. 149–53, 178–85.

101 Cartwright, *Commonwealth in Danger*, p. lxxv.

102 *Address of the British Convention*, p. 86.

103 Jonathan Clark emphasises the links between nonconformity and radical independence: *English Society*, p. 330. See also Black, *The Association*, p. 176.

104 Claeys, *Thomas Paine*, pp. 49, 104.

105 'Address to the National Convention in France' (Derby, 20 November 1792) in Claeys (ed.) *Political Writings of the 1790s*, vol. IV, p. 80.

106 David Williams noted that 'I have had doubts concerning menial servants; on account [of] their dependence on their masters': Dickinson, *Liberty and Property*, p. 228.

107 Claeys, *Thomas Paine*, p. 89. Paine wrote of the latter: '[when] they reassume their original independent character of a man and encounter the world in their own persons, they repossess the full share of freedom appertaining to the character': *A Serious Address to the People of Pennsylvania* (1778) quoted in Ford, 'Political Theory of Thomas Paine', p. 132.

108 Paine, *First Principles*, p. 261.

109 Arianne Chernock has recently highlighted a subcurrent in radical thought wherein female enfranchisement was comprehensible: 'Extending the right of election: men's arguments for women's political representation during the late British Enlightenment' (unpublished paper, Pacific Coast Conference for British Studies: UC Berkeley, March 2004).

110 Hilda Smith, *All Men and Both Sexes: Gender, Politics and the False Universal in England 1640–1832* (Pennsylvania: Pennsylvania University Press, 2002).

111 Mary Wollstonecraft, *A Vindication of the Rights of Men with A Vindication of the Rights of Women and Hints*, ed. Sylvana Tomaselli (Cambridge: Cambridge University Press, 1995), p. 237.

112 G. J. Barker-Benfield, 'Mary Wollstonecraft: eighteenth-century commonwealthwoman', *Journal of the History of Ideas* 50:1 (1989), pp. 95–115.

113 Wollstonecraft, *Vindication*, pp. 78, 132.

6

Anti-Jacobinism and citizenship, 1789–1815

WHEREAS THE CULTURE OF MANLY 'INDEPENDENCE' had a consistent appeal for radicals and reformers from the late eighteenth century onwards, its libertarianism was more problematic for the conservatively inclined. As in the 1770s, however, the 1790s witnessed a contest over the meanings of key social and political concepts in response to revolution abroad and the realities of war. Ideas such as 'independence' were heightened in significance as they came to be associated with opposing sides in an international military and ideological conflict. We have considered radical and reformist responses to events in France after 1789; the Anti-Jacobin perspective upon 'independence' was distinct and requires separate treatment.

In historical writing, the status accorded to loyalism and patriotism during the 1790s and the Napoleonic Wars has tended to illustrate the political condition of British historiography. It was long marginalised, regarded as a distasteful aberration from the onward march of history. Whiggish historians preferred to concern themselves with the progress of constitutional reform;[1] and then the left-leaning academy of the 1960s and 1970s privileged the radicalisation of the working man over sentimental monarchism, tub-thumping nationalism and McCarthyist paranoia.[2] This all changed in the 1980s, as a succession of revisionists portrayed loyal sentiment as genuine and all-pervasive, challenging the assumption that Britain resisted internal change in this period because of Pitt's repressive rule. They demonstrated that the extent of loyalist activity in the 1790s far outweighed that of the radicals, and Linda Colley argued that the Revolutionary and Napoleonic wars were the climax to a long history of conflict by which Britons came to define themselves against the French 'other'. This national consciousness was increasingly identified with the monarch, and contemporary patriotic feeling was so strong that a large proportion of British men declared themselves willing to fight for their country.[3] The work of these authors has placed loyalism and patriotism firmly on the historical map, and has created the impression that they were socially cohesive and contributed to the perpetuation of the British *ancien régime*.

As things stand, the latter view has become almost consensual. There have been calls for a middle ground,[4] but this is missing the point. Loyalism and patriotism may well be recent arrivals on the academic scene, but the debate is unlikely to move forward while its terms remain confused. To begin with, there remains a curious circumspection about defining what 'loyalism' *is*. 'Loyalist' was a contemporary term, but the '-ism' is an invention of the historian, and has often been used as a catch-all for a fairly heterogeneous range of sentiments and activities. Our understanding of 'patriotism' is more nuanced, since commentators have emphasised that devotion to the welfare of one's country was a posture that could be adopted by both conservatives and reformers in this period.[5] What is distorting, however, is the common assumption that loyalism and non-radical patriotism are essentially the same thing where Britain in the 1790s is concerned. In the process of arguing that late Georgians were genuinely attached to both their country and their king, Colley effectively conflates the two. In certain contexts, loyalism can be patriotic and patriotism can be loyal. If, however, 'patriotism' is understood as devotion to one's country, and 'loyalism' is taken to mean allegiance to one's governors (and, by implication, the social and institutional status quo), then two subtly different commitments are involved. This chapter will show that hostile responses to events in France were at first loyal without being patriotic; then predominantly patriotic, while espousing a different sort of loyalty; and later, either patriotic and loyal, or patriotic and potentially disloyal.

The parameters and terms of the debate have also become confused in other ways. Historians remain undecided about what to call this phenomenon. Besides 'loyalism' and 'patriotism', 'conservatism', 'reaction' and 'counter-revolution' are also taken to connote roughly the same thing, when in fact they involve different commitments and exclusions. They are all unsatisfactory in their way. 'Anti-Jacobinism' is probably the most appropriate term with which to discuss the whole period. It is both xenophobic and anti-revolutionary, without necessarily connoting loyalism (as historians often intend it to), and contemporaries continued to employ the term even after Napoleon's rise to power. This is the only common term that can be applied to both the early and late 1790s, which witnessed *anti-Jacobinism* in very different forms.

Much work remains to be done in this field but the new cultural history has been slow to rise to the challenge. This is surprising, given that questions of identity, symbol, ritual and style were central to the anti-Jacobin experience. Throughout the period 1790–1815, competing bodies of tropes and concepts were restated, reworked or even amalgamated with each other, according to the needs of the moment and the commitments of the commentator. Given idioms only dominated public discussion, however, at certain moments: the intermittent quality of anti-Jacobin effusions needs emphasising.[6] A particular brand of loyalism was dominant during 1792–93, and anti-Jacobin patriotism pervaded British discourse in 'waves', largely confined to 1798, 1801 and 1803–5. Considering loyalism and patriotism as idioms can help lend unity to an otherwise amorphous field: I hope further to hone down 'anti-Jacobinism' by tracing the career of a single concept through this fascinating period. This chapter will focus on the changing role of 'independence' in anti-Jacobin commentary and propaganda. The significance and meaning attributed to this idea by different writers at different junctures can shed much light on their conceptions of national character and belonging. In particular, its use serves to illustrate the flexible uses of a patriotic culture and the extent of anti-Jacobinism's libertarian potential. Following Colley's lead, it is possible to conceive of patriotism and volunteering in terms of citizenship, an activity with inclusive, personally empowering implications. Thus we can paradoxically make a case for the libertarian potential of reaction, suggesting that its uncomplicated status in the historiographies of the left (where reaction is successful and a Bad Thing) and of the right (where it is successful and Good) needs re-complicating.

'Independence' is often overlooked as an element of the ideology of anti-Jacobinism. So too are ontological questions. Britons were not just told how to view the Jacobin 'other': proponents of anti-Jacobinism expended considerable effort on instructing ordinary British women and (especially) men how to behave amidst the crisis. Britons were repeatedly told how to *be* loyal, vigilant, patriotic citizens, and were given ample opportunity to act the part. Patriotic citizenship is commonly a highly gendered role, but it was particularly so during the French wars. From the mid-1790s, the idea of 'the independent man' was central to anti-Jacobin identities: why this was not so earlier in the decade, and continued to be contested, requires explanation.

This chapter falls into three parts. The first explores the early hostile responses to events in France, and the persistence of similar themes in the works of Anglican clerics and Evangelical moral reformers: in both cases, the notion of 'independence' was either conspicuously absent or actively contested. The second section then explores the resurgence of this idea in the period 1794–1805, as more strident notions of patriotism were appealed to in times of potential unrest and threatened invasion. This 'anti-Jacobin patriotism' was a qualitatively different phenomenon to the earlier loyalism: sources no longer exclusively dwell upon obeying one's governors, as instead a more active and potentially libertarian model of anti-Jacobin selfhood was prescribed. I will then conclude by suggesting that this opened the door for the culture of patriotism – even anti-Jacobin patriotism – to be employed in a way that was critical of the establishment during the final decade of the wars.

Godliness and obedience

Edmund Burke's *Reflections on the Revolution in France*, regarded by many as the classic statement of British conservatism, was published in 1790. He contrasted the stability of the British social, religious and political order with the chaos of revolutionary France, the benefits of prescriptive constitutionalism with the dangers of speculative innovation, and the chivalric virtue of the elite with the vice of the poor. It was by no means the first hostile response to events in France, but it was certainly in keeping with other early responses to the Revolution.[7] Rather than focusing upon Burke himself, this section will examine the early loyalist pamphlets and newspaper press, before turning to religious writers and moral reformers. It is, however, interesting to note the Burkean nature of their social vision and their response to the Revolution – in which 'independence' as a personal and social value played little or no part. There was little by the way of forthright patriotism in the early 1790s.[8] Reaction in these years concerned itself with countering subversive doctrines and prescribing obedience: it was loyalist but was not patriotic.

In common with Burke, the pro-ministerial and anti-revolutionist pamphlet, periodical and newspaper literature in the period 1792–93 presented a vision of society as organic, interdependent, hierarchical and divinely ordained:

> The Author of our Being has not made us equal – we cannot make ourselves so. We were meant for society, and endowed with different powers and faculties to assist each other; the strong must protect the weak, the weak will contribute to the convenience and accommodation of the strong. It is the superior blessing which God has bestowed on the human race, to unite us together by mutual dependence on each other; from this arise all the comforts and endearments of human life.[9]

In common with many other pamphlets of its type, this address from the Grand Jury of Middlesex counters the egalitarian doctrines of the radicals

and revolutionaries by insisting upon both the inevitability and the beneficial effects of inequality. There will always be rich and poor because
that is God's plan and, without the rich, the poor would be infinitely
worse off. Man cannot exist alone, for he is by nature a social being and
all are mutually dependent upon one another. This point about the interdependence of the ranks was reiterated by John Reeves, at a meeting of the
archetypal loyalist group, the Association for Preserving Liberty and
Property Against Republicans and Levellers, in November 1792:

> By this happy Inequality, and dependence of one man on another,
> employment is found for all, in the several vocations to which they have
> been called by design or accident. This happy Inequality and depen-
> dence is so infinitely diversified in this country, that there is no place
> upon earth where there are so many ways, in which a man by his talents
> and industry may raise himself above his equals.[10]

Reeves argued that these beneficial social bonds would be broken if
Britons accepted the doctrines of the French revolutionaries. There was
little place for 'independence' in this social vision.

The propertied classes were sufficiently anxious that this social message should reach the poor that many pamphlets were especially written
for cheap or free distribution. Their simple message was conveyed
through songs and stories, in a familiar and accessible style appropriated
from popular chapbooks. In this example, produced by Reeves's Association and sold for one penny, John Bull's brother Thomas refutes the revolutionaries' doctrines with a few apparently self-evident truths: 'They
begin with telling us *all Mankind are equal*; but that's a lie, John; for the
Children are not equal to the Mother, nor the Mother to the Father; unless
there is *Petticoat Government*; and such Families never go on well: the
Children are often spoiled, and the Husband brought to a gaol'.[11] Some
historians have highlighted this passage as an example of how loyalist
propaganda was 'constructed to confuse', deliberately scrambling the language of reform.[12] I would argue instead that the message is pretty clear:
the patriarchal family is here a metaphor for a patriarchal and cohesive
social and political order. This was a common device in such literature,
conveying the (paternal) beneficence of inequality and interdependence
and the (feminine) chaos that would result from its alternative. Through
pamphlets such as these, the loyalists of 1792–93 sought to 'counteract the
political poisons that were now so industriously administering to the
lower orders of the people'.[13]

Many religious commentators hostile to the successive regimes in
France remained attached to this loyalist social vision. In particular,

Anglican clergymen sought to get the anti-revolutionary case across. If Old Dissent welcomed the Revolution in its early days, Anglicans were either cautious or concurred with the Methodists in staunch opposition, and records of anti-Revolutionary sermons date from as early as October 1789.[14] Many such sermons were printed and some clergymen wrote tracts containing similar matter. Their message was consistent: man is a sinful, flawed creature and government was instituted by God for his own good, so man should honour his rulers:

> It is the evident doctrine of Scripture, that government is the appoint-
> ment of God, to be a restraint on man's selfishness, and to preserve a
> measure of order in the world, notwithstanding human depravity . . . It
> is our indispensable duty to honour our rulers, and to behave with
> respect and deference towards them. (i. Pet. c. ii. v, 17.)[15]

There was no place for independence, or even ebullient patriotism, in such a prescription. It is hard to imagine that this rather dour, unattractive message of submission was as effective in propaganda terms as the skits modelled on the chapbook genre. It appears to have been a common perception that clergymen produced these conformist tracts in order to better their chance of preferment, rather than out of any genuine zeal.[16]

The Evangelical response to the Revolution was arguably more original and effective. In their view, everything was not as it should be: the poor were licentious and ungodly, and the rich – who should be setting a positive example – were little better. God had punished France for its immorality with chaos, suffering and bloodshed of apocalyptic proportions, and would only judge Britain the victor in the coming struggle if its people turned their backs on their former ways. One of the most striking Evangelical efforts in the 1790s was Hannah More's contributions to the *Cheap Repository of Moral and Religious Tracts*. Susan Pedersen argues that these works should be viewed in the context of moral reformism rather than 1790s loyalism: but, as far as Evangelicals were concerned, these questions were one and the same.[17] Britain's national security was intimately bound up with the godliness, dependent obedience and moral fibre of its people.

The *Cheap Repository* was launched in the mid-1790s. An assortment of prominent churchmen and writers – of whom More was the most prolific – composed a series of stories and ballads aimed at the lower orders. These were then distributed to Sunday schools and the poor by Evangelicals and the gentry, or sold through booksellers and hawkers. These works appropriated both the traditional distribution channels and the style of popular chapbook literature, in order to counter directly the bawdy, licentious, convivial culture that they celebrated. Employing the vivid language and sensational titles of chapbooks, they sought to convey their simple moral message through tales about the lives of everyday people. Very few of the tracts were overtly political – 'Village Politics' and 'The Riot' are the oft-cited examples – but their social and moral teachings had a clear anti-revolutionary objective. The chapbooks that they imitated and opposed celebrated and helped to perpetuate a popular culture that revelled in humour, sociability, irreverence, good fortune, forthrightness and sexual openness; and scorned social place, religious duty and 'respectable' values.[18] They were far from being radical, but their readers were arguably empowered by seeing identifiable characters triumphing in irreverent ways. 'Independence' was primary among the values attributed to chapbook heroes and, as such, plays no part in the diametrically opposed values of the *Cheap Repository*.

More's stories presented a picture of a cohesive and hierarchical social order, in which their heroes are contented with their humble station. As Will Chip the carpenter explains:

'Tis the head that directs, 'tis the heart that supplies
Life, vigour, and motion to hands, feet and eyes.
Though diff'rent our stations, some great and some small,
One labours for each, and each labours for all.

That some must be poorer, this truth I will sing,
Is the law of my Maker, and not of my King.
And the true Rights of Man, and the life of his cause,
Is not equal POSSESSIONS, but equal, just LAWS.[19]

Here we see a bodily metaphor conveying a supposedly commonsensical message about interdependence and social place: the familial metaphor we saw earlier also recurs in the *Tracts*.[20] In addition to social being, More also dealt with questions of self, encouraging the reader to subject 'every sphere of life to moral surveillance'.[21] Conviviality and humour are banished from these works. Hard work and simple living were prescribed, in opposition to the chapbooks' indulgence in fortune and leisure.[22] The heroes of the *Cheap Repository* have domestic and politically conservative priorities, and are wise enough to cherish what they have:

Now do but reflect
What I have to protect,
Then doubt if to fight I shall choose, Sir;
King, Church, babes, and wife,
Laws, Liberty, Life,
Now tell me I've nothing to lose, Sir.[23]

The characters in these stories who avoid disaster and ruin are all godly, Sabbatarian, recognise God's overruling agency and judgement, and place more emphasis on their welfare in the next world than in this.[24]

These stories do not celebrate 'independence', nor do they even employ the term. More avoids the question of independence's place in popular culture in the *Cheap Repository*, but makes her position clear in her *Moral Sketches*. There she condemns social and spiritual independence as fallacious notions in the context of a divine order: 'True dignity, contrary to the common opinion, that it is an inherent excellence, is actually a sense of the want of it; it consists not in our valuing ourselves, but in a continual feeling of our dependence upon God, and an unceasing aim at conformity to his image'. More prescribes humility, an acceptance of human limitations and reliance upon divine favour. She explicitly tries to rid 'dependence' of the negative connotations that it had acquired from eighteenth-century oppositional critiques of place and patronage:

> In dependence on God there is nothing abject; in attendance on Him, nothing servile. He never, like the great ones of the world, receives the suitor with a petrifying frown . . . It is no paradox, then, to assert that dependence on God is the only true freedom – freedom from doubt, and fear, and sin; freedom from human dependence; above all, freedom from dependence on ourselves.[25]

We can see that the spiritual rather than the social independence of the poor was More's primary target, but also that the two were intimately linked within the Evangelical vision of the world.

The religious idiom of loyalism changed remarkably little throughout the period 1789–1815. This is illustrated by the activities of the Society for the Suppression of Vice, established in 1802. In many ways this had a similar objective to the *Cheap Repository Tracts*. Its target was 'vice', in its contemporary sense. Irreligion and the abuse of the Sabbath were condemned and sensual gratification was also a target, but M. J. D. Roberts argues that its primary motivation was to oppose 'disorderly and culturally rebellious behaviour' among the 'traditionally dependent'.[26] The Society continued to flourish into the 1810s, suggesting that the early-1790s loyalist concern with social obedience and moral reform – and its implied rejection of 'independence' as a personal and social value – persisted among many religious commentators throughout the years of the Revolutionary and Napoleonic Wars.

The anti-Jacobin patriot

If religious loyalism remained largely unchanged, the idiom of main-stream secular anti-Jacobinism began to change from 1794. The high-flung metaphysical and intellectual rhetoric about a war-of-ideas had given way to a thoroughly military war with the Old Enemy. In the context of increasing taxes, potential unrest and the prospect of an invasion, it became imperative to rally the people to Britain's defence, and the dour, submissive, pious rhetoric of 1792 was clearly thought to be inadequate to the task. Between 1794 and 1805 a more strident patriotism was appealed to, notably expressed during intermittent 'waves' of anti-Jacobin concern and activity in 1798, 1801 and 1803–5. In particular, the idiom of eighteenth-century 'Country' oppositional patriotism was appropriated to the side of the establishment – a shift that has largely been ignored by historians.[27] This is surprising, since it represents an important change, not only in stylistic but also in ideological terms. Within the context of this later, more John-Bullish patriotism, 'the independent man' was repeatedly appealed to as the ideal model of British manliness, with important implications for questions of citizenship and patriotism's libertarian potential.

As we have seen, loyal Britons in the 1790s were encouraged to see themselves and to act in a particular way. From 1794 these prescriptions became more insistent and took a very different form. The emphasis shifted from passivity, obedience and inward purification to a more ebullient, active and outward-directed patriotism. In particular, men were encouraged to be vigilant, to be always on their guard and not to underestimate their enemy. This was a recurrent theme in loyalist pamphlets at the height of the invasion scare in 1803:

> I will tell you how this perdition, these horrors are to be averted – by feeling the full extent of your danger . . . by recollecting that the high reputation for Greatness, Richness, Valor, Liberty, and Independence, which we are ever ready to bring forth as our Pride and Boast, were gained and established by the Blood of Thousands and Millions of your brave Ancestors, and not by supineness and indolence.[28]

These themes appear time and time again in these sources: the 'horrors' that an invading army will perpetrate; the need for vigilance; the appeal to past battles and the blood of ancestors; and a litany of home-grown freedoms, prosperity and national character.

The emphasis on popular freedom, the resistance of tyranny, active patriotism and 'independent' manliness are symptomatic of the establishment's appropriation of the 'Country' idiom from around 1794. Given its radical, anti-establishment implications, Pittites clearly could not borrow 'Country' patriotism wholesale. As such, while its style remained intact, the focuses of its critique were subtly modified. Loyalist propaganda in the early 1790s had been anxious about the 'patriot' tag, a term employed by sympathisers of the Revolution:

OCH! My Name is PAT RIOT, and I'm never easy
For when all is quiet it turns my head crazy;
So to kick up a dust, by my soul, I delight in –
Then to lay it again – *I fall to without fighting.*
           CHORUS. – *Row, row, row, row, row.*

Nought but Times *topsy-turvy* suit my Constitution,
And all that I want is a *snug* Revolution;
Then in *Rank*, and in *Riches*, I'll *equal* my *Betters*,
And a long list of *Creditors* change into *Debtors* . . .[29]

This song of 1793 is typical: as far as early loyalists were concerned, patriotism was disruptive and self-seeking in its boasted reformism. By contrast, comparable propaganda from 1794 onwards positively revelled in the culture of patriotism. Fundamentally, anti-Jacobin patriotism was not directed against the ruling establishment. George III's ruling style was identifiable and affectionate – Colley has shown how an image of straightforward, rural and domestic virtue developed around him[30] – and Pitt cultivated a 'Great Commoner' image: this made it possible to believe that they were on the side of the people, even *of* the people. Defending his Majesty and his Government could therefore be seen as a patriotic act. As far as targets were concerned, 'Country' patriotism was only part of a longstanding tradition in which the sturdily virtuous English were contrasted with the superstitious, oppressed and either decadent or impoverished French. The radical critique of the supposedly frenchified English ruling class was relatively recent and it proved straightforward to shift attention back to the French themselves. It is interesting to note how these earlier characterisations of the establishment and the Scots were transferred on to the revolutionary French: they are portrayed as monkeylike, effeminate and cringingly dependent.

A consistent patriotic identity emerges from these sources. In particular, personal liberty and national self-determination were conflated in the popular mind. Pro-ministerial propaganda commonly drew attention to Britons' *personal* independence while encouraging them to take pride in and defend their *national* independence. An 1803 pamphlet, for example, gloried in the battles of their ancestors, telling the tale of the famed Finsbury Archers of the sixteenth century:

> The Inhabitants of Shoreditch, Spitalfields, Finsbury, Clerkenwell, &c. &c. that used to compose our Companies, were Tradesmen and manufacturing Hands, the most useful hands in the Kingdom; as it was from those it derived its commercial opulence; and from those it looked for the support of its honor, and independence, as a Nation, in which support their own Independence, their glorious Constitution, every thing dear to Britons, as Men, as legal Subjects, as valuable Members of Society, as Husbands, Fathers, Sons, Brothers, was involved.[31]

As this commentator saw it, the 'independence' of the nation was intimately bound up with their independence 'as Men'. Their specifically masculine stations ('Husbands, Fathers, Sons, Brothers') were at issue here.

The historic character of the Englishman or Briton,[32] we are told, is that of the 'free man' (or 'freeman'):

> The alternative before us is, either to establish for ourselves and for our prosperity the undisturbed enjoyment of happiness and of liberty, or to drag out a miserable and enslaved existence, dependant upon the will of the most arbitrary and iron-hearted tyrant that ever disgraced the human species. Under our glorious constitution we have been born freemen, we have lived freemen; it remains with ourselves to determine whether we shall continue freemen.[33]

A freeman will resist attempts to curtail the freedom on which his self-definition relies, and dependence upon a tyrant is particularly galling to his 'independent' nature. In contrast with the loyalist sources from 1792–93, a proud 'independence' was repeatedly noted as being inherent in all true patriots and was actively encouraged as a model of behaviour. Englishmen have a 'high and independent spirit', for they have 'grown up in the manly habits of independence of mind'.[34] We will repeatedly see how this sincere, forthright culture of masculine 'independence' encouraged an inclusive and participatory model of citizenship and focused attention on 'historic' personal freedoms.

As Linda Colley has demonstrated, war with France encouraged Britons to define themselves against an imaginary French 'other'. The British national character was repeatedly contrasted with that of the French in loyalist propaganda. The Frenchman – 'to whose national character every sensible Briton has a natural antipathy'[35] – was demonised as bestial, cruel, slavishly dependent and easily oppressed by his native tyrants. Napoleon himself was often taken to personify 'French' characteristics in the invasion-scare pamphlets of 1803. The contrast between the Englishman and the Frenchman was realised with particular effectiveness in two dialogues between 'Buonaparte and John Bull'. Whereas Buonaparte detests 'that unmannerly Way you Englishmen have of calling every Thing by its vulgar Name', John Bull revels in the fact that he is straight-talking, 'PLAIN', 'rude' and has 'A WILL OF MY OWN, that will make me as strong as Forty *French Slaves*'.[36] The same emphases recur in 'A Word of Advice to the self-created consul':

> As a plain Man, permit me to give you a Word of Advice, if your Arro-
> gance and Presumption have not put you above It ... your Cruelties,
> your insatiable Thirst for *extensive Dominion, and arbitrary and over-*
> *bearing Power,* has raised up against you *Enemies* in *every Friend to*
> *Virtue, Truth, Religion, Morality, Order, Freedom, and Independence.*[37]

The characteristics of the English and the French are placed at opposite poles of the binary symbolic order of contemporary political culture: freedom against slavery, manly straightforwardness against effeminate cultivation, truth against deceit – and independence against dependence.

French soldiers were portrayed as being slavish and oppressed, fighting only 'to gratify the ambition of one individual'.[38] Anti-Jacobin patriots predictably contrasted this with the virtues of the British regular army and navy. These pamphlets and papers, however, were true to the 'Country' inheritance in that they devoted far more of their attention to Britain's irregular defences, namely the militia, the Independent Companies and the new Volunteers. Whether, as Colley argues, the establishment's anxieties about a popular soldiery resulted in a big effort to 're-imagine plebeian soldiers as potential heroes and patriots' is unclear.[39] Contemporaries continued to idealise the militia and the armed Freeman, and anxieties persisted about the constitutional implications of a standing army, so anti-Jacobins had little difficulty in admiring the new non-professional recruits. The unthinking, impoverished automatons of the French army were contrasted with free virile Britons, who more than made up for their lack of training and arms with valour, strength and a consciousness of their cause:

> *The Briton fights for his Liberty and his Rights,* the Frenchman fights for
> *Buonaparté,* who has robbed him of both! Which, then, in the nature of
> events, will be most zealous, most active, and most terrible in the Field
> of Battle? – the independent supporter of his country's cause, or the
> Slave who trembles lest the arms of his comrades be turned against
> himself . . .?[40]

The military realities may have been very different, but many Englishmen nevertheless had considerable faith in the efficacy of the independent man on the battlefield. Cookson notes that Pitt and Dundas believed in 'the right of possessing arms inherent to every British subject' and were in favour of a 'nation-in-arms' model of national defence in this period.[41] British men were encouraged to train as 'HALF SOLDIERS – THEN British Spirit and Valour will supply the OTHER HALF'.[42] They were encouraged to become heroes.

In Chapter 2, we saw how theatricality was central to English public political culture. The same is true of the culture of anti-Jacobinism in the period 1794–1805. The element of performance inherent in encouraging men to be vigilant, ebullient patriots was not lost on this writer in the *Loyalist* in 1803:

> We are acting a part in the greatest public drama ever represented. We are placed on an exalted stage... We must play our parts well, when so much depends upon us; or we are, one and all, ruined, past redemption. It is not by putting on fine clothes, and strutting across the proscenium, that we shall obtain applause. We must not merely appear heroes and conquerors; we must *be* heroes, and *become* conquerors.[43]

In this passage, the importance of theatricality and 'the hero' in contemporary ontologies is again underlined. The melodramatic hero helped to make loyal conduct comprehensible, encouraging men to be active, courageous, direct and protective towards their (feminine) dependants. Melodrama also served to characterise the French in a recognisably villainous mould. Moreover, this aesthetic located heroism and agency among everyday people, promoting a participatory notion of citizenship.

In the manner of their theatrical heroes, Englishmen were encouraged to show no quarter in the face of the enemy. Loyal subjects sent letters to the Association for Preserving Liberty and Property pledging to confront persons disrespecting the King: this was an example of a melodramatic role accessible to all Britons.[44] In contrast to the loyalist prescriptions of obedience, anti-Jacobin patriotism urged subjects to take an active role in the defence of their sovereign. These sources repeatedly warn men of the horrors that will befall their wives and children if they are not vigilant in their country's cause. Like true heroes of popular theatre, they are expected to rally to their defence, especially when they are threatened with sexual danger:

> [to the tune of 'Rule Britannia']
> Your wives and daughters call you on,
>   To save them from rapacious lust;
>   To save them from rapacious lust;
> By all the glory – the glory you have won,

> Save them – on you alone they trust.
> Then arm, ye Britons, your lovely females save,
> Britons never, never, never, will be slaves.[45]

Tales of the bloodshed, enslavement and rape allegedly perpetrated by the French army on the Continent were often relayed in gothic detail. Napoleon was commonly cast as the 'black', diabolical villain – proud, vengeful and irrationally vicious:

> BUONAPARTE. Yes! and, after turning all your *habitations* into *slaugh-ter-houses*, I will convert your *palaces* and *mansions* into *barracks* for my vicious slaves; your *churches* and *chapels* into *brothels* for their gratification and lust; your *shops, granaries,* and *farm-houses,* into *dog-kennels*; and your *cottages,* into *pigsties!* And *all of you,* the *high* and the *low,* the *rich* and the *poor,* shall speedily feel the vengeance of *my insulted majesty!*[46]

The contempt of the French for social, domestic, familial and communal bonds was repeatedly asserted. In common with the villains of popular theatre, Napoleon and his soldiers were seen to penetrate and disrupt virtuous families and communities (conceived of in the feminine). Manly, independent Britons were offered a heroic role in pledging to rush to the defence of their dependants. In a similar way, defending the national community – commonly portrayed in the feminine through personifications such as 'Britannia' – could be seen as a manly, heroic act in this scheme. There was a clear congruence between anti-Jacobin identities, independent manliness and melodramatic heroism.

Presenting political action within this accessible, populist aesthetic was democratising in its effect. Furthermore, some of the preoccupations of post-1794 patriotism retained the libertarian implications of the 'Country' critique. Like the post-1690 'Country' opposition, anti-Jacobin patriots sought to prevent military despotism (albeit a foreign instead of a domestic one). The language of 'slavery' and 'bondage' recurs in later anti-Jacobin propaganda, notably in biblical commentaries and apocalyptic prophecies which draw direct comparisons between biblical episodes and Britain's current plight.[47] In an address of 19 October 1803, Abraham Rees argued that Britons would need to fight like the Old Testament Jews:

> To the invading army we shall say, 'This is hallowed ground which you are approaching, and which we cannot suffer to be polluted by the vassals of despotism. Our freedom and independence we have derived from our progenitors, ever venerable in our remembrance, who sealed our Magna Charta with their blood; who established for their defence

those bulwarks of "Trial by Jury," the "Habeas Corpus," and the "Bill of Rights," unknown to your country, which, notwithstanding all its boasted reforms, is still, in many respects, the land of slaves.'[48]

Like their radical-patriot predecessors, anti-Jacobin patriots continued to revel in home-grown, constitutional freedoms. Thus, while it bolstered the authority of the existing order, it reiterated the 'freedom and independence' of the ordinary Briton – a conservative argument with decidedly libertarian implications. If radicals and reformers were themselves marginalised, their arguments for change were – arguably more than ever – commonplace in public discourse.

Besides the pervasiveness of the 'Country' idiom, the middle years of the Revolutionary and Napoleonic Wars also had more immediate implications for citizenship. Most obviously, anti-Jacobin patriot propaganda addressed its readers as 'Citizens'.[49] Furthermore, these sources repeatedly emphasise the social inclusivity of the anti-French effort, pointing out that the rich and the poor stand to suffer equally under an occupying army.[50] In contrast to the 1792–93 loyalist brand of social consensus, which prescribed obedience and knowing-one's-place, patriotic appeals emphasised inclusion and even implied a measure of equality. As the Bishop of Llandaff noted, 'we have a British spirit. That spirit is now roused, it pervades the whole country; it animates the nobility, gentry, yeomanry, all orders and descriptions of men'.[51] In being asked to volunteer and be vigilant in their country's cause, an active, participatory notion of citizenship was extended far further down the social ranks than heretofore. All Britons were expected to take an active role in defending 'the rights, the liberties, and independence of British subjects!'[52] As Colley has argued, in encouraging all Britons (or, at least, all adult men) to regard themselves as patriots and citizens, the ruling elite ran the risk of demands for political change in the future.[53] If Britain was indeed the land of liberty, then its 'independent men' would come to expect more from the establishment.

The revival of reform

A third phase may be identified in the history of British anti-Jacobinism. In the mid-1800s the complexion of the war and the domestic political scene began to change. From around 1805, criticisms of the establishment became increasingly vocal and, by 1809, the movement for reform – marginalised and suppressed since the 1790s – had substantially revived. Historians of radicalism and reform have noted this revival, so I shall not re-tell this at length.[54] What is significant to this study, however, is the recapture of the 'patriotic' initiative by critics of the regime, who were still able to maintain their anti-Napoleon, anti-French, pro-war credentials, and who therefore deserve to be included in a study of British anti-Jacobinism.[55] The style and critique of 'Country' patriotism was re-appropriated, first in calls for military, and then for economic and parliamentary reform. In particular, the idea of 'the independent man' was powerfully exploited by critics of the existing order, eager to reassert a 'critical patriot' stance in the cause of reform.

By the mid-1800s, Britons had endured a decade of war and now appeared to face a different enemy. The years of invasion scares and hysteria about fifth columnists were behind them: the war was now a familiar and expensive overseas conflict with a French despot.[56] The slur 'Jacobin' could still be hurled at proponents of reform but, in a far less charged political atmosphere, it had by then become rather tired. Instead, concern about waste, corruption and the conduct of the war began to occupy the centre ground. Philip Harling has shown how the growth of the British war machine was linked to elite 'extravagance' and 'corruption' in people's minds, since the huge tax burden necessary to sustain the war was commonly seen as being misappropriated by greedy placemen.[57] British political culture, therefore, remained firmly within a paradigm of virtue and corruption, and the developing discourse of 'Old Corruption' was symbolically gendered even more elaborately than its 'Country' predecessors. In this context, the moral character of the ruling elite, the royal family, indeed all public men, came under scrutiny in the name of anti-Jacobin patriotism. Even the founder of the Society for the Suppression of Vice was condemned for having a government salary in 1809.[58] Contrary to Colley's rather linear argument that radicals gradually 'vacated the realm of conventional, xenophobic and complacent patriotism, and left it for the state authorities … to occupy', from around 1805 critics of the establishment found it easier again to employ arguments drawn from 'Country' patriotism.[59]

In this context, the dichotomies traditionally employed to describe the British wartime political scene break down completely. Patriotic arguments continued to be used by anti-war radicals, by the anti-radical establishment and by critics of the conduct of the war. It is worth focusing briefly on this latter group, who have been little studied and whose attacks on military corruption within the 'Country' idiom opened the door for a wider onslaught on 'Old Corruption' and the electoral system. Leigh Hunt's *Examiner*, for example, was established in 1808 and from the outset lambasted the establishment by pursuing characteristically 'Country' causes.[60]

Where the conduct of the war was concerned, however, he was not required to relinquish the mantle of wartime patriotism. The moral character of the ruling elite came under scrutiny, particularly the extravagance, connections and military competence of the Duke of York (to whom Hunt quoted Bolingbroke's *Patriot King* on the need to maintain his character and esteem). Placemen and corruption were roundly condemned, especially in the military establishment. Furthermore, Hunt revived the notion of 'the independent man' as the repudiatior of governmental corruption. In an address to the electors of Westminster, he began:

> As a man who thinks entirely for himself, I feel a pleasure and a pride in addressing you. Compelled, like every honest editor of a paper, to gaze even to shivering upon the fogs of ministerial corruption and to explore with hazard and with loathing the pools in which English principles are stagnant, I breathe a new atmosphere in the presence of independent men.[61]

In the remainder of his address he contrasts independent 'purity' with secrecy, opacity and contagion, revelling in the symbolic binaries that recur in anti-corruption stories.

The idea of 'the independent man' as the patriotic scourge of corruption came to the fore in the *Examiner*'s first *cause célèbre*, the Captain Hogan affair. Hogan, a Captain in the 32nd Foot, resigned his commission '*in consequence of the treatment he experienced from the Duke of York*'. He alleged that he had long been passed over for promotion, as he refused to pay the £600 required by certain persons to ease his progress through the ranks. Hogan instead sought an audience with the Duke, where he declared 'I would feel it unworthy of me, as a British officer and as a man, to owe the King's commission to low intrigue or PETTICOAT INFLU-ENCE'. This profession of manliness, however, was to no avail. Hogan resigned his commission in disgust and wrote a pamphlet condemning the Duke and providing proof of the traffic in army commissions. The *Examiner* championed his pamphlet, characterising the Duke as 'the fore-father, if not, the begetter, of these corruptions' – and ended up in court. Hunt, however, claimed to have no regrets. Hogan was portrayed as an independent patriot, willing to martyr himself for the good of the people against a corrupt faction and their networks of patronage: his action was all the more patriotic since this corruption was directly compromising the war effort. Hunt shared the sense of martyrdom. He informed his readers of the ruinous cost of the court proceedings:

> But an honest, an independent, and an ill-treated man shall always be supported in his complaint, so long as there is reason to believe it true,

by the Proprietors of this Paper. As they are brothers by birth, so it is their happiness to be brothers in sentiment, and it will be their pride to be brothers in suffering, if they can do one atom of service to the constitution and help awaken the eyes, the hands, and the hearts of Englishmen to the only effectual means of resistance against the common enemy.[62]

The Duke of York was also the focus of the greatest scandal of the war years, which almost single-handedly passed the patriotic initiative to radical critics and launched the first widespread reform agitation for two decades. As with the Hogan affair, the corruption of the military establishment was at issue, so commentators could criticise the regime without appearing unpatriotic or anti-war. Colonel Gwyllyn Lloyd Wardle was the hero of the affair, and his supporters presented him with a medallion for being 'a most magnanimous, fair, and independent patriot'. Similarly, Harling notes that the reform agitation of 1809–12 – launched largely on the back of the Duke of York affair – was remarkable for 'its adamant professions of loyalism and patriotism'.[63]

In the latter years of the conflict, 'independence' was up for grabs by both supporters and critics of the war and of the ruling establishment. Far fewer anti-Jacobin patriot and loyalist texts were produced in these rather war-weary times, so we must turn instead to other types of source to get an impression of the stylistic state-of-play. At the election for Devon County in 1812, Mr S. Colleton Graves asked the voters, 'will you make an effort to have independent men, who will advocate *peace* and *reform*, and who will oppose *war*, *sinecures*, and *taxes*?' His opponents, however, also claimed to be personally 'independent'. On Graves's defeat, a squib signed 'G' revelled in the defeat of the 'Hampden Club man': 'Huzza! God bless the King, Church, Constitution, and the good Laws of Old England; and those who do not like to live under them, may go and join their friend Buonaparte, at Moscow'.[64] Conservative, constitutionalist, anti-Jacobin patriotism was still a force in the early 1810s, albeit not as all-pervasively as it had been for brief periods a decade before. The *Anti-Gallican Monitor* continued to draw the connection between the Briton's personal independence and national independence, and the need to pursue the war to safeguard them both. In March 1811, for example, it was quick to condemn the 'arbitrary conduct' of the French in subjecting British prisoners of war to forced labour:

> The character and habits of the British sailor will never submit to such tyranny; he is not, by the very nature of his profession, formed for a day labourer: his high spirit of independence and freedom, will lead him to resist them whose command or directions he may be placed under;

and a Frenchman is, of all men, the last whom an English sailor will submit to.[65]

The Francophobia and personal libertarianism of eighteenth-century oppositional patriotism, then, could still be employed to pro-war, pro-establishment ends.

In general, however, the radical-libertarian connotations of 'independence' and 'patriot' were revived from 1805, after the establishment had enjoyed the better of patriotic arguments for a decade. In particular, the later war years added a new impetus to the idea of the 'independent man' as the monitor, critic and repudiatior of the corrupt, oligarchical establishment, and also saw the promotion of a more inclusive notion of male citizenship. These connotations were carried forward into the Age of Reform. Proprietorship of a patriotic culture, however, could never be fixed, and would continue to be contested by critics of the establishment and their opponents: the flexibility of the 'Country' inheritance persisted. This chapter has sought to question the historical right's conflation of patriotism, loyalism and social consensus (with which Linda Colley sits rather uncomfortably). In particular, after the debates surrounding two decades of war, the libertarian idea of 'independence' was more emotive than ever and had a central place in the male Briton's conception of his political and social being. For years to come, 'independence' would be worth struggling over.

Notes

1 As noted by J. Dinwiddy: 'Interpretations of anti-Jacobinism', in M. Philp (ed.), *The French Revolution and British Popular Politics* (Cambridge: Cambridge University Press, 1991), pp. 39–49.

2 E. P. Thompson, for example, dismisses the loyalist demonstrations of 1792: 'these carefully fostered demonstrations of loyalty, however popular the momentary bribery and licence may have made them, have an increasingly artificial air'. Loyalism, in his view, was a 'heresy-hunt' orchestrated by the authorities: *The Making of the English Working Class*, 3rd edn (London: Penguin, 1980), pp. 123, 126.

3 R. B. Dozier, *For King, Constitution and Country: The English Loyalists and the French Revolution* (Lexington: Kentucky University Press, 1983); Linda Colley, 'The apotheosis of George III: loyalty, royalty and the British nation, 1760–1820', *Past and Present* 102 (1984), pp. 94–129; 'Whose nation? Class and national consciousness in Britain 1750–1830', *Past and Present* 113 (1986), pp. 97–117; *Britons: Forging the Nation 1707–1837* (New Haven: Yale University Press, 1992).

4 A. Booth, 'English popular loyalism and the French Revolution', *Bulletin of the Society of Labour History* 54:3 (1989), pp. 26–31.

5 Colley, 'Apotheosis of George III' and 'Whose nation?'; G. Newman, *The Rise of English Nationalism: A Cultural History 1740–1830* (London: Weidenfeld and Nicolson,

1987); H. Cunningham, 'The language of patriotism, 1750–1914', *History Workshop* 12 (1981), pp. 8–25; J. E. Cookson, *The British Armed Nation, 1793–1815* (Oxford: Clarendon, 1997), p. 8.

6   A point made by Cunningham in 'The language of patriotism', p. 13. Cookson explores the military and social ramifications of the war in terms of these 'waves' of activity in his *British Armed Nation*.

7   Robert Hole has shown that some clergymen were delivering hostile sermons from late 1789: 'English sermons and tracts as media of debate on the French Revolution', in Philp (ed.), *The French Revolution*, pp. 18–37 (p. 18).

8   Significantly, Colley's account of how George III came to be the focus of conservative British patriotism does not draw upon a single source between the 1789 thanksgiving and 1795: 'Apotheosis of George III'.

9   'A CHARGE to the *GRAND JURY* of *MIDDLESEX*, 1792. By *WILLIAM MAINWARING*, Esq. CHAIRMAN': handbill (*c.* 1792).

10   *Proceedings of the Association for Preserving Liberty and Property against Republicans and Levellers* (London, 1792), p. 4.

11   *Liberty and Property Preserved Against Republicans and Levellers. A Collection of Tracts* (London, 1792), no. 1, p. 2.

12   Booth, 'English popular loyalism', p. 27.

13   Mr Bosanquet, at a meeting of 'merchants, bankers and traders' at Merchant Taylors' Hall, as reported in the *Evening Mail* 591 (7 December 1792).

14   Hole, 'English sermons and tracts', pp. 18, 23–5.

15   Thomas Scott [chaplain of the Lock Hospital], *An Impartial Statement of the Scripture Doctrine, in respect of Civil Government, and the Duties of Subjects* (London, 1792), pp. 3, 18.

16   For example, the genre is mocked by an anonymous writer in the persona of a *parvenu* priest: 'Polemophilus Brown' [Alexander Geddes?], *A New Year's Gift to the Good People of England, Being a Sermon, or something like a Sermon, in Defence of the Present War* (London, 1798), p. 6.

17   Susan Pedersen, 'Hannah More meets Simple Simon: tracts, chapbooks and popular culture in late eighteenth-century England', *Journal of British Studies* 25 (1986), pp. 84–113.

18   Pedersen, 'Hannah More meets Simple Simon', pp. 86–9, 101–6.

19   Hannah More, 'Will Chip's *True* Rights of Man . . .', in *The Works of Hannah More*, 18 vols (London, 1818), vol. I, p. 322.

20   See, for example: 'Village Politics . . .', in *Works of Hannah More*, vol. I, p. 354.

21   Pedersen, 'Hannah More meets Simple Simon', p. 94.

22   See, for example: 'The Riot . . .', in *Works of Hannah More*, vol. I, pp. 334–9.

23   Hannah More, 'The Ploughman's Ditty; Being an Answer to that foolish Question, What have the POOR to lose? A Question frequently asked during the Alarm of Invasion', in *Works of Hannah More*, vol. I, p. 319.

24   See, for example: 'Village Politics', p. 358; 'The Riot', p. 339.

25   Hannah More, 'False notions of the Dignity of Man, shewn from his helplessness and dependence', in *Works of Hannah More*, vol. V, pp. 295, 296, 300–3. A similar insistence upon the dependence of man on God can be found in the anonymous *Address to true Christians, on the Signs and Duties of the Times*, excerpted in *Loyalist* 12 (1803), pp. 196–200.

26 M. J. D. Roberts, 'The Society for the Suppression of Vice and its early critics, 1802–1812', *Historical Journal* 26:1 (1983), pp. 159–76 (p. 167).

27 Hugh Cunningham describes both eighteenth-century oppositional patriotism, and loyalist rhetoric's sensitivity to radical-patriot concerns, without making the appropriation explicit, in his brief 'The language of patriotism', pp. 11–17. Philip Harling notes the use of 'Country' arguments by post-1808 radicals, but has little to say about their earlier Pittite appropriations: 'Leigh Hunt's *Examiner* and the language of patriotism', *English Historical Review* 444 (1996), pp. 1159–80 (pp. 1177–9).

28 F. Klingberg and S. Hustvedt, *The Warning Drum: The British Home Front Faces Napoleon. Broadsides of 1803* (Berkeley and Los Angeles: California University Press, 1944), no. 1, p. 33.

29 *The Anti-Levelling Songster. Number 1* (London, 1793), p. 10.

30 Colley, 'Apotheosis of George III', pp. 100–3, 125.

31 'The Duke of Shoreditch; or, Barlow's Ghost' (*c.* 1803), in Klingberg and Hustvedt, *Warning Drum*, p. 134. See also 'What have we to fight for?', *Loyalist* 9 (1803), pp. 149–51.

32 The two appear to be interchangeable in these sources. Englishness is synonymous with Britishness, whereas – even in the context of 'Britons' – the Irish, Welsh and Scots are discussed and addressed specifically. For example, the series of open letters addressed 'To the People of Ireland' in successive editions of the *Loyalist* in 1803.

33 'Speech of the Duke of Rutland, at the meeting on Statherne Hill, near Belvoir Castle, August the 25th, 1803', *Loyalist* 19 (1803), p. 316.

34 George Clark, 'An address to the mechanics, artificers, manufacturers, and labourers of England, on the subject of the threatened invasion', *Loyalist* 15 (1803), p. 247; *War with France: The Only Security of Britain, at the present momentous crisis: set forth in an Earnest Address to his fellow-subjects, by An Old Englishman* (London, 1794), p. 10.

35 *War with France*, p. 9.

36 'A second dialogue between Buonaparte and John Bull' (1803), in Klingberg and Hustvedt, *Warning Drum*, no. 25, pp. 107–10.

37 Klingberg and Hustvedt, *Warning Drum*, no. 59, pp. 194–5.

38 'Comparison between France and England' (1803), in Klingberg and Hustvedt, *Warning Drum*, no. 15, p. 251.

39 Colley, *Britons*, p. 284.

40 'Publicola', 'Brave Soldiers, Defenders of Your Country!' (1803), in Klingberg and Hustvedt, *Warning Drum*, no. 49, p. 168.

41 Cookson, *British Armed Nation*, pp. 187, 14.

42 'Publicola', 'Publicola's Postscript to the People of England' (18 August 1803), in Klingberg and Hustvedt, *Warning Drum*, no. 1, p. 34.

43 *Loyalist* 9 (1803), p. 154.

44 M. Morris, *The British Monarchy and the French Revolution* (New Haven: Yale University Press, 1998), p. 155.

45 'Freedom or Slavery. A NEW SONG' (1803), in Klingberg and Hustvedt, *Warning Drum*, no. 36, p. 137.

46 'B. W.', 'A Dialogue between the Corsican Tyrant BUONAPARTE, and an English Farmer', *Loyalist* 7 (1803), p. 126; emphasis added. On the 'black' villain, see M. R. Booth, *English Melodrama* (London: Jenkins, 1965), pp. 18–24.

47 See, for example: L. Mayer, *A Hint to England; Or, A Prophetic Mirror; Containing an Explanation of Prophecy that relates to The French Nation and the Threatened Invasion; Proving BONAPARTE to be The BEAST that arose out of the Earth . . .* (London, 1803).

48 Abraham Rees, *An Antidote to the Alarm of Invasion . . .* (London, 1803), p. 13.

49 For example: 'Citizens of England, You Have Been Told That Bonaparte Will Not Attempt Invasion: *Read the following detailed Account of his Preparations, and ask your-selves whether those who tell you so are your Friends or your Enemies*' (title of an 1803 pamphlet, reprinted in Klingberg and Hustvedt, *Warning Drum*, no. 39, p. 146).

50 'An original letter to the people of England on the threatened invasion: by AN ENGLISHMAN', *Loyalist* 2 (1803), pp. 42–3.

51 R. Watson, 'An extract from a Speech intended to have been spoken in the House of Lords, November 22, 1803', *Loyalist* 19 (1803), p. 308.

52 'To the People of Ireland. – Letter V', *Loyalist* 11 (1803), p. 186.

53 Colley, *Britons*, p. 318.

54 For example: J. Cannon, *Parliamentary Reform 1640–1832* (Cambridge: Cambridge University Press, 1972), ch. 7, 'The aloe of reform', pp. 144–64; J. R. Dinwiddy, *Radicalism and Reform in Britain, 1780–1850* (London: Hambledon Press, 1992).

55 Philip Harling has revised the Colley consensus that the existing order enjoyed a monopoly of patriotic arguments during the French wars, noting the reformist uses of patriotism in the late 1800s. See his 'Leigh Hunt's *Examiner*' and 'The Duke of York Affair (1809) and the complexities of war-time patriotism', *Historical Journal* 39:4 (1996), pp. 963–82.

56 The *Anti-Gallican Monitor and Anti-Corsican Chronicle* was established in 1811. Committed to war with 'the present Tyrant of the Continent', the paper dedicated itself to seeing 'the perfidy and profligacy of the French government exposed; and the true character of its ruler developed' (1:1, p. 4). The paper professed independence of party, but – composed by Perceval's secretary, Herries – was undoubtedly pro-ministry. In contrast with its 1790s predecessors, however, the paper concentrated almost entirely on foreign matters and military events: by then, the war was a less immediate affair.

57 Harling, 'Leigh Hunt's *Examiner*', pp. 1173–9. See also his *The Waning of 'Old Corruption': The Politics of Economical Reform in Britain, 1779–1846* (Oxford: Oxford University Press, 1996).

58 Roberts, 'Society for the Suppression of Vice', p. 171.

59 Colley, 'Apotheosis of George III', p. 128.

60 Harling has noted the congruence between the *Examiner*'s posture and 'Country' ideology: 'Leigh Hunt's *Examiner*', p. 1177.

61 *Examiner* 34 (21 August 1808), pp. 529–31; 43 (23 October 1808), p. 673; 30 (24 July 1808), p. 465.

62 *Examiner*, 43 (23 October 1808), pp. 673–4; 53 (1 January 1809), p. 3.

63 Harling, 'Duke of York Affair', p. 981.

64 *Spirit of Election Wit, at the City of Exeter and County of Devon; together with the Burlesque Election at Ide, in the Year 1812* (Exeter, 1812), pp. 81, 84, 90.

65 *Anti-Gallican Monitor* 9 (24 March 1811), p. 79.

7

Independence versus Old Corruption, 1815–29

BY THE END OF THE NAPOLEONIC WARS, supporters and critics of the establishment had come to associate 'independence' with citizenship: in political terms, 'the independent man' was either the vigilant loyalist patriot, or the critic of the corrupt and ineffective wartime establishment. The political and social definitions of 'independence' would continue to be contested throughout the period 1815–29 and beyond. Radical, reformist and right-wing commentators redefined their notions of independent manliness, positing the independent man as the incorruptible repudiator of all that was felt to be wrong in contemporary social and political life, battling evil from without. The figure of the independent man provided both a structural remedy in political theory and an empowering role in political practice, a part that men could play in the epic drama of virtue against corruption. As this chapter will demonstrate, 'independence' was emphatically a male virtue by this period, a gendering that was further reinforced by radical masculinism, domestic ideology and the vogue for chivalry in late-Georgian culture.

Throughout this period of reappraisal and reinvention, however, the persistence of an older oppositional tradition becomes increasingly apparent. Constitutionalist radicals continued to place their faith in the longstanding ethos of electoral independence, and reformist Whigs similarly moulded their ideology around an idealised notion of the independent citizen-voter. This eighteenth-century idea dominated political culture and thought in this period, despite the political right's objections and attempts by utopian socialists to realign the debate. As we will see in the final chapter, it was this model of electoral independence that prevailed when the opportunity arose to redefine the nature of citizenship in 1830–32: it was in this form that 'independence' completed its transition from being the boast of the politically excluded to becoming the official criterion for political inclusion.

The postwar political landscape resists conventional typologies. The Whig party was divided ideologically and factionally, and the strength of the Liverpool administration belied the splits that would beset the Tory party from the late 1820s. 'Radicalism' is yet more problematic. The years 1815–22 are conventionally portrayed as the heroic apogee of radical activity, and this has fostered a unified understanding of 'radicalism' that is essentially delusive. 'Radical' was a contemporary term but 'radicalism' was not and would have been a conceptual anachronism. A study of the idea of 'independence' in this period highlights the fact that, ideologically speaking, radicals sometimes had more in common with their political opponents than with each other. Given this typological fluidity, it is more productive to examine the competing views of manly independence to which various commentators subscribed, rather than to examine how each political group in turn employed the idea.

By 1815, radicals had developed 'Country' patriotism into the critique of 'Old Corruption': we saw in the previous chapter how protests regarding the management of the war broadened into demands for parliamentary and economic reform. The independent man continued to be regarded as the repudiator of 'the Thing' – the client structure of the political, financial and military establishment – for he was the only type of political actor who could resist the lure of patronage and speak his mind in the cause of truth. All other persons could be rendered dependent, lose their autonomous personality and be enveloped into its conspiracy. Different models of manly independence were proposed in the period following the conclusion of the French wars, as different commentators proposed contrasting ways of combating Corruption. This chapter will focus upon the three such ideas: the independent working man, the gentleman (which was reinvented in the light of the contemporary vogue for all things medieval) and the independent elector. It is first worth concentrating, however, on the radical journalists who did so much to invent the 'Old Corruption' picture, and who themselves proposed new models of manly independence with the aim of rendering Corruption comprehensible and amenable to reform.

The immediate postwar years were characterised by unemployment, high prices and heavy-handed government, and this proved to be fertile ground for radical journalism. A large number of radical papers were established in these years, in spite of the high stamp tax and the threat of legal suppression, and it is worth focusing on three of the most prominent publications. Thomas Wooler's *Black Dwarf* led the field from 1817–23, adopting the persona of a traveller from a strange land in order to sow misrule and to throw the absurdity of British politics into relief: as Leonore

Nattrass has noted, this appropriated a refined Enlightenment convention to subversive ends.[1] As an invisible dwarf, the journal's fictional author was in a unique position to monitor and expose the workings of corruption, as Wooler explained in the 'Prospectus': 'Secure from his invisibility . . . he will be engaged at the same instant, in listening for evil at the portals of the temple, under the canopy of the throne, and in the gallery of the lower house; in weighing the patriotism of our patriots; in comparing the disinterested independence of our journalists . . .'[2] John Wade published our other two examples: the *Gorgon* – the *Black Dwarf*'s main rival – and *The Extraordinary Black Book*. The *Black Book* was serialised between 1820 and 1823, and was published in its entirety in 1831, providing a 600–page directory 'of the expenditure, patronage, influence and abuses of the government, in Church, State, Law and Representation'.[3] In professing to present 'a complete view' and to render the hideous complexity of corruption comprehensible, the *Black Book* is representative of radical writing in these years. The emphasis on visuality is important. Corruption had to be seen and understood before it could be countered: as we have seen, the lauding of openness over secrecy and the straightforward over the complex were important gendered binaries in the values of popular oppositional politics. Furthermore, the 'spectator' was a longstanding trope in Georgian politics. The manly, rational and disinterested ('independent') spectating subject is empowered while his spectacle (in this case, corruption) is objectified and belittled: Foucault reminds us that ocularity was an important technique of power in this period.[4] As Addison and Steele had a century before, postwar radical journalists aped this legitimising perspective.

The *Black Dwarf*, *Gorgon* and *Black Book* outlined comparable diagnoses of England's ills and prescribed similar cures. Consistent with their 'Country' predecessors, Wooler and Wade placed great emphasis on the emasculating effect of networks of patronage and influence. Expenditure on patronage, they argued, wastes taxpayers' money and perverts the disinterestedness of representatives and office-holders. The *Black Book* explains in detail how ministers spend Crown revenues on pensions, emoluments and lucrative offices, creating networks of dependants who obey their command. This constitutes a 'secret machinery' of influence, which renders the national institutions 'partial, oppressive, and aristocratic'.[5] Patronage also has pernicious social and cultural effects. 'Dependence' upon a patron is the antithesis of manliness and virtue, and it is so widespread that it results in a general degeneration and demoralisation, which poses a threat to the sturdy culture of English libertarianism. The *Black Dwarf* blamed this squarely on the current ministry and emphasised the reach of its malign influence:

> The present system is that body of corruption, and the members of the administration are the hands by which it works . . . They hate independence, because they know that the independent detest them . . . They form in reality a political plague, which extinguishes all virtue; and the contagion of their pestilential influence penetrates into every recess . . . The measures by which they have destroyed the independence of the nation and reduced its inhabitants into two classes, the *rich* and the *poor*, may be the invariable precursor of despotism.[6]

The remedy for this state of affairs, explains the *Gorgon*, is to make the people aware of 'the system' by means of 'political information'. Knowledge, as Wade was to explain in a later issue, is power.[7] Radical journalists drew upon the plebeian autodidact ethos and made grand claims for the efficacy of information in the battle against the ignorance of corruption.

Journalists like Wade and Wooler claimed that they were uniquely qualified to impart this knowledge. As Kevin Gilmartin has argued, radical journalists reiterated their manly 'independence' to justify their role.[8] As well as asserting their separateness from privilege and the corrupting establishment, they appropriated independence's empowering and legitimising connotations from mainstream opposition politics. The independent man was the straightforward and disinterested repudiator of corruption: the *Gorgon* prescribed 'bold, manly, and persevering conduct' and praised the 'truly worthy and independent' who supported reform.[9] In particular, radical journalists saw independence in terms of energy and strength of personality. They believed that they epitomised these qualities and that this in itself was sufficient to resist corruption – hence the frequent egotism of Cobbett and his contemporaries.[10] The manly editor-as-Hero engaged in symbolic battle with his monstrous feminine nemesis and would inevitably prevail:

> Corruption has received a blow to heart at which she is abashed and confounded; she has been grappled with at the very seat of infamy and baseness, and laid prostrate at the feet of the people; she has threatened, intimidated, bribed, and calumniated, all have been in vain; she has been vanquished – and by what? *the wrongs of the People proclaimed by an omnipotent* PRESS.[11]

This misogynist rhetoric was indicative of the assertively masculine culture of the radicals, who emphasised the gendered aspects of 'independence' in order to render it more inclusive for humble men (and, in turn, more insistently *exclusive* for women): radicals sought to change independence's traditional preoccupation with rank and wealth, which undermined working men's claims to citizenship. Whereas earlier republicanisms had based personal autonomy and a stable political identity on propertied independence, this radical reworking of independence along the lines of personality, intellect and gender empowered their (often propertyless) readers. Radicals increasingly argued that working men had the potential for independence, and we will now see how the language of 'Old Corruption' converged with the emerging culture of class.

The independent working man

In the hands of the postwar radical journalists, the 'Old Corruption' scheme evolved into a comprehensive social critique. Although the continuities from earlier radical worldviews were marked, their writings were characterised by a thoroughgoing attempt to understand the problems faced in the areas of work, poverty, economic exploitation and social domination in political terms. Radicals gave their political critique a social basis, and politicised the social and economic: it is little wonder that Marxist social historians have repeatedly characterised this period as a heroic age of working-class political thought and activity.[12] Contemporary radicals, however, did not reduce the political to the economic in quite the same way. As with their eighteenth-century predecessors, the Regency radicals worked within the paradigm of virtue and corruption, and were concerned above all with the need to counter political monopoly, self-interest and influence with transparent independent checks. They understood oppression in terms of excessive taxation and the denial of constitutional liberties, pre-eminently political representation. The social component to this critique did not involve a levelling of property and rank, but concerned an understanding of how the politically excluded productive classes were enriching those who had personal connections with the tax-gathering establishment. Inadequate representation, they argued, meant that this establishment was unlikely to reform itself and was, indeed, likely to pass partial and oppressive laws to protect its interests.

In this context, the ideas of 'independence' and 'dependence' took on newly charged meanings. 'Dependence' was applied with increasing bitterness to the parasitic state and the networks of influence and patronage within it; and – by way of an appropriation of the language of economists, liberal Tories and moral reformers – the term also enabled radicals to critique the root causes of escalating pauperism. 'Independence' retained many of its former political associations, but its connotations of financial self-support were given a new political relevance now that radical ideology pitted 'the productive' against 'the tax-eaters', with the implication that the former possessed greater political virtue and entitlement than the latter.

The postwar radicals contrasted the productiveness of the politically excluded working man with the unproductive parasitism of his enemies. The longstanding radical preoccupation with taxation and civil-political liberties spoke to working people who felt hard done by on both counts, and the new emphases on labour and social justice addressed a situation of low wages and mass unemployment. These journals attacked the upper classes for economic dependence upon those who labour, via the networks of the taxgathering 'system'. The *Gorgon* described a three-class society, in which the 'upper' and 'middling' are 'identified with Corruption, and from a principle of self-preservation will resolutely oppose every attempt at Reform':

> Opposed to this phalanx, with interests quite distinct and even incompatible, are arrayed the PRODUCTIVE CLASSES of society . . . who, by their labours increase the funds of the community, as husbandmen, mechanics, labourers, &c.; and are thus termed to distinguish them from the *unproductive* classes, as lawyers, parsons, and aristocrats; which are termed idle consumers, because they waste the produce of the country without giving any thing in return.[13]

Radicals emphasised industry over idleness, playing on the work ethic of popular Protestantism. Working people, argues the *Gorgon*, want only the opportunity to support themselves independently and consider charity ignominious: 'To support men by charity instead of a just equivalent for their labour, is injurious both to the giver and receiver; but when men are allowed the means to maintain themselves by their labour, they receive no favour, consequently it confers neither obligation nor dependence'.[14] They contended that the government was hypocritical to criticise the people for pauperism and lack of independence, when it was they who mismanage the economy and deny them work. Worse still, it was they who lived off the unnecessary taxes with which the people were burdened. Radical journalists appropriated the language of 'pauperism' to attack those in the upper classes who lived off the state via the patronage system. The *Black Dwarf* railed against 'those *splendid paupers* in Pall-Mall and elsewhere, who *forcibly*, and against its consent, rob the nation of millions to support them in wanton extravagance, and the vilest debauchery'. Dependence is indeed degrading, but it is the elevated and not the humble 'paupers' who are guilty of it: 'If men without claim are to be reproached with dependence, bring forth your Ardens, your Camdens, and your host of noble beggars, who, with all the practised impudence of the fraternity, deem the nation obliged to them for dissipating its wealth, and injuring its morals'.[15]

Up to now, we have focused on radical journals as a medium for constituting a political personality for working men, but this period also witnessed unprecedented 'outdoor' political activity by working people. The 'mass platform' orchestrated by populist radical leaders such as Henry Hunt claimed to provide a constitutionally legitimate means for the common people to assert their presence on the national political scene. Through monster meetings, working men could demonstrate several aspects of their claim: through order, they demonstrated their respectability; by parading as trades, they displayed their productivity; and, through sheer numbers, they suggested that they were a force to be reckoned with. 'The people' physically claimed their sovereignty and underlined this claim by demonstrating that they were independent.

Hunt, for one, had firm ideas about the personal independence of the men who came to his meetings. Like Wooler and Wade, he emphasised their desire for working self-sufficiency and contempt for charity, and contrasted their independent productivity with the dependent idleness of the wealthy pensioners, placemen and sinecurists who were supported by their labour.[16] In turn, they had superior political virtue to their tax-eating opponents. At a hostile county meeting in Devizes, Hunt commended the 'independent portion of the meeting' who showed 'fair-play' to the 'diabolical' speeches, then manfully protected him when the authorities attempted to seize him:

> the gallant, brave, and kind-hearted people of Wiltshire surrounded me with an impenetrable phalanx; they formed an irresistible bulwark with their persons, which proved an impregnable barrier against all the assaults of the constables, bullies, and blackguards, that were urged on by the Mayor and his myrmidons – a '*matchless crew*'.[17]

By contrast, his enemies – anyone connected with the system of influence – were castigated with the degrading vocabulary of effeminate passivity: they were described as sodomites, 'tools', 'dirty little toad eaters', 'petty-fogging scoundrels', 'lickspittles' and so on. Consistent with the emphasis on visuality and bodily legibility in Georgian politics, Hunt physically portrays the dependent in the most nightmarish terms.[18]

Hunt's most famous appearance – and the climax of the mass platform – took place at St Peter's Fields in Manchester on 16 August 1819. The Peterloo Massacre has come to be regarded as an iconic moment in the history of the English working class, and its subsequent reporting had a profound impact upon how the working people and the reform movement were perceived. Whereas trial witnesses in support of the yeomanry emphasised the masculine stoutness and aggressiveness of the gathering, contemporary radical accounts underlined its femininity and passivity. This was not only in the presence of women and children, but – almost uniquely in radical history – in the behaviour of the men: they were unarmed, 'peaceable', 'harmless'.[19] It was worth temporarily losing the working man's association with manly independence in order to emphasise that he too was a victim of the state and needed protecting. Hunt, on the other hand, emerged from Peterloo with his manliness intact. As an earlier article on Hunt in the *Manchester Observer* had commented, 'The good old character of an independent country Gentleman is surely there in him'.[20] Radical leaders continued to emphasise the gentility of their independent manliness. As we will now see, however, both they and their opponents were beginning to conceive of 'the gentleman' in new ways in this period.

The chivalrous gentleman

The radical tactic of the 'gentleman leader', already developed by Wilkes and the Associators of the 1780s, came into its own in this period. John Belchem and James Epstein have explored how radicals emphasised the gentlemanly 'independence' of their leaders in order to legitimise their unprecedentedly populist and public activities, to license misrule and to underline the separateness of their platform from interest and conventional party politics.[21] As we will see, many aspects of their political style and critique overlapped with those of the more Romantically inclined right-wing commentators of the day, including their uses of chivalry, gentlemanliness and the idea of a restorable golden age.

The 'Westminster radicals' were far more diverse than the label suggests, and their leading figures emphasised their gentlemanliness in different ways.[22] At the patrician, parliamentary end of the radical spectrum were Sir Francis Burdett and the indefatigable Wyvill, with links to reformist Whigs and to Bentham's circle of philosophic radicals. Their view of political activity was abundantly clear from the nature of the Hampden Clubs of the 1810s. Formed to maintain pressure on hesitant Whig politicians, they maintained their exclusivity by means of a £300 subscription fee, ensuring that their image would be one of 'strong central leadership by wealthy independent gentlemen'.[23] In contrast with journalists like Wooler and Wade, the disinterestedness, civic virtue and claims to natural leadership that Burdett sought to exude were fundamentally predicated upon the 'independence' conferred by property and rank. A print of 1818 by Robert Cruikshank (figure 5) depicts a stately Burdett attacking both government corruption and more extreme radicals such as Hunt and Cochrane: he is defending the impoverished and oppressed people but – as with the Friends of the People of the 1790s – is clearly not *of* the people himself. Here we see the 'independent man' as a classical warrior citizen, protected by the breastplate of 'INDEPENDANCE', 'HONOR' and 'MAGNA CHARTA'. He is armed with the light of 'TRUTH' and a flaming sword bearing the names of his personal Whig and radical allies. 'The independent man' is here a radical pitted against certain other radicals, reminding us that 'radicalism' was not a unified political position, and that contemporaries instead placed their faith in political *independence* as having the capacity to effect change.

The CHAMPION / Westminster defending the People from Ministerial Imps & Reptiles

5   Robert Cruikshank, 'The Champion of Westminster defending the People from Ministerial Imps and Reptiles' (7 July 1818)

At the more populist end of the radical spectrum, men such as Henry Hunt, Admiral Cochrane and Major Cartwright had a very different relationship with the 'gentleman leader' persona. Hunt was born into a Wiltshire farming family and established himself as a gentleman profit-farmer, but his flamboyance and agricultural success resulted in his being ostracised by the county's established landed gentry.[24] Hunt always professed to admire true gentility, and his own pointed gentility was an asset to the movement: Cobbett commended the propriety with which Hunt presented a set of resolutions to the Prince Regent, challenging his detractors to deny that he had acted 'with the spirit and the resolution of an independent man'.[25] There was much that was defiantly *faux* about Hunt's independent gentlemanliness – his white suit and hat, stentorian oratory and tendency to assume control and steal the limelight. As with his journalistic colleagues, Hunt's larger-than-life persona in public and in print – notably in the blatant egotism of his 1822 *Memoirs*[26] – was calculated to emphasise his strength of personality, manly heroism and legitimacy of action and leadership. He was thus a suitable focal point for the monster meetings of the late 1810s, summoning, licensing and vocally spellbinding the people. Under his auspices, the mass crowd constituted itself as a constitutional actor, a force worthy to express its will to parliament.

After the mass meetings of the 1810s, the postwar radicals' next high point was also their last. Their support for Queen Caroline was once viewed with distaste by historians of radicalism: it was marginalised as an 'affair' and radicals were regarded as having demeaned themselves by flirting with monarchism, melodrama and chivalry. More recently, cultural historians have taken the episode very seriously as a pivotal moment in the history of radicalism, popular culture and political aesthetics. Thomas Laqueur opened up the debate in an article of 1982, which argued that its aesthetic was inherently conservative and emasculating, and distracted radicals from the real business of developing a language of secular republicanism.[27] Historians such as Anna Clark have since responded, arguing instead that melodrama was accessible and empowering, and was peculiarly responsive to the plight of the Queen and her supporters since its plots 'revolved around and power'. Melodrama enabled Caroline's male supporters to imagine her as a pure wronged woman and the victim of an aristocratic libertine (George IV), in whose defence they should adopt a chivalric, heroic and protective role.[28] The Caroline agitations enabled radical leaders to emphasise their gentlemanliness, and presented an opportunity for working men to regain their manliness after the symbolically effeminising experience of Peterloo, by asserting their active masculine independent subjectivity in defence of a passive feminine dependent object: championing the Queen's cause was a claim to virtuous citizenship.

Radical activity declined rapidly after the Caroline agitations came to an end in the early 1820s. This was a period of prosperity and of increasing liberalism and co-operation in government. Moreover, as Iain McCalman has argued, the 1820s witnessed a shift in values and political style.[29] With the exception of electoral culture (which remained remarkably resistant to change), the Caroline agitations were the last manifestation of the eighteenth-century tradition of employing patriotic crowd misrule for subversive political ends. In an atmosphere of self-improvement, respectability and campaigns for religious liberties, radical politics would have to find a new aesthetic.

Chivalry and gentility, however, continued to fascinate Romantics on the political right. In the 1820s, the direction that Britain was taking under its Tory government caused disquiet, not just among populist radicals and Whigs, but also conservatively inclined members of the social and political elite. These included the *Quarterly* reviewers, the Lake Poets (who had long since abandoned their enthusiasm for Jacobinism) and 'Ultra' elements of the Tory party, who viewed with dismay what they saw as the breakdown of an organic, hierarchical and cohesive society. This was a concern that they shared with nostalgic restorative radicals such as Francis Burdett, who similarly revered the values of the old society and viewed the aristocracy as the natural champions of the people's cause. In particular, the postwar vogue for chivalry and Romantic medievalism gave a distinctive style and social basis to this critique. In this, and in so much else, they echoed their obvious antecedent Edmund Burke, but their taste for chivalry went beyond a basic reverence for past values. The immense popularity of Walter Scott's novels and Kenelm Digby's *Broad Stone of Honour* fuelled an enthusiasm for a romanticised image of the Middle Ages. The rarified elite fascination with titles, turrets and tournaments has been detailed by Mark Girouard in his *Return to Camelot*, but the political implications of the medievalist style in the 1820s remain largely unexplored.[30]

The Romantic right and their radical contemporaries identified similar social and political threats, blaming the newfangled systems of government finance and influence. Indeed, in the wake of Whig reform in the 1830s Burdett and Cobbett would converge with radical Tories such as Richard Oastler and the Young Englanders, but in the 1820s their political responses were distinct. The Romantic right expressed a paternalistic regard for the social plight of the people but – before Catholic Emancipation convinced men such as the Marquis of Blandford that parliament was dangerously unrepresentative – would not consider enfranchising them. As such, their conception of 'independence' was markedly different to those of the radicals and the Whigs. Manly independence was a value only of the truly noble. Self-ownership and self-sovereignty, the Romantic right maintained, were to be found only among gentlemen, which served to justify their traditional political and social pre-eminence: 'independence' also concerned their superior capacity for feeling, conscientious judgement and leadership. The common people, by contrast, were not fit to exercise 'independence'. When they did, it was socially disruptive; and when they attempted to enter the world of politics, their inherent 'dependence' ensured their corruption by the patronage economy. This was the right's take on 'Old Corruption': government was being entrusted to self-seeking *parvenus*, and should be returned to those who were naturally endowed for its exercise – gentlemen of the old nobility.

The Romantic right adhered to a Burkean conception of the social and political order. Burke argued that 'Men are never in a state of *total* independence of each other. It is not the condition of our nature'.[31] Man is essentially a social creature who is dependent upon others, for he is too weak, too morally and intellectually flawed to exist alone. The ideal society is organic and cohesive, relations between individuals should be interdependent, and individuals should have a firm sense of their place in its necessarily hierarchical scheme. Right-wing commentators in this period generally rejected the novel notion of a divided three-class society in favour of a consensual two-tier model of aristocracy and people, in which the aristocracy are independent and paternalist, and the people are dependent and deferential. In this essentially rural social vision, the squire should be both a political representative and a community leader. In an article in the *Quarterly Review*, Southey outlined his view of what an MP should be:

> men of large landed property, whose families are as old in the country as the oaks upon their estates, having hereditary claims on the confidence of their constituents, – in a word, true English gentlemen, well acquainted with local interests, liable to error like other men, but above all suspicion of sinister motives; perfectly independent, and, unless they are stricken with fatuity, sincerely attached to the existing institutions of the country.[32]

Old families do not just derive a propertied independence from their estates, but are in a sense at one with the land: note the 'oaks' simile, with its suitably Old English overtones. Their constituents recognise this. They have a deferential loyalty and emotional attachment to the local squire – and rank in general – based on generations of benevolence and guidance from his family: the language of 'connexions' is important here, especially in electoral rhetoric. Their commitment is based on an affective attachment to institutions and the social order, an important theme in English conservatism. The resident landowner is the person best 'acquainted with local interests' and the people, aware of this and grateful for their paternal leadership, acknowledge their natural leaders at the polls.

These writers all emphasised the supposed special bond between 'the people' and the nobility, a spirit that was declining and ought to be reinvigorated. Digby, for one, made much of the duties of 'Christian gentlemen' as patrons of the poor.[33] Noblemen were able to take on this fatherly role because of their inherent characteristics: 'independence' did not merely connote financial means, but was a personal quality passed down the generations from ancient times. Robert Plumer Ward explored this 'spirit of independence' at length in *De Vere: Or, The Man of Independence*, the second in a trilogy of 'fashionable' (or 'silver-fork') novels outlining the supposed qualities of the English upper class.[34] The two conflicting passions in the work are ambition and independence – the latter 'bears up the hero under all his little reverses, and is the main cause of much of the action'. De Vere's family has 'a spirit hereditarily independent': they are proud, determined, contemptuous of constraining obligations, and their menfolk are manly. His mother and father, despite inherited debt, refuse to compromise their independence by making a remunerative switch of political allegiance, and resolve instead to move from the ancestral home to the 'moated house'.[35] De Vere enters patrician society in reduced circumstances under the tutelage of his uncle Lord Mowbray, an unprincipled political magnate. Throughout his eventful career, De Vere encounters *parvenus* and melodramatic villains who are determined to thwart his progress, but his strength of character carries him through and the 'good' characters in the novel's black-and-white moral scheme all recognise De Vere's spirit of independence. For Ward, this meant far more than just financial means – although, in order to succeed in society and politics without resorting to a degrading dependence on another, it was an important element. The plot of Disraeli's 1844 novel *Coningsby; Or The New Generation* revolves around the same central conflict, evidently a common dilemma of late-Georgian propriety: how does a young gentleman of modest means get on in the world while maintaining his independence? In both cases this is eventually resolved by a fortuitous inheritance but, in true romance style, we are left with the impression that the family's position has been rightfully restored as a result of the central protagonist's consistency of virtue in the face of adversity.[36]

Ward's *De Vere* reveals an important aspect of the right's conception of 'independence': full selfhood was conditional upon personal autonomy, which was only truly accessible to gentlemen. Only 'independent' subjects were fully human, had full freedom of conscience and were thus capable of acting as full political beings. Throughout *De Vere*, the hero longs for 'a freedom from controul, a consciousness of power derived from one's self alone'. For De Vere, even joining a political party, however honourable, would 'paralyse' him: 'No! in whatever I may engage, I must have the free use of my arms, nor even fear the loss of them. I must be thoroughly *mei juris*, before I could feel that freedom of action, that dignity of independence, which could alone render me capable of serving a party, could I belong to one'.[37] De Vere's notion of full personhood is reliant upon his autonomy, whereby his full freedom of action and conscience are not constrained by another. 'Dependence' of any kind is degrading, even meriting the language of physical paralysis. Digby also explored the idea of 'power derived from one's self alone' in his exploration of the belief-system of chivalry:

> there is a spiritual monarchy, constituting to each man the kingdom of his soul, in which he has to govern according to truth and justice, and to oppose error and evil without regard to the policy of other powers . . . As in the warfare of the middle ages, when each man was regarded as a power, so in the spiritual combats of all times, chivalry requires every man to believe that he is personally called upon to pronounce between error and truth, justice and injustice, vice and virtue.[38]

A conception of self whereby every man is a sovereign power, governing 'the kingdom of his soul' and instinctively judging in the eternal battle of good and evil clearly appealed to the Romantic right. The exercise of individual conscience required both this sense of free will and the appeal to feeling that the Romantics so admired. Leonore Davidoff argues that they promoted this conception of self in reaction to the standardised, rational, abstract individual of classical economy and utilitarian thought. The Romantic hero was the 'idealised individual subject who made his own world'. Significantly, British Romanticism's conception of 'the hero' – the independent subject – was exclusively masculine.[39]

In contrast to the noble and genteel, the right argued that the common people were not naturally independent. William Wordsworth, for example, condemned the radical Whig lawyer Henry Brougham and his allies:

> independence, according to the meaning of their interpretation, is the explosive energy of conceit – making blind havoc with expediency. It is a presumptuous spirit at war with all the passive work of mankind. The independence of which they boast despises habit, and time-honoured forms of subordination; it consists of breaking old ties upon new temptations; in casting off the modest garb of private obligation to strut about in the glittering armour of public virtue.[40]

This variety of independence is needlessly disruptive, 'presumptuous' and vain: the 'churl' was the *bête noire* of the Romantic right.[41] Similarly, these commentators argued that cities posed the greatest threat to traditional society's affective basis, drawing upon 'Country' patriotism's longstanding valorisation of rural virtue over urban vice. Wordsworth noted that 'large towns in great numbers have sprung up, and others have increased tenfold, with little or no dependence upon the gentry and the landed proprietors'. Where 'there is not an attachment to the Church, or the landed aristocracy, *there* the people will dislike both, and be ready, upon such incitements as are perpetually recurring, to join in attempts to overthrow them'.[42]

Given the people's lack of true independence, they should not enter the gentlemanly world of politics. Several of these writers express their anxieties about 'the *parvenu*', the low-bred upstart who sacrifices all notions of principle and self-respect in the interests of 'getting on'. Such men are dependent upon patrons due to their own lack of moral influence and financial means, but their ambition is subtly dangerous. The contemptible Clayton in *De Vere* epitomises the type:

> The qualifications for rising, as he chose to make the attempt, are of far more difficult attainment than are imagined. The devotion of self to the will of another, the immolation of one's comforts by the total surrender of one's independence – the destruction of one's hours – the sacrifice of tastes, opinions, pleasures, and pursuits – the not choosing to say one's soul's one's own, when a patron says otherwise . . . In short, Clayton was from nature a tuft-hunter, from necessity a place-hunter, from habit an actor, from disposition a hypocrite.[43]

For Ward, Clayton's surrender of his independent selfhood, his willing passivity, is the ultimate degradation. Clayton is not fully a man – he is certainly well short of being a gentleman. These contemptible dependants serve to throw those of 'true' nobility, independence and manliness into relief. They are portrayed in the mould of the 'white' villain from Melodrama: pallid, fawning, physically weak yet capable of exerting an insidious power over others, and certain to receive a suitable comeuppance at the denouement.[44] Dependent men like Clayton are villainous, for they seek to upset the natural order by manoeuvring their betters into a position where *they* are dependent upon *them*.[45] This was the Romantic right's take on 'Old Corruption'. It was concerned less with the taxpayers' money that dependants consumed, nor even the inefficacy of an influenced parliament, but with the social status of the people (including, one suspects, many liberal Tory ministers) who were supposedly ousting aristocratic gentlemen from their role of natural social and political leadership. The patronage and finance systems, they argued, encouraged dependence and granted dangerous upstarts access to the machinery of government, with devastating effects on the country: these novel practices were therefore aberrations, and society and politics should be restored to their former ideal state. *De Vere* and *Coningsby* should be read as romance-fantasies of social restitution, in which the independent man – epitomising true, chivalrous nobility – was the heroic repudiator of all that was felt to be wrong with contemporary society.

The independent elector

As such, the Romantic right explicitly rejected the culture of electoral independence that we explored in Chapter 2. Wordsworth's journalistic defences of the Lowther family during the 1818 Westmorland contest epitomised this stance. The Whig carpetbagger Henry Brougham styled himself as the 'Champion of Independence' when he sought to break the family's electoral dominance of the county. Wordsworth responded to this by defending the Lowthers' local influence as the natural consequence of rural society's interdependence, and by denying that local people required emancipating. Furthermore, he questioned Brougham's manliness by insinuating that he was constrained by degrading obligations. 'Mr Brougham's *independence* is a dark *dependence*', he argued, suggesting that the Whig's lack of breeding and personal means, and reliance upon party backers, denied him a political will of his own. With this he contrasted the personal independence of the Lowthers:

> It must unavoidably happen therefore that, at all times, there will be few persons, in such a County, furnished with the stable requisites of property, rank, family and personal fitness, that shall point them out for such an office, and dispose them to covet it, by insuring that degree of public confidence which will make them independent, comfortable, and happy, in discharging the duties which it imposes.

It was obvious, he argued, to entrust the representation of the county to the Lowthers. Freemen were not overawed by property and status, but recognised the benefits of voting for the noble family: indeed, voting in this way reinforced a reciprocal relationship that was socially cohesive and mutually beneficial. For Wordsworth, electoral politics took place within a utopian county society, where benefits flowed down from the old landed nobility.[46]

In this respect, then, radicals significantly diverged from their contemporaries on the political right. The independence of the ordinary voter was at the heart of their ideology. Although radical journalists emphasised the social aspect to the 'Old Corruption' scheme, their critique was primarily political in its nature and traced all ills to the inadequacy of the representative system.[47] The *Black Book* stated its position:

> first, that the House of Commons, as at present constituted, is uncon-
> stitutional and irrational; secondly, that it has been productive of all the
> calamities under which the country now labours; and, lastly, that it is
> utterly impossible any great measure of retrenchment, or any other
> measure materially beneficial to the country, can be carried while it
> remains unreformed.

To improve the accountability and efficacy of MPs, these journals advo-
cated a redistribution of constituencies and 'a real infusion of democratic power'.[48] Wooler's justifications for extending the franchise shed light on his conception of personal 'independence'. He employed the argument of natural law in his advocacy of universal suffrage: 'in a natural state, men are all alike; independent of each other, and consequently all alike equal'. This was universal *male* suffrage, however: 'the foundation of universal suffrage', he argued, is 'that men are alone independent by nature, and that idiots, madmen, women, and children, must in all states be dependent'.[49] Wooler's appropriation of classical republicanism made gender the sole determinant of the independence required for political citizen-
ship, rejecting the established view that it required the possession of property. His argument for wider male enfranchisement, however, was explicitly predicated upon the exclusion of the 'dependent'.

In the absence of a reformed political system, Wooler and Wade placed their faith in the longstanding culture of electoral independence. The *Black Book* employed the independence-versus-oligarchy scheme in its critique of the representation, and listed all the boroughs 'Independent of nomination' in one of its many corruption-busting inventories.[50] The *Gorgon* in particular urged on the independence efforts in Westminster, Middlesex and elsewhere. It praised 'the worthy, the enlightened, and independent electors' and considered it to be 'of great importance to the people, to return as many honest and independent members as may be in their power'.[51] As with electoral independence, radical journalists professed an anti-party creed and sought to realign the meaningless Whig–Tory political dualism into a more relevant two-way contest. Poli-
tics, they argued, should consist of a contest between the people and the

corrupt government, the 'outs' and the 'ins', the independent and the dependent.

Henry Hunt also believed that the remedy for all the nation's social, economic and civil problems was political: parliamentary reform to prevent the parties, 'the Parsons, the placemen, and their dependants' from carrying 'every thing' in opposition to the interests of the people. His scheme for parliamentary reform famously included universal (male) suffrage: 'every Englishman had a right to claim an equal right to the participation in the laws of his country'.[52] Like other radicals, however, he appreciated the existing traditional culture of electoral independence and continued to employ its tactics and idiom in Bristol, Wiltshire, Bridport, the famous metropolitan elections of the 1810s and (from gaol) Somerset.[53] He even countenanced an ironic scheme to buy a rotten borough from the proceeds of a workers' subscription, to parody the anti-independence efforts of the political elite.[54]

The political commentators who placed most emphasis on the idea of the independent elector, however, were the reformist Whigs. Mainstream Whig reformism was kept alive in this period by Lord John Russell and John Lambton (the future 1st Earl of Durham). By placing the idea of the independent elector at the centre of their social and political critique, they echoed the arguments of former Friends of the People like Grey, and offered the Whig aristocracy a role in a reformed political world – a compromise that would powerfully bind the party together in 1830–32. In particular, their parliamentary reform motions between 1819 and 1823 focused the attention of the parliamentary classes on the question in a way that short debates on pro-reform petitions failed to do. By studying these speeches in conjunction with Russell's monumental *Essay on the History of the English Government and Constitution* of 1821, we get an impression of how Whig ideology responded to the extra-parliamentary reformism of these years, and how the idea of the manly independent citizen-voter had an increasingly clear place within it.

When Russell and Durham broached the question of reform in December 1819 – only five months after Peterloo – it was an emotive public issue and one that many among the upper classes associated with plebeian violence. In giving notice of his measure, Lambton was therefore bold to countenance enfranchising 'all copyholders and householders paying direct taxes', even with a view to alleviating the present disturbances.[55] Russell's motion of the following week was more conservative, concentrating upon a limited redistribution rather than the franchise. The abolition of 'small decayed boroughs', he argued, would prevent ambitious and unprincipled men from getting into parliament in order to extract favours from the ministry.[56]

Lambton finally got to have his motion debated in a thin house on 18 April 1821. As promised, he proposed a sweeping measure. He began by updating the Whig *raison d'être*: they had no longer to contend with Crown prerogative, but with an executive that governed through a corrupt majority in the Commons, to which no effective constitutional check could be posed. The remedy to this was to ensure that 'the people may be adequately represented in the legislature', by enfranchising all taxpaying householders, disfranchising decayed boroughs and establishing triennial parliaments. The 'middle and lower orders of society' could safely be entrusted with the vote, given recent increases in intelligence and education, and because they were well informed and vigilant regarding political questions. Rather than being apathetic or subservient, they are animated by 'that independent and intelligent spirit ... which only requires the occurrence of a fit opportunity to prove its existence in all parts of the empire'. Furthermore, taxpayers have a right 'to regulate and control' the legislature through their representative, and their modest property is a guarantee of their reliability: 'It affords the best pledge for his conduct, and renders him independent of that commanding and overbearing influence or temptation, which, if exerted against a poor and dependent man, would prevent the possibility of his bestowing a free and unbiased suffrage'.[57] This 'independent' elective body would choose their members with regard to the general interests of the country, thus re-balancing the constitution.

Russell's *History of the English Government and Constitution* (1821) engaged with Lambton's vision of an 'independent' electorate. This gives us an interesting perspective on the later Reform Act, since his *History* was the most comprehensive theoretical work to be produced by any of the reformers of 1830–32. It included a historical survey of English governments from the time of the Tudors and a thematic analysis of its present state. Here he expressed his optimism regarding the virtues both of 'the people' and the constitution they live under, for it affords liberty with order – the mark of civilisation in its highest state. 'The quality essential to freedom', he argued, was that the people 'should feel a continual jealousy of power' and exercise a 'spirit of enquiry and investigation'. For Russell, this combination of freedom and order, personal libertarianism and self-control, epitomised the peculiarly English quality of 'independence'. Unlike Lambton – yet like the reformers of 1830–32 – he singles out the middle classes as being the repository of this virtue: they are 'the most disinterested, the most independent, and the most unprejudiced of all'.

The great problems with universal suffrage were that it would not allow the voice of the independent middle classes to be heard, and would swamp the electorate with persons who could be manipulated to evil ends:

> It is manifest, that universal suffrage is calculated to produce and nourish violent opinions and servile dependance; to give in times of quiet a general preponderance to wealth, and in times of disturbance, additional power to ambitious demagogues. It is the grave of all temperate liberty, and the parent of tyranny and licence.[58]

His motions of 1822 and 1823 were consistent with this scheme and confronted the issue of wider electoral participation head-on. He argued that an assembly charged with the important task of monitoring the executive should take greater care over the question of who should be entrusted to choose its members. The vote should be entrusted only to 'that class of persons who would be capable of appreciating the merits of their representatives'.[59] He agreed with Blackstone that this electorate should consist of 'free agents': 'there are in this country at least one million of free agents – men perfectly free and independent, who have no vote for a member of parliament, though anxious to acquire the right, and in every way qualified to exercise the functions of electors'. Specifically, the 'middle classes' had a superior claim to the elective right:

> Free alike from the temptations created by want, and from those suggested by indolence, they find, in decent competency and useful occupation, the guardians of their morality . . . Thus forming themselves the best class of the community, and at the same time zealous for the welfare of others, they constitute one of the most solid pillars of the state; and I know not that I could select a better sign of the future prosperity of a country, than the wealth, comfort, and intelligence of the middle orders.

Here we see a leading Whig articulating political reform in terms that would not alienate the sober propensities of the respectable gentry and middling persons of the day, by lauding the virtues of altruism, reliability and industry – a formula that would be reiterated in 1830–32.

There was no doubt, however, that this was *Whig* political reform: 'If I know any thing of Whiggism, the spirit of Whiggism is, to require for the people as much liberty as their hands can safely grasp at the time when it is required'.[60] In the *History* he defined 'political liberty', not as an abstract ideal, but as an identifiable quasi-feudal privilege that is granted from above.[61] Specifically, it is a share of control over that which governs – the vote, in other words. Consistent with the classical model of obligation, an individual who has some control over his governor is independent and free, whereas an individual who is governed unconditionally is dependent and unfree. The only bulwark against oppression on a national scale 'is for the people to retain a share of that supreme power in their own possession'.[62] This political liberty, however, should be granted with care. The Whigs of 1688, he argues, were right to retain 'a certain quantity of borough influence' in order to guarantee the success of the new regime:

> But now, when the people are enlightened, and fully capable of understanding their own interests, the Whigs will act wisely if they yield to the increased intelligence a due share in the return of their representatives. As they formerly retained the boroughs to secure liberty, let them now for the same noble object consent to part with them.[63]

Russell argued that the Whigs, as the people's ancient friends and the trustees of their liberties, were in a unique position to decide when it was safe to cede power to 'the people' and to trust in their independence. In a few years' time they would get their chance.

Radicals and reformers in this period, then, continued to work within very well-established intellectual traditions. Rather than engaging with utilitarianism and liberalism, as historians once supposed,[64] they largely remained committed to restorative, historicist, national constitutionalism. The continuing appeal of 'the independent man' was a symptom of this. Although radicals sought rhetorically to identify this figure with the working man, and Whigs with the middle-class elector, they retained a vision of empowerment based upon manly freedom from obligation, within a world of virtue and corruption.

By way of conclusion, however, it is worth considering one radical current that was able to depart from the traditional model of political entitlement: utopian socialism. Robert Owen, in particular, was interested in political reform, but only in the broader context of his idiosyncratic critique of the organisation of society.[65] His view of character formation (and consequently of gender) was such that human beings were essentially equal and that, with the right education and social circumstances, they could be rendered happy and useful, and inequality and injustice would disappear. His communitarian experiment at New Harmony, Indiana, sought to achieve this in microcosm, and the manifesto of his American years was entitled 'The Declaration of Mental Independence'. Delivered as an address on 4 July 1826, the fiftieth anniversary of the Declaration of Independence, Owen appropriated its title to suggest that *political* independence was only the first step towards achieving a much higher goal, *mental* independence in the perfectly ordered society. In order to establish the 'New Moral World' it was necessary to abolish the trinity of 'monstrous evils' that afflicted contemporary society: private property, 'absurd and irrational systems of religion' and marriage (which, he argued, combined the worst aspects of property and religion). Only thus would the human mind be free, the real promise of 1776; thus would 'rational intelligence, real virtue, and substantial happiness, be permanently established among men: ignorance, poverty, dependence, and vice would be forever banished from the earth'.[66]

Owen therefore retained the neo-classical conviction that dependence upon another precludes individual freedom and self-fulfilment, but he differed significantly from conventional thinking on how the independence/dependence dichotomy was gendered. Owen did not share the beliefs of his radical contemporaries that women's nature, status and role were necessarily different to those of men, and that men's claims could only be pursued at their expense. The dress, work patterns and education of men and women could be equalised and, exposed to the same environmental character-formation, their capacities and natures would be comparable. As Barbara Taylor argues, the Owenite method of ending female dependence was to abolish property and property-in-marriage: familial kinship ties and responsibilities were to be transferred to the level of the community. Partnerships should be based only upon affection and 'female dependency must be replaced by mutual independence and respect'.[67] In practice, females' relative status at New Harmony was far from equal and participation in 'male' work and politics was accompanied by the expectation that they would perform all of the 'female' domestic duties. Nevertheless, Owen's ideas represented a significant departure from contemporary social thinking. In particular, 'independence' became a matter of nurture and not of nature: Owen was one of the few thinkers in the anglophone political canon to assert that 'independence' was not reliant upon one's Englishness or manliness.

Owen did not have a truly popular following until the 1830s, by which time he had largely abandoned utopian communitarianism in favour of trade unionism, labour exchanges and co-operation, activities far closer to mainstream working-class culture. English radicalism and reform remained predominantly within a tradition of neo-classicism, constitutionalism and national particularism. As such, the vision of citizenship that predominated was that of the Whig reformers and the mainstream radicals, one that built upon the enduring tradition of independent manliness. Whigs and radicals may have disagreed over the precise definition of 'independence' – particularly when it came to questions of property, social influence and class – but they agreed on the fundamentals. The electoral citizen was independent of political obligations, a condition that was increasingly predicated upon his male status and his manly personal qualities. The final chapter of this story will now explore how this vision of independent manliness made its way on to the statute books in 1830–32.

Notes

1 Leonore Nattrass, *William Cobbett: The Politics of Style* (Cambridge: Cambridge University Press, 1995), p. 214.
2 'Prospectus', from *The Black Dwarf, A London Weekly Publication by T. J. Wooler* (1817).
3 John Wade, *The Extraordinary Black Book* (1831), collected edn (Shannon: Irish University Press, 1971), title page.
4 Kristina Straub, *Sexual Suspects: Eighteenth-Century Players and Sexual Ideology* (Princeton: Princeton University Press, 1992), pp. 3–23: 'Ocular Affairs: the gendering of eighteenth-century spectacle'.
5 *Black Book*, pp. 119, 142, 223.
6 *Black Dwarf* (12 March 1817).
7 *The Gorgon, A Weekly Political Publication* 1 (23 May 1818), p. 1; 24 (31 October 1818), p. 189.
8 Kevin Gilmartin, *Print Politics: The Press and Radical Opposition in Early Nineteenth-Century England* (Cambridge: Cambridge University Press, 1996), pp. 33–5.
9 *Gorgon* 24 (31 October 1818), p. 188; 5 (20 June 1818), p. 35.
10 Gilmartin, *Print Politics*, pp. 35, 40.
11 Referring to the late Westminster election: *Gorgon* 8 (11 July 1818), p. 57.
12 E. P. Thompson characterises the period 1815–19 (ch. 15) as that of 'Demagogues and Martyrs' and the 1820s (ch. 16) as 'Class consciousness' – the summation – in *The Making of the English Working Class* (1963), 4th edn (London: Penguin, 1991).
13 *Gorgon* 12 (8 August 1818), p. 90. See also *Black Dwarf* (30 April 1817).
14 *Gorgon* 26 (14 November 1818), p. 204.
15 *Black Dwarf* (12 February 1817). See also *Gorgon* 32 (26 December 1818), p. 254; *Black Dwarf* (26 February 1817).
16 Henry Hunt, *Memoirs of Henry Hunt, Esq. Written by Himself, in His Majesty's Jail at Ilchester, in the County of Somerset*, 3 vols (Bath: Chivers, 1967), vol. III, pp. 327, 219.
17 Hunt, *Memoirs*, vol. III, pp. 467–8.
18 For example: Hunt, *Memoirs*, vol. III, pp. 583, 458, 466, 316–18.
19 *Trial of Henry Hunt, and others, for conspiracy and riot, at Manchester on the 16th of August last . . .* (Manchester, [1820?]), pp. 18–19, 23–6.
20 *Manchester Observer* (6 February 1819).
21 John Belchem and James Epstein, 'The nineteenth-century gentleman leader revisited', *Social History* 22:2 (1997), pp. 174–93 (pp. 180–2); see also Louise Edwards, 'Popular Politics in the North West of England 1815–21' (unpublished doctoral thesis, University of Manchester, 1998), pp. 116–19.
22 W. Thomas, *The Philosophic Radicals: Nine Studies in Theory and Practice 1817–1841* (Oxford: Clarendon Press, 1979), p. 57.

23 John Belchem, 'Orator' Hunt: Henry Hunt and English Working-class Radicalism (Oxford: Clarendon, 1985), p. 53; Frank O'Gorman, The Long Eighteenth Century: British Political and Social History 1688–1832 (London: Arnold, 1997), pp. 248–9.

24 Belchem, 'Orator' Hunt, pp. 14–16.

25 Hunt, Memoirs, vol. III, pp. 236–41, 352.

26 Belchem, 'Orator' Hunt, pp. 8, 133.

27 Thomas Laqueur, 'The Queen Caroline Affair: politics as art in the reign of George IV', Journal of Modern History 54 (1982), pp. 417–66.

28 Anna Clark, 'Queen Caroline and the sexual politics of popular culture in London, 1820', Representations 31 (1990), pp. 47–62.

29 I. McCalman, Radical Underworld: Prophets, Revolutionaries and Pornographers in London, 1795–1840 (Cambridge: Cambridge University Press, 1988), p. 181.

30 Mark Girouard, The Return to Camelot: Chivalry and the English Gentleman (New Haven: Yale University Press, 1981).

31 Quoted in P. Fussell, The Rhetorical World of Augustan Humanism: Ethics and Imagery from Swift to Burke (Oxford: Oxford University Press, 1965), p. 35.

32 Quarterly Review (October 1817), pp. 255–6.

33 Kenelm Henry Digby, The Broad Stone of Honour: Or, The True Sense and Practice of Chivalry (1829 enlarged version), 5 vols (London, 1877), vol. I, p. 4.

34 Robert Plumer Ward, De Vere: Or, The Man of Independence, 4 vols (London, 1827). Its companions are Tremaine: Or, The Man of Refinement (1825) and De Clifford: Or, The Constant Man (1841).

35 Ward, De Vere, vol. I, pp. xii, 52, 47–50.

36 Hayden White discusses the romance form in Metahistory: The Historical Imagination in Nineteenth-Century Europe (Baltimore: Johns Hopkins University Press, 1973), pp. 8–10.

37 Ward, De Vere, vol. IV, p. 56; vol. III, p. 278.

38 Digby, Broad Stone of Honour, vol. I, pp. 118–19.

39 L. Davidoff, 'Regarding some "Old Husband's Tales": public and private in feminist history', in Worlds Between: Historical Perspectives on Gender and Class (Cambridge: Polity, 1995), pp. 227–76 (p. 234).

40 William Wordsworth, 'Two Addresses to the Freeholders of Westmorland', in The Prose Works of William Wordsworth, ed. W. Owen and J. Smyser, 3 vols (Oxford: Oxford University Press, 1974), vol. III, pp. 149–93 (p. 170).

41 Samuel Taylor Coleridge, Lay Sermons (1816–17), ed. Derwent Coleridge (London, 1852), p. 158.

42 Wordsworth, 'Two Addresses', p. 249.

43 Ward, De Vere, vol. I, pp. 137–8.

44 M. R. Booth, English Melodrama (London: Jenkins, 1965), ch. 1.

45 'Thus had this high-born and wealthy nobleman sunk under that most revolting and bitter of all slaveries, that of feeling himself in the power of his dependant' (vol. III, p. 130).

46 Wordsworth, 'Two Addresses', pp. 182, 156, 186.

47 As Gareth Stedman Jones reminds us in his seminal essay 'Rethinking Chartism', in Languages of Class (Cambridge: Cambridge University Press, 1983), pp. 94–177.

48 Black Book, pp. 225, 228.

49 Black Dwarf (4 June 1817).

50 *Black Book*, p. 246.

51 *Gorgon* 8 (11 July 1818), p. 60; 5 (20 June 1818), p. 38.

52 Hunt, *Memoirs*, vol. III, p. 307; *Trial of Henry Hunt*, p. 27.

53 See, for example, his 'Address to the independent Freeholders of the County of Wilts' (1806), reprinted in *Memoirs*, vol. II, pp. 222–4. John Belchem claims that Hunt 'progressed rapidly through "independence" to radicalism' in his early career, but this suggests that 'independence' was inferior to or incompatible with radicalism: *'Orator' Hunt*, pp. 3, 24.

54 'To the Working Classes of England' handbill (Manchester, 1819).

55 Lambton (Commons, 6 December 1819): *The Parliamentary Debates . . . of T. C. Hansard*, 41 vols (London, 1820), vol. XLI, p. 757.

56 Russell (Commons, 14 December 1819): *Hansard*, vol. XLI, pp. 1096–7.

57 *Hansard*, New Series, vol. V, pp. 362–7, 373–4.

58 Lord John Russell, *An Essay on the History of the English Government and Constitution, from the reign of Henry VII to the present time* (1821), 2nd edn (London, 1823), pp. 470, x, 232, 320, 338, 352.

59 Russell (Commons, 24 April 1823): *Hansard*, New Series, vol. VIII, p. 1263.

60 Russell (Commons, 25 April 1822): *Hansard*, New Series, vol. VII, pp. 60, 55, 86.

61 A. Kriegel, 'Liberty and Whiggery in early nineteenth-century England', *Journal of Modern History* 52:2 (1980), pp. 253–78.

62 Russell, *History*, pp. 115, 148.

63 Russell (Commons, 25 April 1822): *Hansard*, New Series, vol. VII, p. 86.

64 Thomas, *Philosophic Radicals*, pp. 95–6.

65 For instance: Robert Owen, *Address to the Agriculturalists, Mechanics and Manufacturers . . .* (Bury, 1827).

66 Robert Owen, 'Declaration of Mental Independence': delivered at New Harmony, Indiana, 4 July 1826, and subsequently printed in the *New Harmony Gazette*. Reproduced in O. C. Jolsson, *Robert Owen in the United States* (New York: Humanities Press, 1970).

67 Barbara Taylor, *Eve and the New Jerusalem: Socialism and Feminism in the Nineteenth Century* (London: Virago, 1983), pp. 49, 36–7.

Independence and the reform debates, 1830–32

THIS ACCOUNT CONCLUDES with the First Reform Act. Historians have conventionally regarded the parliamentary debates on reform as a defining episode in the story of modern Britain, and the date 1832 as a watershed. Whiggish historians portrayed an epic struggle featuring heroic protagonists, who steered Britain away from revolution and into an era of democracy and social consensus; and Tory scholars identified the end of the *ancien régime*. Beyond political history, 1832 is often taken to signify the end of the 'long eighteenth century' and the beginning of a new social world dominated by a confident middle class. Gender history does not conventionally hinge on such strict period-isations, but in many ways this high-political event is the conclusion to the story of how the idea of 'manly independence' changed between the mid-eighteenth and the mid-nineteenth centuries. The language of 'independence' dominated the reform debates. Although it does not feature in the wording of the Act itself, this way of thinking played an important part in its formulation: a totemic piece of legislation that in many ways defined the subsequent social and political order.

Whenever commentators have noted that the framers of the Bill intended that voters should be 'independent', it has usually been in a lim-ited sense, connoting the amount of property a voter was held to require in order to avoid being bribed or coerced.[1] Little attention has been paid to considerations of gender, respectability, intellectual capacity or iden-tity; or to the fact that this complex idea had the long heritage that I have outlined above. Only two little-known articles from the 1970s by Richard Davis and Harold Ellis have made the link between the 'independence' discussed in 1832 and the idea of the 'independent elector', with its origins in eighteenth-century political culture.[2] This suggests that there are important connections between Whig parliamentary reform and the culture of electoral independence described in Chapter 2. As well as sharing a vibrant culture, their respective critiques had much in common. Both causes argued that so long as the Commons was filled with members who were self-interested, incapable or dependent upon powerful patrons, it could not be expected to provide an effective counterweight to the executive or to legislate for the general good. The return of MPs should rely only upon the free choice of the people: it is the electors who should decide whether candidates for the Commons possess the requisite ability, manly character and patriotism. This was not a levelling critique or an attempt to turn MPs into delegates. Rather, it was an opportunity for the common people to recognise their natural leaders, to express approbation at the just exercise of authority or to protest at its abuse. We will see how this ethos influenced the reformers of 1830–32.

As far as the question of 'independence' in English political rationalities is concerned, the Reform Act was not the end of the story, but it was both a culmination and a turning point. The year 1830 was the first time that an opposition had become a government on a platform of parliamentary reform and was capable of carrying it. From this point, the critique of the political 'outs' informed the governing rationality of the 'ins'. 'The independent man', instead of monitoring and standing up to the establishment from without, became the preferred unit of political inclusion. As well as marking a shift in the political location of this language, 1832 marks an important moment in the evolution of its meaning and function. Throughout this book, I have demonstrated how this idea was employed to negotiate the crucial question of who was fit to participate in politics. By the 1830s, it was possible to limit official entry to the public political sphere to 'independent men' and to codify mass participation along these lines. In the reform debates, 'independence' connoted the qualities of enfranchised citizens, and the electorate was imagined as a polity of 'independent men'. From 1832, this was the criterion for citizenship and the state to which the non-enfranchised should aspire, and historians of Victorian Britain have shown how later Reform Acts gradually expanded the definition of 'the independent' to justify entrusting the vote to further groups of people.[3] The role that 'independence' played in the formation of the First Reform Act, however, has yet to be adequately explored – and it is to this that we will now turn.

As Lord John Russell noted in a letter to Lord Durham in 1834, the Whig plan of parliamentary reform 'contained hardly any thing new'.[4] The reform motions that had been tabled in the Commons since Wilkes's in 1776 had differed only in degree – the length of parliaments, the extent of redistribution and (most tellingly) the breadth of the franchise. We get our first systematic view of what the Whigs of the 1830s sought to accomplish in the provisional plan produced by the committee of Russell, Durham, Duncannon and Graham. This document is pervaded by the language of 'independence'. Comprehensive reform, they argue, is required to remove 'all rational grounds of complaint from the minds of the intelligent and the independent portion of the community'.[5] It proposes vesting the right of voting in householders of £20 per annum and establishing vote by ballot. This was impracticable, for in some boroughs the proposed constituency was found to be very small. In the eventual Bill the qualification was set at £10 and open voting continued, but their original plan gives an indication of their intention to enfranchise men of standing and means who would vote autonomously rather than with regard to the wishes of a powerful superior, even to the extent of being entrusted with secret voting. The £20 constituency, they argued, would form 'a constituent body including all the intelligence and respectability of the independent classes of society'. It would prevent 'those scenes of corruption and political profligacy which too often occur where the right of voting is vested in those whose want of education and state of dependence render them quite unfitted for its exercise'.[6] Independence may have been quantified by property for the sake of convenience, but it was not just a question of its ownership: the autonomy connoted by 'independence' related to questions of 'education', 'intelligence', 'respectability' and moral fitness. In order to prevent 'corruption and political profligacy', the Act was built around a very specific conception of the citizen.

In the subsequent debates in the Commons and the Lords, the nature of the voter was placed under exhaustive scrutiny. A broad consensus emerged that the voter should be 'independent', and the independence/dependence dichotomy was employed to negotiate the question of who could safely be admitted to the official political sphere. The meanings of this conceptual binary, however, were contested by supporters and opponents of the measure and a number of positions emerged that were characterised by their perspectives on 'the independent man': those of the Romantic right, the liberals, the radicals and the Whigs. These habits of thought did not correspond to party lines and could even result in contradictory responses to reform, reminding us of the organisational looseness and ideological diversity both of party groupings in this period and of the opposing sides in the reform crisis. This survey of the parliamentary debates also gives us an opportunity to conclude our narrative with a summary of the late-Georgian political spectrum at this crucial juncture in the history of citizenship.

The Romantic right

In general, what may be termed the parliamentary right – comprehending both the Ultra Tories and those who had stuck by Wellington in opposition to reform – were suspicious about independent behaviour among the common people. They were committed to an organic, cohesive, hierarchical and interdependent conception of the social order, a romanticised vision of rural society in which the squirearchy were the natural social and political leaders in their communities. In contrast with the Romantic medievalists of the 1820s, the post-Emancipation parliamentary right of the 1830s were prepared to accept that 'independence' existed in a safe and laudable form among certain sections of the people – but they had very specific groups in mind. As far as they were concerned, independent manliness among the common people was associated with the bracing rural virtue and patriotic self-respect of the yeoman, the freeman or the peasant. The Romantic right believed that such men had a natural alliance with the ancient landed aristocracy against their traditional enemies of industrialists, financiers, degenerate city dwellers, non-Anglicans, republicans, utilitarians and court politicians.

In contrast to the 'independent' guardians of the soil, the £10 constituency smacked of the urban petty-bourgeoisie, their other great bugbear. The Earl of Winchilsea enquired whether anyone could be found 'to contend that that class of persons were independent? Surely not. [T]hey would be ruled by the worst enemies of the country'.[7] In general – and in marked contrast with the Whigs – speakers of this political persuasion had a low opinion of the people's capacity for virtue. A succession of Tory lords cast doubts on the capacity, responsibility and disinterestedness of the humble voter. The Duke of Buccleugh reported that the people of Scotland believed reform meant 'no more excisemen, – no more gaugers; that they should have free trade; that whiskey would be cheap, &c'.[8] More gravely, Winchilsea warned that 'the people would be invested with a preponderating power, which, judging from the invariable result of all similar experiments, would lead to the destruction of the Constitution'.[9]

The right was more confident that voters in counties and rural constituencies would vote for suitable candidates. To the dismay of the Whigs, the Marquis of Chandos appeared to have succeeded in swamping the county electorate with men who were likely to be docile towards landed proprietors, by forcing through an amendment enfranchising £50 tenants-at-will. Milton and Althorp protested that such men would be utterly dependent upon their landlords, but Chandos's supporters responded with the traditional image of the independent man as honest, rustic, loyal and defiant. In contrast to urban shopkeepers, they argued, 'the franchise could not be trusted to a more independent body than the Yeomen whom the Amendment would include'.[10] In areas such as this, the right hoped that what they saw as a cohesive, consensual social order – 'where all the relations and dependencies of social life were in a happier state'[11] – would be unaffected by the Bill. The period 1830–32 witnessed the continuation of an established debate about types of constituency and influence.[12] Whereas the Whigs maintained that all the interests of the community would be represented by enabling the people to select enlightened and disinterested governors, Tories were adamant that the dominant interest in any given constituency would prevail. Therefore, they argued, it was imperative to ensure that there were enough exclusively landed constituencies (that would inevitably return loyal patricians) to counterbalance the urban centres (that would inevitably return demagogues).

Alternatively, the same ethos produced a very different response among Ultras like the Marquis of Blandford. In order to counter these same forces, it was desirable to enfranchise 'the people' in its broadest sense, trusting that their independence and traditional prejudices would result in the return of the sort of MPs who would never have emancipated the Catholics. His own reform plan of February 1830 and his subsequent support for the Whigs' measure were justified in these terms.[13]

The liberals

The diametric opposite of the Romantic right's rationality was that of the liberals. It is difficult to gauge the liberal position on reform from the parliamentary debates: 'Liberal' was not yet a parliamentary label, and those who were committed to a recognisably 'liberal' view of government, economics and society operated from within the existing parties. Of these, the 'liberalism' of the liberal Tories did not extend to electoral reform, whereas the liberals in the reform coalition did not have prominent voices.[14] The liberally inclined 'Young Whigs' like Milton and Althorp tended to toe the Whig line, but in their opposition to the Chandos clause we can get an idea of the liberal conception of independence. They responded to the rustic Romanticism of the right with a dryly functional consideration: did tenant farmers' agreements with their landlords curtail their autonomy? Althorp sought systematically to debunk independence:

Few men knew more about them, or had a higher opinion of their intelligence and integrity. But the question was, were they in such a situation
as would ensure the same independence as to their votes as might be
expected from freeholders? The Committee were not now called upon
to decide upon their respectability, but whether they were in that situation which would make them independent county electors.[15]

For liberals like Althorp, the ideal citizenry consisted of free actors under
a uniform franchise, with all the interests of the community amalgamated
together. Contemporary political economists conceived of the social
domain as a geometrical spatial grid – a recognisably modern abstraction
– populated by functionally equivalent, economically quantifiable individuals.[16] In the liberal view of personal freedom, 'independence' concerned only the individual's ability to resist constraint and his basic
(economic) capacity for self-determination.

Failure to meet the criterion of economic self-sufficiency also disqualified an individual from citizenship: significantly, when Althorp was
chairing the Committee he allowed the Tory William Praed's amendment
excluding recipients of parochial relief to pass without any debate.[17] In
this respect, the Reform Act should be considered in conjunction with the
New Poor Law that followed three years later. Men who could (or would)
not support themselves and their families by their own labours were
dependent, and therefore lacked a full civil, legal and political personality: only independent men could be citizens. Much of the stigma associated with pauperism derived from this essentially political discourse
about freedom and personal virtue. The harsher side of liberal self-help
played its part in the ethos of the Bill.

The radicals

Although radical MPs were prepared to unite behind the Bill, it is not possible to talk in terms of a single 'radical' rationality in the parliaments of
1830–32. If radical members had a more populist and zealous personal
style, their ideologies were often merely extensions of those of their more
mainstream parliamentary colleagues. Burdett (like the young Disraeli)
had much in common with the Romantic right and soon turned Tory;
whereas Hobhouse, Brougham and Durham reconciled their idiosyncratic views with membership of the Whig party. The most sustained and
distinctive radical voices in the reform debates were those of Daniel
O'Connell and Henry Hunt. O'Connell led the Irish Catholic bloc and
attuned his radicalism to the pressing needs of Ireland, whereas Hunt
provided the main link between the Commons' debates and the tradition

of extra-parliamentary plebeian radicalism. Both men proposed far-reaching reform plans of their own, including universal suffrage.

Hunt's proposed amendment 'that all persons being householders, and paying rates and taxes, should be entitled to vote for Members of Parliament' was defeated by 123 to 1 in the Committee stage. Nevertheless, his criticism of how the uniform property qualification failed to accommodate regional wealth variations – a common practical objection, by both supporters and opponents of the Bill – reveals his attachment to the Whiggish notion of political entitlement:

> Its operation would be most unequal, for in London there were no houses under 10*l.* per annum, while in the other towns of England, the average rents of the houses of the working classes were from 5*l.* to 7*l.*; and yet many of the inhabitants of the latter class of houses were in a far higher state of comfort and independence, and better qualified to vote, than those who occupied 10*l.* houses in the metropolis.

In spite of his declaration that 'every man was entitled to vote', his view of political fitness was qualitative. Voters in a 'higher state' of 'independence' were 'better qualified to vote': even some radicals argued that property and situation affected an individual's capacity for conscientious autonomy.[18]

In May 1830 – before the reform debates started in earnest – O'Connell took the opportunity to propose his own comprehensive plan. He too proposed universal suffrage and made a case for its constitutionality by citing authorities such as Blackstone, noting that lawyer's proviso that everyone 'whose wills may be supposed independent' was entitled to vote.[19] He interpreted this dictum in accordance with his own distaste for property qualifications, and with his greater faith in the humble than in the high:

> But even riches were not a sufficient assurance for independence of conduct. If the poor man had natural wants, the rich man had artificial wants – wants which became the more painfully pressing and craving under apparent repletion. Who could look at the opulent classes of society and not see how frequently such was the case? . . . Who had not frequently been compelled to regard with scorn the creatures who doated on stars, and garters, and ribands, and feathers, and other frippery; – and who for such things sacrificed the noblest possession of a human being – independence.

The only sure way 'of making every man, however poor, independent' was the ballot: 'As the rights of all Englishmen were equal, so also ought to be their votes, and ballot would render them so'.[20] While undoubtedly idealising independence, in common with the liberals he stripped it down to the question of an individual's relation to sources of influence and coercion where political qualification was concerned. Unlike most liberals, though, he saw its egalitarian implications: significantly, the radical-utilitarian *Westminster Review* reached identical conclusions on this issue.[21]

The majority of the political world, however, would not accept the ballot. Open voting was regarded as manly and English, so was successfully defended within the traditional language of 'independence'. In the Manichean moral world of electoral independence, the masculine virtues of openness, sincerity and defiance – epitomised by the practice of open voting – were diametrically opposed to the vice of secrecy. Secret voting was widely regarded to be unmanly, suspect in public life and (worse) a characteristic of foreign political systems. Furthermore, the Whigs claimed that the ballot was destructive to character, conducive to perjury and – as we will see – contrary to the operation of the legitimate moral, intellectual and social influences that they sought to promote within the electoral system.[22]

The Whigs

The Reform Act was emphatically a Whig measure. As Peter Mandler has argued, the Whig style of government befitted the challenges of the 1830s: aristocratic self-confidence, party cohesion, benevolence and flamboyance were needed to carry sweeping social and political reform.[23] The Reform Act, in particular, fitted their self-image and self-appointed role. As the ancient friends of the people and the designers of the Revolution Settlement, the Whigs had ensured that the people's political liberty had been kept in trust effectively, until such time as it could safely be bestowed from above.[24] As Russell's father had written to Lord Grenville in 1817, 'The People look to Conciliation, temper, and kindness from the Government': it was this variety of paternal liberality that informed the Reform Bill.[25]

We have seen how the Whigs had a specific idea of the voter in mind. In particular, the Whig conception of personal 'independence' was more expressly *political* than those of their opponents and drew connotations from over a century of oppositional critiques and electoral culture. Central to this is the question of how the Whigs used the language of class. The reform debates were pervaded by a three-tiered social vision, to the extent that Dror Wahrman suggests they were central to the linguistic process by which Britons came to perceive their society as being divided into three classes.[26] The Whigs systematically exploited the common contemporary association of the social middle with virtue and responsibility in their justification of the £10 franchise. Durham, for instance, praised their 'skill, talent, political intelligence, and wealth' and argued that 'the emancipation of the middle classes' was a leading principle of the Bill.[27] The association of 'independence' with the virtues of the middle class was common in contemporary discourse.[28] At Manchester's first election under the new franchise, one of the speakers at the Whigs' celebratory dinner praised 'the virtue, the patriotism, the firmness, and the independence of the middle class of electors'.[29] Moreover, this discursive link was reinforced during the reform debates, to the extent that even opponents of the Bill were forced to negotiate their objections within its terms. Lord Wynford, for example, associated 'independence' with the social middle, but doubted whether this social stratum would in fact be given due political weight by the £10 franchise:

> No doubt it would be well to give the right of electing Representatives to the upper and middle classes of society – persons too independent to be accessible to corruption ... He would confer the right on all who were gifted with knowledge to perceive its value, and possessed of property to pronounce their opinions with independence.[30]

The Whigs, however, considered 'independence' and class in political terms. Arguably they did not use the term 'middle classes' in a sociological sense at all: what they meant by this was the eighteenth-century idea of the 'independent electorate', positioned between the populace and the nobility.[31] Or, more precisely, between the *dependent* populace on the one hand and the networks of aristocratic and Crown clientage on the other: the social middle was the stratum that supposedly possessed the greatest independence from compromising obligation. As we have seen, this political discourse was fundamentally gendered. Women's historians have long appreciated that gender and class are mutually constitutive cultural categories. The notion of manly 'independence' contributed to the construction of Georgian understandings of a 'middle class' (and, indeed, to the pervasive masculinism of much class discourse). The Whigs argued that these manly, middle-class, independent electors had the personal qualities and private means to resist bribery and corruption, and were enlightened and responsible enough to select their natural leaders from the ranks above them. The Whig party, of course, had long cast themselves in this role and trusted that 'the independent' would favour *them* with their votes.

This conception of electoral behaviour should be placed in the context of the Whig view of influence and social relations. This contrasted markedly with the automatic community deference (or worrying lack thereof) posited by the right, and with the ideal of unrestrained individual equivalence sought by doctrinaire liberals and radical utilitarians. The distinction between 'legitimate' and 'illegitimate' influence pervaded the Whigs' attempts to justify the Bill. They argued that the influences of bribery, coercion and 'nomination' were illegitimate: the disfranchisement of 'rotten' and 'close' boroughs, new electoral procedures and – centrally – the creation of 'an independent and excellent constituency'[32] were held to counteract them. Significantly, although all sides denounced the venality of electors, effectual curbs on electoral treating had to wait a further half-century until the Corrupt Practices Act (which, not coincidentally, coincided with the final demise of the Whigs). The Whigs did not seek to end all social and electoral influence. Although electors should be independent, this was in the context of a hierarchical political society where the legitimate influence of intellect, rank and leadership held sway. As Palmerston argued, the Whigs sought actively to promote 'an influence arising from good conduct and prosperity of demeanour on the one side, and respect and deference on the other; and which was as honourable to those who exercised it, as to those who acknowledged its authority'.[33] This corresponded with the social values of electoral independence: the Whigs realised that this ethos of electoral independence was the best hope for the aristocracy in a changing world, giving them a political role based on their supposed ability and enlightened disinterestedness, and on the mutual respect of elector and elected. The objections of Whigs like Russell to the ballot are comprehensible in this context. He feared that a man voting secretly would be licensed to ignore these legitimate considerations: 'If it would prevent the exercise of an improper influence over the good, it would also prevent the operation of a beneficial influence over the bad'.[34] Voting, Whigs argued, was a public trust and open voting offered a constitutional check to individual irresponsibility. Casting a vote in open rejection of legitimate influence was one thing; doing so with the secrecy of the ballot was quite another. The Whigs regarded the former as the action of an independent man, rejecting the claims of radicals – who did not recognise this kind of influence to be desirable or relevant – that only the ballot guaranteed the elector's independence.

So who was the ideal citizen of 1832? Fundamentally, he was an adult male – the only group held to have the capacity for independence. Although women had in practice long been prevented from voting by local custom, the Reform Act formally excluded them for the first time and it would be a further century before their disqualifying association with 'dependence' was fully overturned in this respect.[35] This exclusion of women from active citizenship was never discussed in the parliamentary debates on reform. There was a suggestion that women were not considered as political beings in a debate on the admissibility of petitions, when anti-reformers insinuated that women had signed certain pro-reform petitions, thus rendering them unconstitutional:

> The Earl of *Mansfield* denied that this petition emanated from a meeting of the county of Perth, properly convened. He admitted, that it was numerously signed, but it was signed by the inhabitants of Perthshire only, male and female, for he had been assured that a number of women attended the meeting, and had actually signed the petition.[36]

Women may have been 'inhabitants' of the county, but they did not qualify as citizens.

More pervasively, considerations of manliness and patriarchy recur in the debates. As Grey argued, being the man of the household – even a £10 one – entailed a degree of responsibility and respectability:

> they are persons who in my opinion, from the very circumstance of their occupying a 10*l.* house . . . have given a sort of guarantee of their holding a certain station in life – who thereby exhibit an open sign of their possessing some property – who have given a pledge to the community for their good conduct – and who for the most part are married men and the fathers of families.[37]

Like earlier reformers, the Whigs of 1830–32 valorised the male stations of father, husband and householder. Citizenship and household mastery were fundamentally linked, and both were held up as stations to which all men should aspire. In a sense, the public role of independent men was predicated upon having people dependent upon them. In common with the Whig view of leadership, the Whig view of citizenship involved manly, enlightened and disinterested action *on behalf of others*. Their mastery over others was testament to their self-mastery, and the fact of their having people to support, protect and represent was a basic guarantee of their reliability and selflessness. Although it only came to dominate English reformist rationales from the 1770s, the household – as a fundamental unit of the political world, and as a gendered model of obligation, virtue and power – altered remarkably little from classical republicanism through to Whig reform.

As we have seen, the citizen of 1832 supposedly possessed sufficient property and standing to avoid being placed in a state of obligation that would affect his vote. Like the 'independent' voters in the boroughs, he was also expected to possess a degree of the manly stoicism and fearlessness of the freeborn Englishman, to resist the intimidation of mobs or overmighty nobles, and to disdain the lure of the demagogue. He was still called upon to cast his vote openly, although new electoral procedures made this rather less fearsome a task than it had once been. As Vernon argues, measures such as electoral registration, the introduction of multiple polling places and the power to alter the time of the nomination, poll and declaration served to curtail the vital and participatory culture of election contests.[38] The reformed political world was rendered appropriate for the early Victorian version of the independent man, just as the unreformed had been for his predecessor.

Lastly, electoral culture's stress on conscientiousness was amplified, but with a new emphasis on intelligence and education. Throughout the reform debates, supporters of the Bill lauded the moral and intellectual improvement of the people, and the Whigs in particular expressed an active desire that the people should consider and discuss public questions.[39] Like their Whig leaders, the 'independent' citizenry had the capacity for enlightened disinterestedness. Victorian Liberals would later amplify these imperatives, making social respectability, moral seriousness and personal accomplishments important aspects of active political citizenship. From 1832 working men who aspired to the franchise were encouraged to elevate themselves, and the culture of autodidacticism and self-improvement would be central to the claims of such men well into the age of Gladstonian Liberalism.[40]

The Reform Act of 1832, therefore, should be viewed in the broadest cultural and historical perspective. Far from being the 'modernising' measure of Whig historiography, the reformers of the 1830s were drawing upon long-established notions of political virtue and entitlement, a rationale that hinged on the crucial notion of the independent man. Only by attending to contemporary understandings of gender, obligation and virtue can we comprehend how citizenship was conceived of by nineteenth-century legislators, and experienced by nineteenth-century citizens themselves. Nor was the Act an unqualified step forward in terms of political inclusion, since 'dependent' groups such as women and paupers were excluded from official electoral politics by its provisions. The reformers of 1832 – like so many of their predecessors – believed that politics should be a world only for independent men.

Notes

1 For example: M. Brock, *The Great Reform Act* (London: Hutchinson, 1973), p. 143.
2 R. W. Davis, 'Deference and aristocracy in the time of the Great Reform Act', *American Historical Review* 81 (1976), pp. 532–9; H. A. Ellis, 'Aristocratic influence and electoral independence: the Whig model of parliamentary reform, 1792–1832', *Journal of Modern History* 51:4 (1979) On Demand Supplement, pp. D1251–76.

3 Patrick Joyce, *Democratic Subjects: The Self and the Social in Nineteenth-Century England* (Cambridge: Cambridge University Press, 1994); Catherine Hall, Keith McClelland and Jane Rendall, *Defining the Victorian Nation: Class, Race, Gender and the Reform Act of 1867* (Cambridge: Cambridge University Press, 2000).

4 Russell to Durham (19 October 1834): *Early Correspondence of Lord John Russell, 1805–1840*, ed. R. Russell, 2 vols (London, 1913), vol. I, pp. 51–4 (p. 53).

5 The report is printed in full in *The Reform Act, 1832: The Correspondence of the Late Earl Grey with His Majesty King William IV and with Sir Herbert Taylor*, ed. H. Grey, 2 vols (London, 1867), vol. I, Appendix A pp. 461–3 (p. 462).

6 *Correspondence of the Late Earl Grey*, p. 462–3.

7 Earl of Winchilsea (Lords, 4 October 1831): *Hansard's Parliamentary Debates*, 3rd series (London, 1831), vol. VII, p. 1141.

8 Duke of Buccleugh (Lords, 14 April 1831): *Hansard*, 3rd series, vol. III, pp. 1320–1.

9 Earl of Winchilsea (Lords, 4 October 1831): *Hansard*, 3rd series, vol. VII, p. 1142.

10 Sir Charles Burrell (Commons, 18 August 1831): *Hansard*, 3rd series, vol. VI, p. 283.

11 Earl of Haddington, presenting an anti-reform petition from Edinburgh (Lords, 14 April 1831), 3rd series, vol. II, p. 1316.

12 J. Milton-Smith, 'Earl Grey's Cabinet and the objects of Parliamentary Reform', *Historical Journal* 15:1 (1972), pp. 55–74 (p. 66).

13 See, for example: (Commons, 18 February 1830) *Hansard*, 2nd series, vol. XXII, pp. 678–98; (Commons, 21 November 1830), *Hansard*, 3rd series, vol. I, pp. 65–8.

14 Peter Mandler, *Aristocratic Government in the Age of Reform: Whigs and Liberals, 1830–52* (Oxford: Oxford University Press, 1990), p. 72.

15 Althorp (Commons, 18 August 1831): *Hansard*, 3rd series, vol. VI, pp. 280–1.

16 Mary Poovey, *Making a Social Body: British Cultural Formation 1830–1864* (Chicago: Chicago University Press, 1996).

17 William Mackworth Praed (Commons, 26 August 1831): *Hansard*, 3rd series, vol. VI, p. 686.

18 Henry Hunt (Commons, 24 August 1831): *Hansard*, 3rd series, vol. VI, pp. 553, 554.

19 From: William Blackstone, *Commentaries on the Laws of England*, 4 vols (Oxford, 1765), vol. I, p. 165.

20 Daniel O'Connell (Commons, 28 May 1830): *Hansard*, 2nd series, vol. XXIV, pp. 1210, 1214.

21 *Westminster Review* 25 (July 1830).

22 Henry Brougham (Commons, 28 May 1830): *Hansard*, 2nd series, vol. XXIV, pp. 1251–2; Lord John Russell (Commons, 1 March 1831): *Hansard*, 3rd series, vol. II, p. 1084.

23 Mandler, *Aristocratic Government*, p. 8.

24 Ian Newbould, *Whiggery and Reform, 1830–41: The Politics of Government* (Stanford: Stanford University Press, 1990), p. 2; A. Kriegel, 'Liberty and Whiggery in early nineteenth-century England', *Journal of Modern History* 52:2 (1980), pp. 253–78 (p. 275).

25 Bedford to Grenville (9 February 1817): *Early Correspondence of Lord John Russell*, vol. I, p. 185.

26 D. Wahrman, *Imagining the Middle Class: The Political Representation of Class in Britain 1780–1840* (Cambridge: Cambridge University Press, 1995).

27 Durham (Lords, 14 April 1832): *Hansard*, 3rd series, vol. XII, pp. 356, 363.

28 Leonore Davidoff and Catherine Hall, *Family Fortunes: Men and Women of the English Middle Class, 1780–1850* (London: Hutchinson, 1987), p. 199 and *passim*.

29 *Report of the Speeches at the Great Dinner in the Theatre, Manchester, to celebrate the election of Mark Phillips, Esq. & the Right Hon. C. Poulett Thompson* (Manchester, n.d.), p. 7.

30 Lord Wynford (Lords, 7 October 1831), *Hansard*, 3rd series, vol. VIII, p. 196.

31 Davis, 'Deference and aristocracy', p. 538; Ellis, 'Aristocratic influence', p. D1254 and *passim*.

32 Durham, quoted in Davis, 'Deference and aristocracy', p. 536.

33 Palmerston (Commons, 3 March 1831): *Hansard*, 3rd series, vol. III, p. 1326.

34 Russell (Commons, 1 March 1831): *Hansard*, 3rd series, vol. III, p. 1084.

35 Anna Clark, 'Gender, class and the constitution: franchise reform in England, 1832–1928', in J. Vernon (ed.), *Re-Reading the Constitution: New Narratives in the Political History of England's Long Nineteenth Century* (Cambridge: Cambridge University Press, 1996), pp. 239–53.

36 (Lords, 26 January 1832): *Hansard*, 3rd series, vol. IX, p. 830.

37 Earl Grey (Lords, 9 April 1832): *Hansard*, 3rd series, vol. XII, p. 19.

38 James Vernon, *Politics and the People: A Study in English Political Culture 1815–1867* (Cambridge: Cambridge University Press, 1993), pp. 99–101.

39 Earl Grey (Lords, 18 April 1831): *Hansard*, 3rd series, vol. III, p. 1478; Mandler, *Aristocratic Government*, p. 37.

40 Joyce, *Democratic Subjects*; David Vincent, *Bread, Knowledge and Freedom: A Study of Nineteenth-Century Working Class Autobiography* (London: Europa, 1981).

Conclusion

Why were Georgians so fascinated with the idea of 'the independent man'? As we have seen, different historians have offered contrasting hypotheses. Women's historians attribute 'independence' to misogyny and the reinforcement of patriarchal power, in the context of the 'emergence of separate spheres'. Social historians are inclined to place it in the context of the 'rise of the middle class', as middling men sought 'independence' from patrician patronage and deference structures. Other social historians prioritise changing ideas about work and economics: Geoffrey Best notes that independence 'was the main social consequence of the vulgarisation of the creed of classical economics in a Protestant country'.[1] John Tosh, on the other hand, has argued that we need to take all of these aspects on board if we are to understand nineteenth-century masculinities, since they were formed in the interconnections between home, work and all-male association: 'some notion of complementarity is always implied by that key nineteenth-century indicator of masculinity achieved, "independence", combining as it did dignified work, sole maintenance of the family, and free association on terms of equality with other men'.[2] Many of these considerations are indeed important. Much of the power of the idea of 'independence' derived from its allusive range: it drew upon meanings from a variety of contexts, which could emotively be employed in a range of situations. I would argue, though, that the primary reason for the cultural power of the idea of 'the independent man' was *political*. When Georgian men claimed to be 'independent', they were drawing upon a political culture that privileged freedom from obligation, self-ownership, patriotism, straightforward manliness and constitutional balance.

There were many reasons why these considerations were all-pervasive in Georgian political culture. As we have seen, English commentators revered classical and Renaissance political thought, and this often informed their perspective upon contemporary questions. From the mid-seventeenth century, English political theorists increasingly thought in terms of mixed balanced constitutionalism, whereby the 'independence' of institutions and political actors was fundamental to the preservation of freedom and good government. Furthermore, the classical 'familial model' of independence and dependence pervaded Georgian thought. This fostered an understanding of liberty, virtue and power that was inescapably gendered. An individual who depended upon the will of another was absolutely unfree, was liable to be corrupted and even lacked an autonomous personality of their own. Within the familial scheme, only the father and master was 'independent', so liberty, virtue and power were gendered in the masculine.

This critique of obligation was particularly appropriate to a state and a society pervaded by relations of clientage. The end of the seventeenth century saw the establishment of a large permanent military establishment, new financial institutions and networks of government patronage, which cumulatively multiplied the number of persons who held office or wealth at the pleasure of the executive. It was during this 'first age of party' that 'independence' became a ubiquitous feature of opposition argument, as persons excluded from power and favour employed the classical critique of obligation and constitutional balance in order to assert the depravity of the 'ins' and the moral superiority of the 'outs'. Only 'the independent', they argued, were able to speak freely and to act for the good of all ('the Country'), because those who wielded power and those who depended upon them would inevitably be corrupted. It is likely that 'independence' also took on its electoral significance in this period since, after the Triennial Act of 1694, frequent elections enabled the development of a distinctive and continuous electoral culture. By the 1760s the culture of electoral independence was highly developed, and it remained remarkably consistent up to 1832 and beyond.[3]

In the eighteenth century, 'independence' was often the boast of those who regarded themselves as the nation's natural legislators, and who kicked against centralisation, professionalisation and the newly moneyed. The idea of 'the independent man' meshed with the localised, amateur, gentlemanly ethos upon which so much of English political, governmental, military and legal life relied. 'Independence', however, proved to be a highly adaptable form of opposition argument. John Wilkes's claim to 'independence' was again that of an ambitious gentleman who made a virtue of the fact that he did not have his snout in the trough, but the Wilkite phenomenon – combined with ideas imported from revolutionary America – opened the door to wider interpretations of political entitlement. Wilkes's focus upon the rights of freeborn Englishmen, and the subversively empowering implications of Wilkite street theatre, were democratic in their implications. However much his personal image was repellent to reformers in later, more morally censorious decades, they too would conceive of citizenship in more inclusive terms by expanding the parameters of 'independence'. By the 1790s, many plebeian radicals were able to make political claims for *all* men, on the basis of their 'independent', rights-bearing personalities.

'Independence', however, would not always be the boast of the excluded. Pitt the Elder had already demonstrated that this anti-ministerial stance could be carried into office and, in the later 1790s, his son's wartime establishment appropriated the oppositional aesthetic of 'Country' patriotism in order to motivate the population against the threatened invasion. The independent man was re-imagined as the vigilant anti-Jacobin patriot. Preaching a participatory model of national citizenship to men from all walks of life, however, arguably served to highlight the inequity of the current system of electoral citizenship. Although Pitt the Younger is usually credited with having succeeded in suppressing political reformism in the 1790s, the arguments of his propagandists made political reform more difficult to reject thereafter. Furthermore, concerns about the size and ineffectiveness of the wartime establishment refocused attention upon 'Old Corruption', of which 'the independent man' remained the incorruptible repudiator.

When the political reform movement revived in the first two decades of the nineteenth century, working men participated on an unprecedented scale. Many radicals reconfigured the basis for electoral citizenship along the lines of gender in order to pursue their claim: manhood and not wealth or station, they argued, could be the only natural qualification for the vote. Reform, when it came, would not be so far-reaching, but would be based around a model of the citizen that owed much to the idea of manly independence. The voter of 1832 was a householder, a property owner and a male, who was conscientious, free and able to recognise his natural leaders because he was independent. The Reform Act, therefore, should be regarded in the context of two centuries of debate about the implications of 'independence'. In this broader chronological perspective, 1832 becomes the pivotal moment in the transformation of the idea of 'the independent man': what had started out as an elitist critique of political exclusion had become the criterion for political inclusion.

This study ends with 1832, but it is far from being the end of the story. The First Reform Act established the parameters for later politics and, throughout the coming century, persons excluded from official political life would make a case for their inclusion by claiming to be 'independent'. Chartism represents a continuation of the eighteenth-century radical critique of political exclusion, and promoted the enfranchisement of 'independent' working men along similar lines.[4] Eugenio Biagini has demonstrated the striking continuities between the cultures of radicalism and Gladstonian popular liberalism, and there are now a number of studies arguing that the 1867 Reform Act was predicated upon an attempt to enfranchise the 'independent' portion of the male working class.[5] There is evidence that men excluded by this measure emphasised their manly 'independence' in agitating for the Third Reform Act,[6] and it would be instructive to explore how far the arguments surrounding the Ballot Act and the Corrupt Practices Act were conducted in these terms.

Fundamentally, the debate over what sorts of persons should be entrusted with the vote was only resolved with the full enfranchisement of women in 1928. Feminists such as Mary Wollstonecraft, Robert Owen and William Thompson had long argued that the cultures of male independence and female dependence were artificial, and that both sexes should be given the opportunity to realise the 'independence' upon which their political personality relied. The suffragists' case for female electoral citizenship, however, was a lot more complex than a simple repudiation of the male independence / female dependence dichotomy. Whereas some propertied women argued that they were *more* independent than many of the men enfranchised in 1884, other suffragists sought to work *within* the 'separate spheres' discourse, arguing that the political world would benefit from their 'feminine' qualities, and that the specific interests of wives, mothers and single women required protection through direct representation.[7] 'Virtual representation' was challenged without overturning sexual difference, suggesting that Edwardians thought about the relationship between gender and political rights in a different way to their forebears. This paradigm shift also contributed to the depoliticisation of the notion of 'manly independence' by the twentieth century: when the prospect of universal suffrage loomed, it was clear that political entitlement was no longer the qualitative business that it had once been. This serves to remind us that the late-Georgian and Victorian periods represent a unique moment in British history when electoral citizenship was something that had to be *earned* by demonstrated social, political and moral worth – considerations that were evaluated in fundamentally gendered terms via the notion of 'independence'.

It is clear that 'independence' in the Victorian period increasingly becomes a question of race. We have seen how the 'independent' political character of the English was often conceived of in proto-racial ways, particularly with regard to Saxon origins, and in opposition to certain foreign 'others'. Nevertheless, the 'independent man' was rarely contrasted with non-European races in the eighteenth century. The political language of 'slavery' employed classical and biblical reference points, thus eliding the contrast between contemporary chattel slavery and domestic claims for political emancipation – however incongruous this may have appeared, particularly in the American context. It was only in the mid-nineteenth century, in the context of race science and anxieties about the empire, that the black became a significant 'other' for the independent Englishman. Catherine Hall has examined this development, arguing that the Second Reform Act defined the citizen in terms of race as well as gender and class.[8]

This study of 'the independent man' has highlighted other areas that need further work. It has become clear that the current historiography underestimates the cultural pervasiveness and endurance of the 'Country' (and later 'Old Corruption') worldview. This was not merely a high-political critique or pragmatic rhetoric, but offered a comprehensive model of society and politics, measures of good and evil, and stories of decline and redemption. 'Country' patriotism provided the characteristic aesthetic of Georgian political life, and elements of it endured well into the Victorian period: what is *Bleak House*, if it is not a gothic portrayal of the foetidity, the complexity and the inhumanity of 'the Thing'? A fuller appreciation of the 'Country' critique would help us to understand how critiques of political and social exclusion modified – and yet remained remarkably consistent in their key elements – from the English Civil War until Victorian Liberalism. Fundamentally, the idea of 'the independent man' remained powerful because this neo-classical worldview remained powerful. The dominance of neo-classical thinking is striking in late Georgian political culture, particularly in terms of balanced constitutionalism, citizenship and notions of patriotism and public virtue – considerations that were inescapably gendered when viewed through a classical lens. Feminist political scholars have long appreciated the misogynistic and exclusionary implications of classical republicanism, but tend to assert that it was supplanted over the course of the eighteenth century by Lockean liberalism.[9] The continued prominence of 'the independent man' and the 'Country' critique, however, suggests that classicism endured well beyond this – a fact with profound implications for the statuses of men and women.

Why, then, was manly independence politically important? It was not as a result of objective developments in the realms of society, economics or gender, although it undoubtedly took on emotive meanings from all of these discourses. Manly independence was politically powerful because it was itself a political idea. Indeed, Georgian conceptions of their society, economy and gender relations were significantly influenced by it. Rather than the passive reflector of these realms, political discourse contributed to their very constitution.

Politics, therefore, has a significance beyond its traditional parameters, but British political studies remains a resolutely conservative business.[10]

Whereas a vigorous debate has taken place in social history about the implications of postmodernism,[11] political studies' response largely remains that of miscomprehension or latent hostility. Fears of political disengagement and dangerous relativism, however, are unfounded. Political historians have much to gain from a greater self-reflexivity regarding their own methods, and a greater sensitivity to the perspectives of those whom they study. Fundamentally, they should be aware that politics is not a natural thing to do. Political conduct, communication and subjectivity are not transhistorical 'givens'. To assume that they are, and to approach Georgian political life with essentially twenty-first-century categories, would be wholly anachronistic. Only by understanding the contemporary cultural context, and by reflecting critically upon the question of how contemporaries engaged with it, can politics in the past be comprehensible.

In this study I have sought to demonstrate that the fundamental question in English political life over the eighteenth and nineteenth centuries was that of who was considered fit to be admitted to full citizenship: what sorts of persons should be given the vote? As Sandra Stanley Holton argues, historians need a fuller understanding of 'the cultural, symbolic significance of the vote in our society, a significance which requires the historian to look beyond its potential, or otherwise, for effecting change'.[12] This intervention from the perspective of women's suffrage history highlights the inadequacy of the conception of citizenship that still dominates mainstream political history. Political studies needs to develop a more nuanced understanding of the political self, and this requires an interdisciplinary methodology, with insights from gender studies, literary studies, performance studies and post-structuralist cultural theory, to name but four such approaches. Indeed, given the current emphasis upon cultural constructivism, the need to understand historical context is paramount, so political history is well situated to become a meeting place for interdisciplinary cultural studies.

The histories of masculinity and politics, in particular, should be closely allied, and productive links are beginning to be developed from both sides.[13] Thus far, however, little of this engagement has taken place before the Victorian period: this is surprising, given that eighteenth-century gender historians have already forged productive links with the 'public' histories of work, nationalism and the law (besides the more predictable focuses upon 'private' sexuality and the family).[14] To date, the best studies of masculinity in Georgian politics have taken place in broader cultural histories that have tellingly integrated the question of male political subjectivity into broader studies of gender, class and race.[15] Georgian politics needs a gender perspective, and vice versa, because the central political questions of citizenship and electoral entitlement were highly gendered, in terms of both the exclusion of women and the exclusion of certain sorts of men. It is worth taking stock at this point and considering some of the ways in which this study of 'the independent man' opens up further potential links between the histories of masculinity and politics.

'Independence' was almost universally regarded as a male quality in this period. Within the classical understanding of liberty and virtue, to which Georgian culture owed so much, only the male household head could be in a position of independence. This was the basic 'familial model', but understandings of what constituted his 'independence' were far from static. As we have seen, over the eighteenth and nineteenth centuries, important shifts took place in the definition of the independent man, which had profound implications for understandings of citizenship. 'Independence' was initially identified with the possession of certain types of property, with high rank, and with the acquirements that, through leisure, they enabled. 'Independence' was not achieved through work, but through its avoidance. From the late eighteenth century, however, there was a shift of emphasis from these exterior acquirements that were available only to the few, to 'inner' qualities that were accessible to all men. The cults of male sensibility, manly simplicity, Romanticism and sincerity instead evaluated men in terms of their inner 'truth'. We saw in Chapter 5 how 'independence' was increasingly viewed in terms of abstention rather than opulence, of selflessness rather than bombastic shows of public spirit, of humility rather than self-aggrandisement, and of industry rather than leisure. Tobias Smollett's 'Ode to Independence' was a particularly prescient expression of this.[16] By the 1790s, many radicals were arguing in terms of inherent rights rather than artificial privileges: rights were both provided by, and guaranteed the integrity of, the independent personality.

When radicals pursued this claim, however, they did so in terms of the rights of *men*. 'Independence', which was once associated with certain sorts of elite men, was increasingly being identified with maleness *per se*. Committed to a classical paradigm that identified liberty and virtue with the absence of obligation – but not yet prepared, with Robert Owen, to reconfigure the relations between the sexes – they took it to its logical conclusion in order to conceive of male entitlement in the broadest terms. To return to Thomas Wooler's dictum:

> in a natural state, men are all alike; independent of each other, and consequently all alike equal, and this state is called natural equality, or equality of birth; on this equality is founded universal suffrage. [But]

men are alone independent by nature, and . . . idiots, madmen, women, and children must in all states be dependent.[17]

By retaining 'independence' as the basis for political empowerment, and by conceiving of 'independence' solely in terms of gender (besides age and basic mental capacity), they pursued the political claims of men at the expense of women. Indeed, there was a marked strain of misogyny in late-Georgian radical culture. The radical claim involved a hardening of the boundaries between (independent) men and (dependent) women.

When the official definition of citizenship was revised in the nineteenth century, political entitlement was initially conceived of in more narrow social terms. The Reform Act of 1832, however, was designed around a fundamentally gendered conception of the citizen. Women were officially excluded from electoral citizenship, whereas the citizen was not only male but was evaluated in terms of his maleness. The 'independent' citizen was the head of a household, of modest station and property, and capable of supporting, protecting and representing his non-manly dependants: although this benchmark excluded many men, it was presented as one to which all men could aspire. As I have suggested above, further Reform Acts expanded the definition of what it meant to be an independent man until, with the Third in 1884, political 'independence' was identified with manhood itself.

Over two centuries, therefore, 'independence' shifts from being the apogee of manliness to becoming equated with maleness. 'Independence' is always masculine and evaluative, but it comes to be associated less with rank, and more with biological sex. This is congruent with Thomas Laqueur's account of the transition from a 'one-sex' to a 'two-sex' model over the same period, one of the few established chronologies in the history of masculinity. In early modern wordviews, he argues, gender difference was conceived of in qualitative rather than binary terms. Men and women were held to have essentially the same bodies, but men had a superior balance of heat, fluids and humours. Gender difference was incremental: men occupied a higher place on the Chain of Being, but gender distinctions were slippery and men could fall into effeminacy or hermaphroditism. Manhood was therefore at the top of a continuum. Over the eighteenth century, however, the bodies and natures of men and women were increasingly conceptualised as separate and different. Men were identified with strength and rationality, whereas women were conceptualised as passive, non-rational and reproductive.[18] Thus, whereas 'independence' was once associated with the pinnacle of the gender scale, it was increasingly identified with manhood itself, to the exclusion of a 'dependent' femininity.

Hence we see the late-Georgian attempts to establish firm bound-aries between male 'independence' and female or effeminate 'dependence'. The example of attitudes towards male same-sex desire is instructive here. In Stuart England, the sexes were conceived of in more androgynous terms, and there was little sense that heterosexuality and homosexuality were exclusive poles of male identity and behaviour. Male intimacy was relatively unproblematic, and sodomy – which was often associated with vigorous male libertinism – was a mortal sin but not a sexual deviance.[19] John Wilkes's libertinism in the 1760s was, by contrast, emphatically heterosexual. When he accused his enemies of being sodomites, however, he was largely implying that – within the Roman paradigm – they were exercising a power over each other that was unnatural between men, since the passive partner was in a position of dependence. By the time of the Regency, attitudes had changed further. When Henry Hunt responded to some hecklers at the 1819 Westminster election he had a different object in view:

> One day, when I was about to address the people at the close of the poll, the gang began their accustomed attack, and vociferated the most revolting, obscene, and truly horrid observations, relating to my wife; upon which I turned round and asked, if it were possible for such lan-guage to proceed from the mouth of any one who possessed the char-acter of a man? And I added, that it did appear to me more than palpable, that no one would resort to such cowardly, base, and horrid language, but some monster that was connected with a gang like that of the Vere-street notoriety.

By associating his opponents with a group of men who had recently been tried at the Old Bailey for 'unnatural crimes', Hunt sought to deny that they were men at all, and thus their claims to have 'independent' political personalities.[20] He, on the other hand, simultaneously affirmed his man-liness by rushing to defend the honour of his wife – the dependant whom, as an independent man, he was bound to protect.

Gender and politics were therefore inseparable in the eighteenth and nineteenth centuries. There is a widespread appreciation nowadays that gender is important in political contexts, but the relationship between gender and politics should be two-way: we need to put politics back into our understanding of gender change in this period. The fact that a par-ticular section of the political spectrum was trumpeting models of man-liness and domesticity reminds us that the 'separate spheres' ideology of the Georgian middling sorts was political in motivation. Their supposed adherence to idealised gender roles was an argument for constitutional reform since, they argued, their moral superiority and 'natural' familial responsibilities merited political inclusion. The frequent masculinism and misogyny of late-Georgian reformism arguably had lasting implications for the British left. One of the paradoxes of Victorian and Edwardian politics is that many women – and even many feminists – often found a more natural home in the supposedly less 'progressive' Conservative party.[21]

Is the Georgian cult of 'the independent man' still with us? Racism, misogyny and homophobia are still features of British life, and it is likely their cultural roots are deep since we have inherited a world structured by eighteenth-century categories. It could even be argued that the Georgian apotheosis of 'the independent man' has left us today with constraining masculine norms.[22] Men today still privilege financial and emotional self-sufficiency over intimacy and fulfilment, and an (ironically very stylised) plainness over any legitimate aspiration to cultivation. It would be wrong to assume that there is a 'natural', pre-constructed masculinity to which we can return, but the constructivist emphasis in contemporary cultural studies does at least hold out the prospect that norms can change. Contrary to the stories that Georgians told about it, the history of masculine independence does not involve the restoration of a past golden age, but it may yet have a happy ending.

Notes

1 Geoffrey Best, *Mid-Victorian Britain, 1815–75* (London: Fontana, 1979), p. 280.
2 John Tosh, 'What should historians do with masculinity? Reflections on nineteenth-century Britain', *History Workshop Journal* 38 (1994), pp. 179–202 (p. 188).
3 Frank O'Gorman, *Voters, Patrons, and Parties: The Unreformed Electorate of Hanoverian England* (Oxford: Oxford University Press, 1989), p. 285.
4 Gareth Stedman Jones, 'Rethinking Chartism', in *Languages of Class* (Cambridge: Cambridge University Press, 1983), pp. 94–177.
5 E. Biagini, *Liberty, Retrenchment and Reform: Popular Liberalism in the Age of Gladstone 1860–1880* (Cambridge: Cambridge University Press, 1992); C. Hall, K. McClelland and J. Rendall, *Defining the Victorian Nation: Class, Race, Gender, and the British Reform Act of 1867* (Cambridge: Cambridge University Press, 2000).
6 Biagini, *Liberty, Retrenchment and Reform*, p. 278.
7 Sandra Stanley Holton, *Feminism and Democracy: Women's Suffrage and Reform Politics in Britain 1900–1918* (Cambridge: Cambridge University Press, 1986).
8 C. Hall, 'Rethinking imperial histories: the Reform Act of 1867', *New Left Review* 208 (1994), pp. 3–29.
9 Carole Pateman, *The Sexual Contract: Aspects of Patriarchal Liberalism* (Stanford: Stanford University Press, 1988).
10 See, for example, Michael Bentley's attack on James Vernon in 'Victorian politics and the linguistic turn', *Historical Journal* 42:3 (1999), pp. 883–902.

11 See, for example, the debate upon 'Social history and its discontents', *Social History* 17:2 (1992); 18:1 (1993); 19:1 (1994); 20:1 (1995).

12 Holton, *Feminism and Democracy*, p. 3.

13 S. Dudink, K. Hagemann and J. Tosh (eds), *Masculinities in Politics and War: Gendering Modern History* (Manchester: Manchester University Press, 2004).

14 See, for example, the essays collected in T. Hitchcock and M. Cohen (eds), *English Masculinities, 1660–1800* (Harlow: Longman, 1999).

15 Anna Clark, *The Struggle for the Breeches: Gender and the Making of the British Working Class* (London: Rivers Owen, 1995); Leonore Davidoff, *Worlds Between: Historical Perspectives on Gender and Class* (Cambridge: Polity, 1995); Catherine Hall, *White, Male and Middle Class: Explorations in Feminism and History* (Cambridge: Polity, 1992).

16 I explore this theme in further detail in 'Tobias Smollett's "Ode to Independence" and Georgian political culture', *British Journal for Eighteenth-Century Studies* 26:1 (2003), pp. 27–39.

17 *Black Dwarf* (4 June 1817).

18 T. Laqueur, *Making Sex: Body and Gender from the Greeks to Freud* (Cambridge: Harvard University Press, 1990).

19 T. Hitchcock, *English Sexualities, 1700–1800* (Basingstoke: Macmillan, 1997), p. 5.

20 Henry Hunt, *Memoirs of Henry Hunt, Esq. Written by Himself, In His Majesty's Jail at Ilchester, in the County of Somerset*, 3 vols (London, 1822; reprinted Bath: Chivers, 1967), vol. III, pp. 582–3.

21 Martin Pugh, *The Tories and the People, 1880–1935* (Oxford: Blackwell, 1985).

22 V. Seidler, *Rediscovering Masculinity: Reason, Language and Sexuality* (London: Routledge, 1989).

Select bibliography

This select bibliography lists key books and articles only. For electoral, press, parliamentary, pamphlet and unpublished sources, please refer to the notes.

Primary sources

The Battle of the Quills: Or, Wilkes Attacked and Defended (London, 1768).

Blackstone, William, *Commentaries on the Laws of England* (Oxford, 1765–69).

Bolingbroke, Henry St John, Viscount, *Letters on the Spirit of Patriotism and on the Idea of a Patriot King*, ed. A. Hassall (Oxford: Clarendon, 1926).

Brown, John, *An Estimate of the Manners and Principles of the Times* (London, 1757).

Bulwer-Lytton, Edward, *England and the English* (London, 1833).

Burke, Edmund, *The Writings and Speeches of Edmund Burke*, eds P. Langford *et al.*, 9 vols (Oxford: Clarendon Press, 1981).

Carr, Sir John, *Descriptive Travels in the Southern and Eastern Parts of Spain and the Balearic Isles, in the Year 1809* (London, 1811).

Cartwright, John, *The Commonwealth in Danger* (London, 1795).

Chesterfield, Philip Stanhope, 4th Earl, *Characters*, ed. A. McKenzie (Los Angeles: William Andrews Clark Memorial Library, 1990).

Cobbett, William, *Advice to Young Men, and (Incidentally) to Young Women, in the Middle and Higher Ranks of Life* (London, 1878).

Dickinson, John, *Letters from a Farmer in Pennsylvania* (Philadelphia, 1768).

Digby, Kenelm, *The Broad Stone of Honour; or, The True Sense and Practice of Chivalry*, 5 vols (London, 1877).

Ensor, George, *The Independent Man: or, An Essay on the Formation and Development of those Principles and Faculties of the Human Mind which Constitute Moral and Intellectual Existence*, 2 vols (London, 1806).

[Ferguson, Adam], *Reflections Previous to the Establishment of a Militia* (London, 1756).

Franklin, Benjamin, *Benjamin Franklin's Letters to the Press, 1758–1775*, ed. V. Crane (Chapel Hill: North Carolina University Press, 1950).

[Gordon, Thomas], *The Character of an Independent Whig* (London, 1719).

Gordon, William, *The History of the Rise, Progress, and Establishment, of the Independence of the United States of America*, 4 vols (London, 1788).

Grey, H. (ed.), *The Reform Act, 1832: The Correspondence of the Late Earl Grey with His Majesty King William IV and with Sir Herbert Taylor*, 2 vols (London, 1867).

Harrington, James, *The Commonwealth of Oceana and A System of Politics*, ed. J. G. A. Pocock (Cambridge: Cambridge University Press, 1992).

Holcroft, Thomas [and Hazlitt, William], *The Life of Thomas Holcroft*, ed. E. Colby, 2 vols (London: Constable, 1925).

Hume, David, *Political Essays*, ed. K. Haakonssen (Cambridge: Cambridge University Press, 1994).

Hunt, Henry, *Memoirs of Henry Hunt, Esq. Written by Himself, in his Majesty's Jail at Ilchester, in the County of Somerset*, 3 vols (Bath: Chivers, 1967).

Jefferson, Thomas, *Notes on the State of Virginia* (1787), ed. W. Peden (Chapel Hill: North Carolina University Press, 1955).

A Letter from a Person of Quality, To His Friend in the Country (1675).

Locke, John, *Two Treatises of Government*, ed. Peter Laslett (Cambridge: Cambridge University Press, 1960).

Macaulay, Thomas Babington, *The History of England from the Accession of James the Second*, ed. C. Frith, 6 vols (London: Macmillan, 1913–15).

MacPhail, Hugh Buchanan, *Lyrics: Love, Freedom and Manly Independence* (Glasgow, 1856).

Mill, James, 'Essay on Government' (1820), in *Utilitarian Logic and Politics*, eds J. Lively and J. Rees (Oxford: Clarendon, 1978).

A Modest Address to the People of Great Britain (London, 1756).

More, Hannah, *The Works of Hannah More*, 18 vols (London, 1818).

Oldfield, T. H. B., *The Representative History of Great Britain and Ireland*, 3 vols (London, 1816).

Paine, Thomas, *The Writings of Thomas Paine*, ed. M. Conway, 4 vols (New York: AMS, 1967).

Price, Richard, *Political Writings*, ed. D. Thomas (Cambridge: Cambridge University Press, 1991).

Russell, Lord John, *An Essay on the History of the English Government and Constitution, from the reign of Henry VII, to the present time*, 2nd edn (London, 1823).

Sandford, Elizabeth, *Woman, in Her Social and Domestic Character*, 5th edn (London, 1837).

Siddons, Henry, *Practical Illustrations of Rhetorical Gesture and Action; Adapted to the English Drama* (London, 1822).

Sidney, Algernon, *Discourses Concerning Government*, ed. T. West (Indianapolis: Liberty, 1990).

Smollett, Tobias, *A Complete History of England*, 4 vols (London, 1757–58).

—— *Poems, Plays, and* The Briton, ed. O. Brack and L. Chilton, with introductions by B. Gassman (Athens: Georgia University Press, 1993).

State Tracts: Being a Collection of Several Treatises Relating to Government (London, 1689).

[Stuart, Daniel], *Peace and Reform, against War and Corruption* (London, 1794).

Wade, J., *The Extraordinary Black Book* (Shannon: Irish University Press, 1971).

Walker, John, *The Academic Speaker . . . To Which is Prefixed, Elements of Gesture*, 3rd edn (London, 1797).

Ward, Robert Plumer, *De Vere: Or, The Man of Independence*, 4 vols (London, 1827).

Wilkes, John, *English Liberty: Being a Collection of Interesting Tracts, From the Year 1762 to 1769, Containing the Private Correspondence, Public Letters, Speeches, and Addresses, of John Wilkes, Esq.* (London, n.d.).

—— *The Correspondence of the Late John Wilkes with his Friends*, ed. John Almon, 5 vols (London, 1805).

Wilson, James, *The Works of James Wilson*, ed. R. G. McCloskey, 2 vols (Cambridge: Harvard University Press, 1995).

Wollstonecraft, Mary, *A Vindication of the Rights of Men with A Vindication of the Rights of Women and Hints*, ed. Sylvana Tomaselli (Cambridge: Cambridge University Press, 1995).

Wordsworth, William, *The Prose Works of William Wordsworth*, ed. W. Owen and J. Smyser, 3 vols (Oxford: Oxford University Press, 1974).

Wyvill, Christopher, *Political Papers, Chiefly Respecting the Attempt of the County of York, and other Considerable Districts, Commenced in 1779, and Continued during several subsequent years, to effect a Reformation of the Parliament of Great Britain*, 3 vols (York, 1794).

—— *The Correspondence of the Rev. C. Wyvill with the Right Honourable William Pitt*, 2 vols (Newcastle, 1796–97).

Secondary works

Bailyn, Bernard, *The Ideological Origins of the American Revolution* (Cambridge: Harvard University Press, 1967).

Barker, Hannah and Chalus, Elaine (eds.), *Gender in Eighteenth-Century England: Roles, Representations and Responsibilities* (London: Longman, 1997).

Barker-Benfield, J. G., *The Culture of Sensibility: Sex and Society in Eighteenth-Century Britain* (Chicago: Chicago University Press, 1992).

Belchem, John, *'Orator' Hunt: Henry Hunt and English Working-class Radicalism* (Oxford: Clarendon, 1985).

Belchem, John and Epstein, James, 'The nineteenth-century gentleman leader revisited', *Social History* 22:2 (1997), pp. 174–93.

Black, Eugene C., *The Association: British Extraparliamentary Political Organisation, 1769–1793* (Cambridge: Harvard University Press, 1963).

Brock, Michael, *The Great Reform Act* (London: Hutchinson, 1973).

Bushman, Richard, *King and People in Provincial Massachusetts* (Chapel Hill: North Carolina University Press, 1985).

Cannon, John, *Parliamentary Reform 1640–1832* (Cambridge: Cambridge University Press, 1972).

Carter, Philip, *Men and the Emergence of Polite Society, Britain 1660–1800* (Harlow: Longman, 2001).

Claeys, Gregory, *Thomas Paine: Social and Political Thought* (Boston: Unwin Hyman, 1989).

Clark, Anna, 'Queen Caroline and the sexual politics of popular culture in London, 1820', *Representations* 31 (1990), pp. 47–62.

—— The Struggle for the Breeches: Gender and the Making of the British Working Class (London: Rivers Owen, 1995).

Colley, Linda, In Defiance of Oligarchy: The Tory Party 1714–60 (Cambridge: Cambridge University Press, 1982).

—— Britons: Forging the Nation 1707–1837 (New Haven: Yale University Press, 1992).

Collini, Stefan, 'The idea of "character" in Victorian political thought', Transactions of the Royal Historical Society 35 (1985), pp. 29–50.

Cookson, J. E., The British Armed Nation, 1793–1815 (Oxford: Clarendon, 1997).

Cunningham, Hugh, 'The language of patriotism, 1750–1914', History Workshop 12 (1981), pp. 8–25.

Davidoff, Leonore, Worlds Between: Historical Perspectives on Gender and Class (Cambridge: Polity, 1995).

Davidoff, Leonore, and Hall, Catherine, Family Fortunes: Men and Women of the English Middle Class, 1780–1850 (London: Routledge, 1987).

Davis, R. W., 'Deference and aristocracy at the time of the Great Reform Act', American Historical Review 81 (1976), pp. 532–9.

Dickinson, H. T., Liberty and Property: Political Ideology in Eighteenth-Century Britain (London: Weidenfeld and Nicolson, 1977).

Dudink, S., Hagemann, K., and Tosh, J. (eds.), Masculinities in Politics and War: Gendering Modern History (Manchester: Manchester University Press, 2004).

Ellis, Harold A., 'Aristocratic influence and electoral independence: the Whig model of parliamentary reform 1792–1832', Journal of Modern History 51:4 (1979) On Demand Supplement, pp. D1251–76.

Fliegelman, Jay, Declaring Independence: Jefferson, Natural Language, and the Culture of Performance (Stanford: Stanford University Press, 1993).

Foord, A. S., His Majesty's Opposition 1714–1830 (Oxford: Clarendon, 1964).

Gilmartin, Kevin, Print Politics: The Press and Radical Opposition in Early Nineteenth-Century England (Cambridge: Cambridge University Press, 1996).

Girouard, Mark, The Return to Camelot: Chivalry and the English Gentleman (New Haven: Yale University Press, 1981).

Hall, Catherine, White, Male and Middle Class: Explorations in Feminism and History (Cambridge: Polity, 1992).

Hall, C., McClelland, K., and Rendall, J., Defining the Victorian Nation: Class, Race, Gender and the British Reform Act of 1867 (Cambridge: Cambridge University Press, 2000).

Hampsher-Monk, Iain, 'Civic humanism and parliamentary reform: the case of the Society of the Friends of the People', Journal of British Studies 18:2 (1978), pp. 70–89.

Harling, Philip, The Waning of 'Old Corruption': The Politics of Economical Reform in Britain, 1779–1846 (Oxford: Oxford University Press, 1996).

Harrison, G., 'Wordsworth's leech gatherer: liminal power and the "Spirit of Independence"', Journal of English Literary History 56 (1989), pp. 327–50.

Hitchcock, Tim and Cohen, Michèle (eds), *English Masculinities 1660–1800* (London: Longman, 1999).

Innes, Joanna, 'Politics and morals: the reformation of manners movement in later eighteenth-century England', in E. Hellmuth (ed.), *The Transformation of Political Culture* (Oxford: Oxford University Press, 1990), pp. 57–118.

Joyce, Patrick, *Democratic Subjects: The Self and the Social in Nineteenth-Century England* (Cambridge: Cambridge University Press, 1994).

Langford, Paul, *Englishness Identified: Manners and Character 1650–1850* (Oxford: Oxford University Press, 2000).

Laqueur, Thomas, *Making Sex: Body and Gender from the Greeks to Freud* (Cambridge: Harvard University Press, 1990).

McCalman, I., *Radical Underworld: Prophets, Revolutionaries and Pornographers in London, 1795–1840* (Cambridge: Cambridge University Press, 1988).

McClelland, Keith, 'Some thoughts on masculinity and the "representative artisan" in Britain, 1850–1880', *Gender and History* 1:2 (1989), pp. 164–77.

McCormack, Matthew, 'Tobias Smollett's "Ode to Independence" and Georgian political culture', *British Journal for Eighteenth-Century Studies* 26:1 (2003), pp. 27–39.

Macpherson, C. B., *The Political Theory of Possessive Individualism: Hobbes to Locke* (Oxford: Clarendon, 1962).

Mandler, Peter, *Aristocratic Government in the Age of Reform: Whigs and Liberals, 1830–52* (Oxford: Oxford University Press, 1990).

Namier, L., *Collected Essays*, Vol. II: *Crossroads of Power* (London: Hamish Hamilton, 1962).

Newman, Gerald, *The Rise of English Nationalism: A Cultural History 1740–1830* (London: Weidenfeld and Nicolson, 1987).

O'Gorman, Frank, *Voters, Patrons and Parties: The Unreformed Electorate of Hanoverian England* (Oxford: Oxford University Press, 1989).

Pateman, Carole, *The Sexual Contract: Aspects of Patriarchal Liberalism* (Stanford: Stanford University Press, 1988).

Peters, Marie, 'The *Monitor* on the constitution, 1755–65: new light on the ideological origins of English radicalism', *English Historical Review* 86 (1971), pp. 706–27.

—— *Pitt and Popularity: The Patriot Minister and London Opinion during the Seven Years' War* (Oxford: Clarendon, 1980).

Pocock, J. G. A., *Politics, Language and Time* (London: Methuen, 1971).

—— *The Machiavellian Moment: Florentine Political Thought and the Atlantic Republican Tradition* (Princeton: Princeton University Press, 1975).

—— *Virtue, Commerce, and History: Essays on Political Thought and History, Chiefly in the Eighteenth Century* (Cambridge: Cambridge University Press, 1985).

Robbins, Caroline, *The Eighteenth-Century Commonwealthman* (Cambridge: Harvard University Press, 1959).

Sainsbury, John, *Disaffected Patriots: London Supporters of Revolutionary America 1769–1782* (Kingston: McGill-Queen's University Press, 1987).

—— 'Wilkes and libertinism', *Studies in Eighteenth-Century Culture* 26 (1998), pp. 151–74.

Skinner, Quentin, *Liberty Before Liberalism* (Cambridge: Cambridge University Press, 1998).

Sweet, Rosemary, 'Freemen and Independence in English Borough Politics c.1770–1830', *Past and Present* 161 (1998), pp. 84–115.

Thomas, P. D. G., *John Wilkes: A Friend to Liberty* (Oxford: Oxford University Press, 1996).

Tosh, John, 'What should historians do with masculinity? Reflections on nineteenth century Britain', *History Workshop Journal* 38 (1994), pp. 179–202.

—— *A Man's Place: Masculinity and the Middle-Class Home in Victorian England* (New Haven: Yale University Press, 1999).

—— 'Gentlemanly politeness and manly simplicity in Victorian England', *Transactions of the Royal Historical Society* 12 (2002), pp. 455–72.

Vernon, James, *Politics and the People: A Study in English Political Culture 1815–1867* (Cambridge: Cambridge University Press, 1993).

—— (ed.), *Re-Reading the Constitution: New Narratives in the Political History of England's Long Nineteenth Century* (Cambridge: Cambridge University Press, 1996).

Vickery, Amanda, 'Golden age to separate spheres? A review of the categories and chronology of English women's history', *Historical Journal* 36:2 (1993), pp. 383–414.

Wahrman, Dror, *Imagining the Middle Class: The Political Representation of Class in Britain 1780–1840* (Cambridge: Cambridge University Press, 1995).

Index

CPSIA information can be obtained
at www.ICGtesting.com
Printed in the USA
FFHW010846011218
49702157-54111FF